EXPLORING OXFORD

For Alexander Jones
who enhances Oxford
by growing up there
and for Joan Ramsey
who honoured Oxford
by retiring there

EXPLORING OXFORD

Michael De-la-Noy

HEADLINE

Copyright © 1991 Michael De-la-Noy (text)
Copyright © 1991 Tony Hutchings (photographs)

Maps drawn by Sue Aldridge, Oxford Illustrators Ltd

First published in 1991
by HEADLINE BOOK PUBLISHING PLC

10 9 8 7 6 5 4 3 2 1

British Library Cataloguing in Publication Data

De-la-Noy, Michael 1934–
Exploring Oxford.
1. Walking recreations
I. Title
914.25740485

ISBN 0–7472–0386–5

Typeset by Medcalf Type Ltd, Bicester, Oxon

Printed and bound in Great Britain by
Richard Clay Ltd, Bungay, Suffolk

HEADLINE BOOK PUBLISHING PLC
Headline House
79 Great Titchfield Street
London W1P 7FN

CONTENTS

LIST OF PLATES

A first visit to Oxford is a thing to remember for life.

Abel Hayward's *Penny Guide to Oxford*

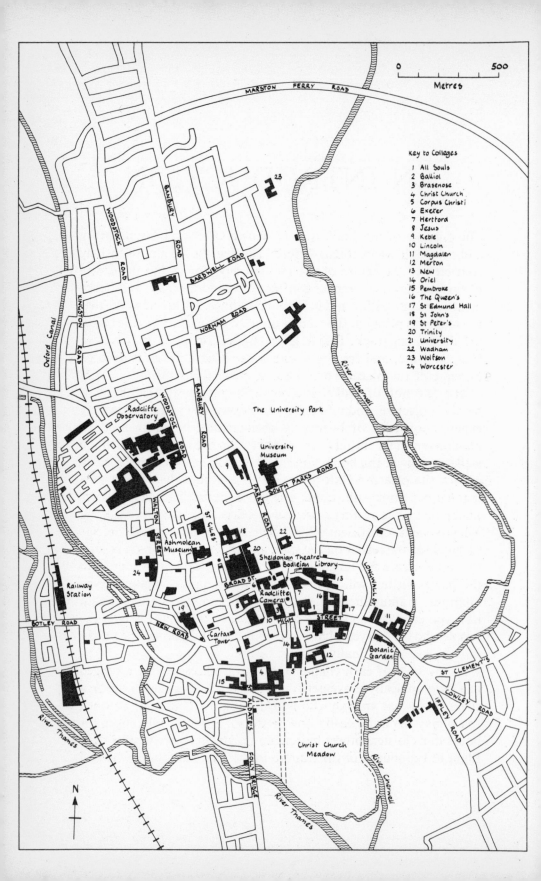

500

Metres

0

MARSTON FERRY ROAD

Key to Colleges

1 All Souls
2 Balliol
3 Brasenose
4 Christ Church
5 Corpus Christi
6 Exeter
7 Hertford
8 Jesus
9 Keble
10 Lincoln
11 Magdalen
12 Merton
13 New
14 Oriel
15 Pembroke
16 The Queen's
17 St Edmund Hall
18 St John's
19 St Peter's
20 Trinity
21 University
22 Wadham
23 Wolfson
24 Worcester

Oxford Canal

WOODSTOCK ROAD

BANBURY ROAD

KINGSTON ROAD

BARDWELL ROAD

NORHAM ROAD

River Cherwell

Radcliffe
Observatory

The University Park

WOODSTOCK ROAD

BANBURY ROAD

University
Museum

PARKS ROAD

SOUTH PARKS ROAD

WALTON STREET

ST GILES

9

Ashmolean
Museum

18

22

20

LONGWALL ST

24

2

Sheldonian Theatre
Bodleian Library

Railway
Station

BROAD ST.

6

13

19

Radcliffe
Camera

7

16

BOTLEY ROAD

NEW ROAD

8

3

17

11

Botanic
Garden

10 HIGH STREET

21

Cartax
Tower

5

14

12

ST CLEMENT'S

River Thames

15

4

ST ALDATES

Christ Church
Meadow

IFFLEY ROAD

COWLEY ROAD

FOLLY BRIDGE

River Cherwell

N

River Thames

AN INTRODUCTION

The purpose of this book is to provide a selection of exploratory and enjoyable walks round Oxford. These walks are almost entirely restricted to the centre of the modern city, for within the centre of Oxford lies the compact confines of the University, and hence most of its interesting and beautiful buildings. Aware however that a visitor with plenty of time may wish to be directed to specific places off the beaten track, I have given a selection of such venues in Chapter Nine, and for those with a car, Chapter Ten is devoted to some of the places worth visiting outside Oxford.

The selection of walks, and hence the places written about, is highly subjective, and reflects more my own taste than it does any expert knowledge of history or architecture. No walk need be undertaken in its entirety, or, of course, in the order in which the walks appear in the book. Indeed, the book has been designed to convey the pleasure Oxford has to offer rather than to act as a manual or, worse still, as yet one more 'definitive' guide. Hence I hope that while visiting a particular college, for instance, the book will provide just sufficient information about its history and contents to enlighten the reader on the spot, and that when he or she repairs to a pub or café for lunch, some of the anecdotes associated with the places visited will provide light — perhaps sometimes even hilarious — amusement. For while bricks and stones and wrought iron and carved wood can achieve a lot, in the end it is only the people who for 700 years have eaten and slept and learned and taught in this place who finally bring it to life.

At the start of each chapter is a list of places to visit arranged in a geographically convenient order; there is also a map of the area covered, so that anyone who wishes to skip a college or an open space may see quite easily how to do so. Some people linger for hours in a cloister, others hasten along, afraid they will miss their flight to Edinburgh or the train to Bath. There are those who will

1

not enter a museum if paid, others who have to be dragged out at closing time. So every walk is voluntary, so to speak, and to try to assist those short of time or for whom Shanks's pony is an alien mode of transport I have listed, in alphabetical order, each venue – again, entirely subjectively – in one of three categories, Highly Recommended, Recommended and Optional.

Also, at the start of each chapter, opening times are listed. You will notice that colleges vary in the facilities they offer to visitors: some are open all day, some only in the afternoon; some will always show off their chapel and Hall, some keep one or other, and sometimes both, permanently locked. Remember too that when undergraduates are not in residence, some colleges close their chapel or Hall when the college is being used for a conference or a summer school, and repairs may account for unexpected closures. Most Halls are closed to visitors while lunch is being served. If the tables are to be laid for a special dinner that, too, may curtail visits. A chapel may be the scene for a wedding or a memorial service; Merton College choir may be making a recording; a television crew may be filming.

It would have been enormously confusing to arrange each walk so as to coincide with opening times, and not everyone sets off first thing in the morning or immediately after lunch. So when planning your own itinerary it is worth checking at the start of the appropriate chapter to make sure you are going to arrive at a particular place when it is open. With a little ingenuity it is perfectly possible to dodge around, using the walks as mapped out here merely as a series of suggestions, improvising upon their layout for yourself.

It will be perfectly apparent that some chapters are longer than others, which does not necessarily mean that in distance covered the walks vary a great deal, merely that within a reasonable walk there are sometimes more, sometimes fewer interesting places to see. But you do not have to see them all. Chapter One, for example, may at first glance appear to contain an unduly crowded itinerary, but not everybody will be drawn to the Town Hall, the Museum of Modern Art or the Civic Information Office; their juxtaposition simply reflects the lie of the land. Chapter Two only contains one college, Chapter Eight, four; but no one has to enter all four colleges unless they wish. They just happen to be conveniently grouped together.

While writing this book I have received courtesy and help from

2

too many college porters to name. I have also received especially valued assistance from Professor Sir Richard Southwood, the Vice-Chancellor; Mr George Bridges; the junior chaplain at Magdalen College, the Reverend Peter Eaton; Mr Edmund Lazarus; the headmaster of Christ Church Cathedral School, Mr Hugh MacDonald; Mrs Margaret Paul, the chaplain of Pembroke College, the Reverend John Platt; Mr Robert Robinson, who supplied an amusing analysis of his novel *Landscape with Dead Dons*; the Principal of Pusey House, the Reverend Philip Ursell; and the Oxford County Hall Archivists.

Unless otherwise stated, all the photographs were taken specially for this book by Tony Hutchings. His enthusiasm for the project and his skills as a photographer made it a privilege as well as a pleasure to work with him.

Michael De-la-Noy
Oxford, 1990

PLACES TO SEE

HIGHLY RECOMMENDED:

Chapter

RECOMMENDED:

Chapter

One	Christ Church Meadow
Five	Exeter College
Five	Jesus College
Five	Lincoln College, especially John Wesley's room
One	Pembroke College, especially the chapel
Six	The Queen's College
Nine	Radcliffe Observatory
Four	St Mary Magdalen
Four	St Michael's Church, specifically the Saxon Tower
Eight	University College, especially the chapel and the Shelley memorial
Three	University Museum
Three	Wadham College, especially the garden

OPTIONAL:

Chapter

Five	All Souls College
Six	Balliol College
One	Bate Collection of Historical Instruments
Nine	Canal Towpath
One	Carfax Tower
Five	Covered Market
One	Folly House
Six	Hertford College
Two	Holywell Cemetery
Two	Holywell Music Room
Three	Keble College
Six	Museum of the History of Science
One	Museum of Modern Art
One	Museum of Oxford
Eight	Oriel College
Nine	Oxford University Press
Nine	Park Town
Three	Parsons Pleasure
Nine	Pitt Rivers Museum (Balfour Building)
Four	Pusey House
Nine	Radcliffe Infirmary

One	St Aldate Church
Nine	St Barnabas & St Paul's
Nine	St Bartholomew's Chapel
Six	St Edmund Hall
Nine	St Sepulchre's Cemetery
One	Town Hall
Three	University Park
Nine	Worcester College

PLACES TO VISIT OUTSIDE OXFORD

PLACES AT WHICH TO EAT

HISTORICALLY SPEAKING

Oxford is a university city, so if you do not care for bicycles or undergraduates you had best stay away. Without the University there is no reason to think that Oxford — said by some to be in the centre of England, but this would perhaps be true if it was situated 120 miles further north — would ever have become anything more than a modest, and probably not very distinguished, market town. No one knows how precisely to date the origins of the University or to account for its location. Myths abound, however. King Alfred was for many years seriously reputed to have been the founder; an even less likely candidate has been someone called King Mempricius, whose other claim to fame was that he was 'surrounded by a large pack of wolves, and being torn and devoured by them, ended his existence in a horrible manner'.

What is known for sure is that the town of Oxford, first mentioned in AD 912, is far older than the University. Edmund Ironside, who reigned briefly in 1016, died, at the age of twenty-seven, in Oxford; so did King Canute's son, Harold I. And charters were granted by Henry I and Henry II. What also seems pretty certain is that Oxford quite simply took its name from a ford in the River Thames where oxen crossed.

The three earliest Oxford colleges, Merton, University College and Balliol, which all still vie for the distinction of being the very first, were not founded until the thirteenth century. Yet Robert Grosseteste, who lived from 1175 to 1253, is credited with being the University's first Chancellor, and as he died a decade before even the three earliest colleges claim to have come into existence his dates give a clue about the nature of the embryonic seat of learning: it consisted originally of halls of residence in which students lived but were not necessarily taught, and it was many of these halls, often connected with religious establishments, which eventually became incorporated colleges.

11

Like many of his contemporaries, Robert Grosseteste was both immensely learned and a firm believer in angels. Matthew Paris, the thirteenth-century monk and historian, described him as 'the corrector of monks, the director of priests, the supporter of scholars, the preacher to the people, the persecutor of the incontinent and the sedulous student of all scripture'. Soon after Grosseteste's appointment, Dominicans, Franciscans, Carmelites and Augustinians established religious houses in the area, and between 1273 and 1477 Dominicans from Provence, Aragon, Rome, Bohemia, Spain, Germany, Poland and Saxony left their homes to settle or study in Oxford.

Throughout Europe it was the Church that kept culture alive during the Dark Ages, supported by a vast wealth which enabled it to build monasteries and abbeys. These served in part as enclosures for learned men, and it is not surprising to find that the earliest Oxford colleges were religious foundations. New College and Magdalen have cloisters reminiscent of cathedral or monastic cloisters; rooms for scholars were ranged round a quadrangle, as they might have been in a religious house; a common refectory was provided, now called a Hall, in which to dine as a community; and invariably each college was supplied with a chapel. Until the Great War, attendance at chapel was compulsory, and in the old pre-Reformation tradition of the clergy, until the middle of the nineteenth century no Fellow (literally someone elected to the fellowship or membership of a college) might marry.

The earliest founders of Oxford's colleges, generally rather earnest and pious men, were very clear about their intentions. Walter de Merton, who endowed Merton College in 1264, decreed, 'There shall be a constant succession of scholars devoted to the study of letters, who shall be bound to employ themselves in the study of Arts or Philosophy, the Canons or Theology'. One member of the 'collegiate body' was to 'have the care of the students in grammar', and there was to be a 'Superior', to be called – in Merton's case – the Warden, 'who must be a man of circumspection in spiritual and temporal affairs'. One person in every chamber, where scholars were resident, 'of more mature age than the others', was to make a report to the Warden 'of their morals and advancement in learning'. The scholars were to eat together, and to 'dress as nearly alike as possible'. As in most monasteries, meals were eaten in silence, while someone read extracts from improving literature. In their chambers, the scholars of Merton were to 'abstain from noise and interruption of their fellows'. And they were to speak only in Latin.

There has been no consistency in terminology adopted by Oxford's colleges. New College, like Merton and Wadham, has a Warden, Trinity and St John's a President, Exeter a Rector, University College a Master, Worcester a Provost. All this, needless to say, is simply a trick to confuse outsiders. Like boys at Eton whose three annual terms are quite illogically referred to as Halfs, undergraduates at Oxford (they intensely dislike being referred to these days as scholars, even those who happen to be on a scholarship) enjoy a private language. They Come Up, Go Down, sit for Greats, Littlego and Moderations, get Gated and Rusticated, Sport their Oakes (which is not quite such a devious occupation as it sounds) and even employ their own version of Screwing.

Because they were founded and endowed by rich clerics and merchants, Oxford's colleges were constructed on a scale far in excess of any domestic buildings other than the country houses of the very prosperous, and inevitably they came to dominate not just the skyline but the entire environs of the town which, until fairly recent times, was quite small. The original medieval city merely ran east from the top of Cornmarket to approximately the end of Holywell Street, south to Deadman's Walk, which forms the southern boundary of Merton College, west to St Ebbe's and north back to St Michael's Street. Within the walls of this minimal space were eventually crammed fifteen colleges. Balliol, Magdalen and St John's were built outside the city walls which, certainly in the case of St John's and Magdalen, explains why they have so much land. Even today the University owns a quarter of the city, and some of the colleges, whose farms and meadowlands have been built upon and now produce an enormous income in rents, are exceedingly rich.

By the fourteenth century there was no question who had gained the ascendancy; the University was lording it over the town, amassing privileges which became the cause of frictions some of which exist to this day. Tales of skirmishes between undergraduates and lads from the town still occasionally enliven the local newspapers, but '17 Held in Booze Battle' turns out to be small beer compared to the riots that broke out in the Middle Ages, and even as recently as 1832.

The most notorious fight commenced on 10 February 1355, when

13

a group of scholars entered the Swyndlestock Tavern at Carfax, on the corner of what is now Queen Street and St Aldate's, 'and there took a quart of wine and threw the said wine in the face of John Croidon, taverner, and then with the said quart pot beat the said John without reason'. It sounds all too familiar, a pointless punch-up that got completely out of hand. Mayhem ensued, the town authorities rang the bells at Carfax, the students retaliated by calling out reinforcements from the tower of the University Church in the High Street, and 'thousands of wild country folk' came 'screaming in, thronged and hooded, carrying a black flag and crying: "Havoc! havoc! smyt fast, give gode knocks!" ' So many 'gode knocks' were given that at the end of a three-day battle sixty-three students lay dead; others, less fortunate perhaps, were said to have been buried in dung-hills. For some perverse reason this frightful event was hailed as a victory for the University, perhaps because until 1825 the mayor – he is now a Lord Mayor – and sixty-three citizens were compelled to go in procession, in penitence, to the University Church, to bow before the Vice-Chancellor and to pay a fine of a penny each.

But brawling was endemic to the Middle Ages. In February 1298, 'when the bailiff was at Carfax carrying his mace, as is due, there came some clerks of the University to fight and disturb the peace, and laid hands on the bailiff and trampled on him and took away his mace; whereupon hue and cry was raised'. The prevalence of 'Stews and Brothel-Houses' apparently led to a good many disturbances. French students, 'whose infamous Lust had engag'd them in their Quarrels', were particularly held to blame, and when things got so bad during the reign of Henry III that 'the foul Disease' was said to have been contracted 'almost in an Epidemical Manner', the Pope sent a cardinal to Oxford 'to reform the Corruptions of the Place'. He stayed at the great abbey in Osney (then spelt Oseney), a few yards south of the present railway station, now the site of a cemetery; it boasted the third largest tower in England, and once had an abbot called Hokenotton.

All went well until a body of scholars called at the abbey to welcome the cardinal, only to be refused admittance by the porter. So they forced their way in, and 'many Blows ensued on both sides'. A poor Irish scholar waiting at the gate for alms had scalding water thrown over him, whereupon a Welshman 'shot the Cook dead through the body, which caused an uproar throughout the House'.

The area to the west of the town is still known as Osney, and the abbey, of which there remains practically no trace, played a major role in the history of Oxford. In 1542 its last abbot, Robert King, became Oxford's first bishop. Its bell, Great Tom, is now hung at Christ Church, and during the Civil War Charles I plundered much of the ruined church to fortify the city.

Divisions between Town and University grew so acute that by the early sixteenth century the students had acquired a kind of diplomatic immunity from civil prosecution and punishment, with the University Chancellor empowered not only to try cases of misdemeanour by his students but to exercise legal authority over the 'townysmen' as well. For example: 'If the officer of the universitie do first arest the brekars of the peace withyn the towne and suburbes of Oxforde, althoo nether parte be of the privilege yett ye correction and punyshment therof shall perteyne onlie to ye chauncellar.'

Further, 'The chauncellar in causis determinable before hym may punyshe obstinate persons and transgressors whether they be of the universite or of the towne'.

The Chancellor was given power to compel 'both scolars and townysmen' to pave the streets 'and kepe them cleyne' (today it costs the city council £600,000 a year just to sweep up the rubbish); and he even had authority to 'banyshe incontinent & viciose women'.

Not every case dealt with by the Chancellor was of a criminal nature. Some involved civil disputes, and for some time he had been in the habit of sorting these out in a more amiable manner than is often the case today. In 1465 it was pronounced that 'Richard Lancaster, canon, and Simon Marshall, on the one side, and John Marshall, schoolmaster, and his wife on the other, shall not abuse or make faces at each other, shall forgive each other for all past offences, and at their joint charges provide an entertainment in St Mary's College, the one party to provide a goose and measure of wine, the other bread and beer'.

Indeed, by this time Oxford had acquired two reputations which may have fluctuated since but neither of which it has ever wholly lost: for commonsense and generous hospitality. Erasmus, the fastidious Dutch humanist much given to investigating scholarly institutions (he even found Windsor Castle more like a house of the Muses than a court), arrived in Oxford in 1499, where he stayed

15

for three months, reporting afterwards that he had met with 'so much kindness, and so much learning, not hacknied and trivial, but deep, accurate, ancient'. And as for his experience of a college dinner: 'Nothing was wanting. A choice time, a choice place, no arrangements neglected. The good cheer would have satisfied Epicurus; the table-talk would have pleased Pythagorus. The guests might have peopled an Academy, and not mearly made up a dinner party.'

Although by the early sixteenth century Oxford University was not yet large in terms of the numbers of colleges it was eventually to contain (in 1945 there were still only twenty-five colleges; by 1990 there were thirty-five), its influence after barely 300 years was so considerable that in 1530 Henry VIII, desperate to justify his desire for a divorce from Katherine of Aragon, sought the opinion of the University, who incurred the royal wrath by declining, at first, to pronounce in his favour. And the establishment of the Church of England, resulting in Henry's break with Rome, was only the first of a succession of religious disputes, some tragic, some creative, in which Oxford was to become involved.

In cooperation with Cambridge theologians, Oxford declared Nicholas Ridley, Bishop of London, and Hugh Latimer, Bishop of Worcester, heretics when they declined to forsake the Protestant cause on the accession of Henry's Catholic daughter, Mary I, and on 16 October 1555 both bishops were burnt at the stake in the middle of what is now Broad Street. The Archbishop of Canterbury, Thomas Cranmer, was condemned to death too, but while awaiting the Pope's permission to be burnt he recanted his alleged heresies. Much good did it do him. He was submitted to a degrading sermon in the University Church, preached by Henry Cole, Warden of New College, who promised nonetheless that after his death a Requiem Mass would be said for him 'in all the churches of Oxford'.

Cranmer was seen openly to weep, and then he stunned the assembly by recanting his recantations, declaring the Pope to be 'Christ's enemy and Antichrist'. He too was taken to Broad Street to be burnt (cars in their thousands daily drive over the very spot), stretching into the flames his right hand, which he said had written contrary to his heart. It was 300 years before a memorial, designed by Gilbert Scott, was erected to the memory of the bishops who died in Oxford for their faith, and then it was placed not in Broad

Street but in St Giles', perhaps because there it would attract the attention of so many visitors as they arrived from both the Banbury and the Woodstock Roads. The cost of these barbaric and blasphemous executions – the wood for the fire and the labour charges – came to eleven shillings and fourpence.

Changes in the religious allegiance of sovereigns began to cause a certain amount of schizophrenia in Oxford. Some fourteen years after Mary's death, a contingent from Lincoln College rang the bells at All Hallows, which brought the mayor round to accuse them of popery. Oh no, they explained, they were only practising. When that failed to satisfy the mayor, a quick-witted member of the college 'answered that they runge not for Queen Marie's dirige but for joy of Queen Elizabeth's coronation'.

If religious disputes were not the cause of distress then the plague was, striking down scholars, teachers and townsfolk alike. It was said that in 1577, 300 people died in three days alone. Some, 'occasioned by the rage of their disease and pain, would beat their keepers and nurses, and drive them from their presence. Others like mad men would run about the streets, markets, lanes, and other places. Some again would leap headlong into deep waters.' The physicians fled, 'not to avoid trouble, which more and more came upon them, but to save themselves and theirs'. No college escaped loss, either by death or through 'Doctors and Heads of Houses' escaping to the country for safety, many colleges retaining property outside Oxford for that very purpose; and in order to apportion blame it was widely rumoured that the plague had been invented by Roman Catholics, 'who used the Art Magick in the design'.

Another future Archbishop of Canterbury who was destined to be executed, William Laud, became Chancellor of the University in 1630 (he was formerly President of St John's), and Oxford had good cause to be grateful to him. He untangled and redefined the jumble of rules and regulations that had accumulated by the early years of the seventeenth century, and looking in detail at everything from Personal Appearance to Divine Truth he drew up a new, coherent code of conduct by which the University was to be governed until 1864. He said he hoped that God would so bless his work 'that it may much improve the honour and good government of that place, a thing very necessary in this life both for Church and Commonwealth'.

17

A student under the age of eighteen who entered any inn or eating-house where tobacco or drink was sold was to be flogged in public. 'Scholars and graduates of all conditions' were to keep away from houses 'where women of ill or suspected fame or harlots are kept or harboured'. And in future no student was to carry 'either offensive or defensive arms, such as swords, poignards, daggers (commonly called stilettos), dirks, bows and arrows, guns, or warlike weapons or implements', unless they were going on a journey. But they were still permitted to carry bows and arrows 'for fair amusement's sake'.

One momentous historical event was to cause a serious rift between the town of Oxford and the University: during the Civil War the town took the side of Parliament, the University that of the King, and it was at Christ Church in Oxford, where Charles I had stayed in 1635, entertained with a comedy performed in the Hall, that he set up his court in 1642, following the indecisive Battle of Edgehill and his failure to take London. For four years, while not campaigning, he lived at the deanery, and Christ Church has acted as a magnet for aristocrats and wealth ever since. Even before the fighting had begun, the King was writing to the Vice-Chancellor asking for money, revenues from the royal mint having been cut off, and Convocation provided £860. Hearing of this 'wicked purpose and intention', Parliament warned individual colleges not to send any more, but they disobeyed, and thanks to the Civil War the treasures of many colleges were sadly depleted. They gave the King most of their silver plate, which was melted down for coinage and minted in New Inn Hall Street; examples can be seen in the Museum of Oxford. Magdalen College contributed the largest weight of silver. Then came All Souls, Queen's, Trinity, Christ Church and Brasenose, at that time referred to, even in official documents, as Brazen Nose. Jesus, Oriel, Lincoln, University College, Balliol and Merton, where the Queen, Henrietta-Maria, was to take up residence in 1643 on her return from Holland, all chipped in.

The King's headstrong but gallant nephew, Prince Rupert, moved in to St John's College, where in 1636 he had nominally been entered as an undergraduate. The Principal Secretary of State, Sir Edward Nicholas, and his family and staff took over Pembroke, so as to be as near as possible to the King, who had to put up with the Great Quadrangle at Christ Church − Tom Quad − being used to pen cattle. All Souls became an arsenal. Yet amid all the billeting of

18

troops and evidence of warlike preparations, Oxford became as much a reflection of Windsor Castle or Greenwich Palace as a military barracks. Charles appointed a Master of Revels; plays and musical entertainments were staged; discreet love affairs were conducted in the college gardens; and duels were fought almost every day. Prince Rupert had to separate two demented contestants with a pole-axe.

The invasion of the colleges by ladies of the court met, needless to say, with opposition. 'Madam,' Dr Ralph Kettell, the President of Trinity, said to Lady Thynne, 'your husband and father I bred up here, and I knew your grandfather; I know you to be a gentlewoman, I will not say you are a whore; but gett you gonne for a very woman'.

When Cromwell's forces won the war it was a bitter blow to the Royalists of Oxford, and scores of Fellows were ousted from their colleges. Following a Parliamentary Visitation, Thomas Goodwin, a Puritan of unyielding ilk, was installed as President of Magdalen. He seems to have had little concern for the academic progress of the students in his charge. He proceeded to examine one scholar with 'a religious Horror in his Countenance. The young man trembled', and according to an article published sixty years later, recalling the dismal days of the Commonwealth (in 1647 Parliament had even abolished Christmas), 'his Fears increased when, instead of being asked what Progress he had made in Learning, he was examined how he abounded in Grace. His Latin and Greek stood him in little stead; he was to give an account only of the State of his Soul, whether he was of the Number of the Elect'. It seems 'the whole examination was summed up with one short question, namely, whether he was prepared for death'.

In 1681, twenty-one years after the Restoration, Charles II, so the diarist Anthony Wood tells us, paid a visit to Oxford, when 'All the way the king passed were such shoutings, acclamations, and ringing of bells, made by loyall hearts and smart lads of the layetie of Oxon, the aire was so much pierced that the clouds seemed to divide'. (Oxon, sometimes today used as an abbreviation for Oxfordshire, was in common usage for Oxford itself, and still constitutes the signature of the diocesan bishop.) Along with so many in England, Oxonians had given themselves up to pleasure and idleness as a restorative after the dreary years of Puritanism. 'Why,' asked Anthony Wood, 'doth solid and serious learning decline, and few or none follow it now in the university? Answer: because of coffee-houses, where they spend all their time; and in entertainments at their chambers, where their studies are become places for victulars, also great drinking at taverns and ale-houses.' In 1650, Wood noted, 'Jacob a Jew opened a coffey house at the Angel in the parish of St Peter in the East'. In 1654 'Cirques Jobson, a Jew and Jacobite . . . sold coffey in oxon in an house between Edmund Hall and Queen Coll corner'. And by the following year 'Arthur Tillyard, apothecary and great royalist, sold coffey publikly in his house against All Soules Coll'.

Wood had been told – but can it have been true? – that there were 370 taverns in the town, and it may have been their prevalence that led to disgraceful conduct amongst the seventeenth-century aristocracy. On 6 June 1681 Anthony Wood recorded an 'outrage committed on the old Lady Lovelace at Hunt's dore against the Crowne Tavern between 8 and 9 at night by Mr Leopold Finch son of the earl of Winchelsey [the Hon. Leopold Finch was one of fourteen children of the 3rd Earl of Winchilsea], lord Bulkley, two gentlemen commoners (Lutterel was one), and four students – all of Ch.Ch. [Christ Church]. They pluck'd her out of her coach, and called her ''old protesting bitch''; broke windowes that night, and done many misdemenaours . . . The townsmen and other envious people report that they should say that they called her ''*Protestant* bitch''. The bishop extremely troubled at it. They had been drinking at the Crowne Tavern.' (A Gentleman Commoner, a term no longer in use, was a student generally thought – and most probably by himself – to have been of aristocratic birth.)

It only required Charles II, good humoured, pragmatic and civilised as he was, to die without producing any legitimate children for confusion and uncertainty to break out again as soon as his incompetent Roman Catholic brother succeeded as James II. James decided it was high time Magdalen had a Catholic President, but quite apart from the fact that the college statutes forbad it the Fellows decided it was a bad idea in principle, and elected their own candidate, John Hough. 'You have always been a stubborn and turbulent college,' the King told them, having summoned them to meet him at Christ Church. 'Repair to your chapel and elect the Bishop of Oxford or else you must expect to feel the weight of my hand.'

They declined to elect the Bishop, Samuel Parker, so James faced them with a Royal Commission, escorted to Oxford by three troop of horse. The Commission ordered John Hough to leave the college, and then the Bishop of Chester, a member of the Commission, complained that 'when we came into the chapel there was no table, when we went into the Hall, no carpet'. He even had to endure a scholar in a bookshop cocking a snook at him. But the Bishop of Chester and his co-religionists won, the Fellows agreed at last to accept the Bishop of Oxford as their President, and the Fellows in their turn were sneered at, for cowardice. In fact, like so many of James II's undertakings, affairs were rapidly turning into a charade. Not content with his ever-increasing loss of popularity, he demanded that the Fellows should make amends by 'acknowledging their contempt for his Sacred majesty in Person, imploring his majesty's Pardon, and laying themselves at his Feet'.

At this the Fellows finally stuck their own heels in. In some mysterious manner the key to the President's Lodgings vanished, and when the Commissioners ordered that the house should be broken into so that the Bishop of Oxford could take up residence, the locksmith who was summoned to do the job ran away. In the end the Commissioners themselves had to break down the door. Twenty-five Fellows were expelled, but within a year the King had more or less come to his senses and all the Fellows were reinstated. So too was John Hough, but not before the King's unhappy nominee, the Bishop of Oxford, had left the President's Lodgings as compliantly as he had entered – in his coffin.

Hough did rather well, becoming successively Bishop of Oxford, Lichfield and Worcester, and there was a nice sequel to James's embarrassing skirmish with Magdalen College when in 1814 the Prince Regent, later George IV, drove into Oxford, and inquired of the politician and satirist John Croker, 'Is that Magdalen Tower?'

'Yes, Your Royal Highness,' Croker replied, 'that's the tower against which James II broke his head.'

Not only did Oxford witness its share of religious controversy, it gave birth to new religious movements destined to alter the whole complexion of Christian worship for millions of people. The first of these was Methodism. John Wesley, one of its founders, matriculated in 1720 and was a Fellow of Lincoln College from 1726 to 1751. In 1729, at a period when many Anglican parsons were busy building large rectories and hunting to hounds, he and a few

21

friends, together with his brother Charles, began to spend three or four evenings a week together. They read the classics and theology, paid visits to prisoners held in the Norman castle (only a fragment of the castle stands today, ironically to the east of Paradise Street, the original 'paradise' being the garden belonging to the Grey Friars, who now have a house in St Giles'), and began to observe the fasts of the Church, 'the general neglect of which we can by no means apprehend to be a lawful excuse for neglecting them', as Wesley himself explained. It was a damning indication of the laxity into which even formal Anglican observance had fallen that by performing such unexceptional activities as reading, fasting and doing good works the Wesleys and their friends should have been dubbed members of the Holy Club. But by 1768 Methodism was so firmly established as a dissenting Church that six Methodists at St Edmund Hall – James Matthews, Thomas Jones, Joseph Shipman, Erasmus Middleton, Benjamin Kay and Thomas Grove – were hauled before the Vice-Chancellor accused of not believing in the Thirty-Nine Articles of the Church of England, assent to which was compulsory at Oxford at this time, and all were expelled.

Samuel Johnson, who had studied at Pembroke, was beside himself with glee. He thought the punishment 'extremely just and proper. What have they to do at a university who are not willing to be taught,' he demanded of James Boswell, 'but will presume to teach? Where is religion to be learnt, but at a university? Sir, they were examined and found to be mighty ignorant fellows.'

'But was it not hard, Sir, to expel them,' replied Boswell. 'For I am told they were good beings.'

'I believe they might be good beings,' was Johnson's typically unassailable riposte, 'but they were not fit to be in the University of Oxford. A cow is a very good animal in a field, but we turn her out of a garden.'

The method of examining students at Oxford in Johnson's time, whether in matters pertaining to the Thirty-Nine Articles or Latin or Greek, was always conducted orally. There were no written examinations either for entry to the University or for a degree, and many farcical oral examinations took place. Lord Eldon, whose name was John Scott before he became Lord Chancellor, recalled that in 1770 his examination in Hebrew and History consisted of the following dialogue:

22

Examiner: What is the Hebrew for the place of a skull?
Scott: Golgotha.
Examiner: Who founded University College?
Scott (wisely sticking to the myth): King Alfred.
Examiner: Very well, sir, you are competent for your degree.

The great historian Edward Gibbon painted a lackadaisical picture of teaching in eighteenth-century Oxford in his *Memoirs*, published in 1792. In 1752, when he was still only fourteen (in the Middle Ages boys often went to university younger than that; in 1667 John Evelyn sent his son to Trinity at the age of twelve, and in 1760 Jeremy Bentham, too, was only twelve when he went up to Queen's), Gibbon matriculated at Magdalen College, where he remained for fourteen months. Those fourteen months, he said, were to prove 'the most idle and unprofitable of my whole life'. He described the Fellows of Magdalen in his time as 'decent, easy men, who supinely enjoyed the gifts of the founder; their days were filled by a series of uniform employments; the chapel and the hall, the coffee house and the common room, till they retired, weary and well satisfied, to a long slumber'.

Gibbon's account of affairs is born out by James Harris, later Earl of Malmesbury, who was an undergraduate from 1763 to 1765. 'The two years of my life I look back to as most unprofitably spent were those I passed at Merton,' he wrote in a letter in 1800. 'The discipline of the University happened at this particular moment to be so lax that a Gentleman Commoner was under no restraint, and never called upon to attend either lectures, or chapel, or hall. My tutor, an excellent and worthy man, according to the practice of all tutors at that moment gave himself no concern about his pupils. I never saw him but during a fortnight, when I took it into my head to be taught trigonometry.'

The Bishop of Salisbury, Gilbert Burnet, had been lamenting that the universities at the turn of the century, especially Oxford, had been 'unhappily successful in corrupting the principles of those who were sent to be bred in them', a view endorsed by Daniel Defoe, who wrote in 1728 that young men were sent to university 'not to study, but to drink; not for furniture for the head, but a feather for the cap, merely to say they have been at Oxford or Cambridge, as if the air of these places inspired knowledge without application'.

It was alleged by John Burgeon, Dean of Chichester, that 'the undergraduates rose early, but spent their days in idleness. Practically, the colleges were without discipline. Tutors gave no lectures. It is difficult to divine how a studiously-disposed youth was to learn anything.'

But these were fairly wild generalisations. Colleges have always been a law unto themselves, in standards of education as in so much else, and differences of opinion and experience abound. John Wesley, from whom, it is true, we would expect an exceptional dedication to duty, remained permanently in residence with his pupils at Lincoln. 'I should have thought myself little better than a highwayman if I had not teached them every day in the year but Sundays', he explained. Reporting progress to his former headmaster, one young student, Benjamin Marshall, claimed he was up each day before dawn, had studied Tograeus by nine o'clock and called upon his Philosophy tutor by ten. After lunch he buried his head in the Koran, and at four o'clock would be hard at work on Aristotle's *Rhetoric*. After dinner he read Horace. His day, he said, ended with prayers at nine, when he would 'return thanks for such success as has been secured'.

If this account is true, it only goes to show that some scholars go to Oxford to work, even if others are there to play. Some, of course, do both.

Among the welcome diversions from study in eighteenth-century Oxford was a visit paid to the city in 1786 by George III. Fortunately Fanny Burney, that wry chronicler of Farmer George's dreary court, was on hand to record the event, for she was Assistant Keeper of the Wardrobe to Queen Charlotte.

'The Vice-chancellor and professors begged for the honour of kissing the King's hand,' she wrote in her diary. 'The sight, at times, was very ridiculous. Some of the worthy collegiates, unused to such ceremonies, and unaccustomed to such a presence, the moment they had kissed the king's hand, turned their backs to him, and walked away as in any common room; others, attempting to do better, did still worse, by tottering and stumbling, and falling foul of those behind them; some, ashamed to kneel, took the King's hand straight up to their mouths; others, equally off guard, plumped down on both knees, and could hardly get up again; and many, in their confusion, fairly arose by pulling His Majesty's hand to raise them.'

Written examinations for an Honours degree were introduced at

24

the beginning of the nineteenth century, a move that was to herald the high earnestness of mid-Victorian Oxford, when dons in general (a don, from the Latin *dominus*, is the generic term for any university teacher), and the holders of professorial chairs in particular, were themselves decked out with academic honours. Serious research in a multitude of disciplines began to take place, tutors not only supervised undergraduates' work but went for long and often silent walks with them, and a certain rigidity in social life, against which the Gay Young Things of the 1920s were to rebel so noisily, set in.

But Oxford, like many a microcosm of society, is working hard one minute, slacking the next, drunk one night, sober again in the morning. Already it seems that by the first quarter of the nineteenth century much of the excessively riotous conduct brought on by alcohol that we identify with eighteenth-century Oxford was, for the time being at any rate, in decline. In 1825 a book called *Hints for Oxford* appeared. 'We do not consider it necessary to remonstrate with our readers on the subject of hard drinking,' it declared, 'as we are aware that this vice has of itself very much decayed in the University. The change is fortunate in many respects, and will tend greatly to put a stop to riot and disorder.'

Yet rioting was far from dead. The Reform Bill of 1832 led to furious fights, the University Proctors – officers elected since medieval times in rotation from the colleges, with certain disciplinary powers – being chased up Cornmarket by gangs from the town, and into Broad Street. When the Master of Balliol, told that a member of Oriel College had been killed, put on his gown, opened the front door of his Lodgings, and began, 'My deluded friends . . .' a stone 'was pitched into the middle of his body and he fell back into the arms of his servants, crying out, "Close the door!" '

A quarter of a century later things had quietened down considerably. Under the patrician influence of Prince Albert, Royal Commissions began to flourish, and in 1850 a Royal Commission was appointed by the House of Commons, chaired by the Bishop of Norwich, to investigate the University of Oxford. Visitors to the various colleges, among them the Bishop of Exeter, saw this as an infringement of their own responsibilities, and five did not even trouble to acknowledge the Commission's inquiries. James Garbett, Professor of Poetry, spoke for many who were complacently satisfied with Oxford's tradition of *laissez-faire* scholarship when he wrote, 'I cannot aid in an object which I condemn, and an inquisition against which I protest . . . We crave peace and you give us chaos.' The Keeper of the Archives, P. B. Duncan, sent what the Commissioners must have found a particularly infuriating response, dressed up as it was in such sweet reasonableness. 'There is nothing in which I should feel more pride and delight in doing than in giving any useful information for the improvement of my beloved University, were it in my power to suggest anything worthy of your attention for its advantage.'

Despite all the obstructions placed in its way, the Royal Commission did produce a report, which led in 1854 to an Act of Parliament which did much to enhance the standards of study by welding the autonomous collection of individual colleges more into a harmonious body, and after more than 200 years the 1636 Statutes of Archbishop Laud were laid to rest. Two innovations which resulted were permission for Fellows to marry and, far more important, abolition of the University Test, which had formerly obliged everyone at Oxford to belong to the Church of England. A decade later the Church of England itself attempted to rationalise its finances by pooling the resources of cathedrals and parishes, some of which were enormously well endowed, some in great poverty, but what the Commission failed to advise was a similar pooling of financial resources for the University, so that today the University as a whole is continually appealing for funds, largely because certain colleges, like St Peter's and Worcester, are relatively poor, while others hardly know how to spend all their income.

A sardonic account of the way in which an undergraduate's affirmation of the Thirty-Nine Articles used to be put to the test was penned in 1834 by G. V. Cox in *Black Gowns and Red Coats*. 'The Dean of the College invites the young man to breakfast – a couple of articles are read – then succeeds a *wadding* of cold meat – an interlayer of boiled eggs (if indeed the Dean is to be munificent) divides the third and fourth; the doctrine of Predestination requires to be swallowed down with a cup of tea, and the Dean reads the newspaper, while the candidate reads the remainder. Is this an indecent farce, or is it not? If it is, why is it not discontinued? Answer: because it is an old custom.'

The great reformation that swept over Victorian Oxford was both liberal in intent, widening the facilities of the University as never before, and also somewhat stifling in practice, for education is not

26

just about stuffing one's head with facts; being alive to experience often proves as useful a start in life as any, and many of the new breed of Oxford dons were found, by some, to be altogether too learned and earnest. Something of that valuable balance between academic study and profitable idleness was upset. Six years before the dawn of the twentieth century an anonymous poem appeared in the *Oxford Magazine*.

> The days of port and peace are gone,
> I am a modern Oxford Don;
> No more I haunt the candle's gloom,
> The cosy chairs of Common-Room;
> No more the senior man discourses,
> Of wine, of women fair and horses,
> Tells with cracked voice and mellow pride
> Old stories of the covert-side,
> Or with sad sigh dim forms recalls
> Whose grey slabs line the cloister walls.
> Student and hunter both are fled,
> All their age is 'lapped in lead.'

In the nineteenth century Oxford was struggling to come to terms with modern scientific investigation, and the emotional and intellectual controversy caused by an inevitable clash with conventional religious wisdom was volcanic. The first Professor of Geology (the chair had been endowed in 1819 by the Prince Regent), Canon William Buckland, found himself at the heart of the storm, being both a cleric and a scientist, and he gave rise to two brilliant lines of parody:

> Some doubts were once expressed about the Flood,
> Buckland arose, and all was clear – as mud.

Buckland was a great believer in practical experience, and was said to have eaten his way through the entire animal kingdom, proclaiming the mole the nastiest thing he had ever tasted until he tried a blue-bottle. No doubt with his tongue in his cheek, John Ruskin said he had always regretted that a prior engagement had not made it possible for him to accept an invitation to breakfast with Professor Buckland, for he had quite expected to be served some delicacy such as mice on toast. The most amazing story recounted about Buckland concerned the day he paid a visit to Nuneham Courtenay, the riverside family home of Edward Harcourt, Archbishop of York, a few miles south of Oxford, when he was shown the heart of one of the kings of France, preserved in a silver casket. 'I have eaten some strange things,' said the Professor, 'but never the heart of a king', and loath to let the opportunity slip by, popped it into his mouth and swallowed it. A print of Professor Buckland lecturing to an attentive audience can be seen in the Museum of the History of Science in Broad Street.

It was a great period for Oxford eccentrics. The Professor of Ecclesiastical History, Robert Hussey, was told his toe had to be amputated. 'Very well, cut it off,' he said, 'but be good enough not to disturb me by talking while you do it, as I have a lecture to prepare.' Robert Nettleship of Balliol College once got as far as admitting to a positive response when he said, 'Not that it may not be. Possibly it is.' Benjamin Jowett of Balliol, himself ordained, told the redoubtable Margot Asquith, 'You must believe in God, my child, despite what the clergymen tell you'.

In 1887, writing in the *National Review*, someone called T. E. Kebbel reflected on the loss of sartorial rectitude. 'Thirty years ago,' he recalled, 'no man was ever seen in the streets of Oxford after lunch without being dressed as he would have been in Pall Mall. Tail coats were sometimes worn in these days in the morning, and the fast men still wore cutaways. But the correct thing for the quiet gentlemanly undergraduate was black frock-coat, and tall hat, with the neatest of gloves and boots, and in this costume he went out for his country walk.'

Garb of this nature was contemporary with the equally great period for Oxford clerics, a period that was to witness the development, some 100 years after Oxford had given birth to Methodism, of what became known as the Oxford Movement (not to be confused with Frank Buckman's quasi-religious twentieth-century Oxford Group); this was the rediscovery, by those on the high wing of the Church of England, of the paramountcy of the sacraments. The three instigators of the Oxford Movement were Edward Pusey, so precociously brilliant that he was appointed Regius Professor of Hebrew at the age of twenty-eight, a post he held for fifty-two years (he was also later a canon of Christ Church Cathedral); John Keble, a poet (of sorts) as well as a priest, in whose memory and name Oxford acquired one of its most architecturally distinctive, and controversial, colleges; and John Newman, a complex Christian leader, vicar from 1828 to 1843 of the University Church of St Mary the Virgin. In 1845, to the shock and grief of many of his Anglican friends, Newman toppled into the arms of Rome, and later became a cardinal.

The Oxford Movement was also known as the Tractarian Movement, for it preached its messages not only through sermons – Newman's services were packed out – but through written tracts, demanding freedom for the Church of England from State interference, and suggesting there was nothing incompatible between belief in Roman Catholic doctrine and subscribing to the Thirty-Nine Articles. Much that resulted from the Oxford Movement remains permanent, not just in Oxford but throughout the world-wide Anglican Communion: emphasis upon the Eucharist as the central service on Sunday, the use of vestments (until 1964 officially illegal: the Church of St Thomas in Becket Street, Oxford, which possesses, on its twelfth-century south side, the oldest door in the city, was the first parish church to reintroduce Mass vestments since the Reformation), and the return of sacramental confession.

In addition to Keble College, Oxford's personal inheritance from the Oxford Movement includes Pusey House in St Giles' and the first post-Reformation monastic community to be founded in England, the Cowley Fathers. One unhappy result of the Oxford Movement was to create in-fighting between Anglicans, and Evangelical colleges began nervously to guard their undergraduates from indoctrination by popish practices, for Newman's conversion to Rome was regarded, by his friends, as a catastrophic and inexplicable desertion, and by his opponents as clear proof that an excess of religious enthusiasm would be bound to lead to victory for the Scarlet Woman.

On 15 June 1841 the youthful and recently wed Prince Albert went to Oxford to receive an address at Commemoration, but although Queen Victoria could scarcely bear to let him out of her sight, she was compelled to spend the day alone, to her 'great grief', in the beautiful surroundings of Nuneham Courtenay. The Prince was 'enthusiastically received,' the Queen told her uncle, King Leopold of the Belgians, 'but the students . . . had the bad taste to show their party feeling in groans and hisses when the name of a Whig was mentioned, which they ought not to have done in my husband's presence'.

Eighteen years later, when Victoria's lacklustre heir, the Prince of Wales, was at Christ Church, she wrote to her eldest daughter to say that 'Dear Papa . . . has gone to Oxford to see how Bertie is going on in that old monkish place, which I have a horror of'. Nothing could better illustrate the masculine nature of Oxford than Victoria's exclusion from the junketings in 1841. Not only were the colleges inhabited entirely by male undergraduates, until dons were permitted to marry few women graced the Fellows' Gardens or Masters' Lodgings. It is true that in the wake of the Reformation the first Dean of Christ Church, Richard Cox, and one of the canons had married, but this was regarded as deeply shocking at the time.

'How often did I wish myself transported to the blissful region of the common room fire-side! Delightful retreat, where never female shewed her head since the days of the founder!' Vicesimus Knox had sighed contentedly in 1782. 'A woman is a creature that cannot reason and pokes the fire from the top' was the view expressed by Richard Whately of Oriel College, and it may be no coincidence that Oriel was the last college in Oxford to admit women. 'Inferior to us God made you and our inferiors to the end of time you will remain', women in the congregation at New College chapel were reliably informed during a sermon in 1884, sentiments that are by no means exceptional among some clergy even today.

But half-way through Queen Victoria's reign women started with success to invade — as most men saw it — what had been an exclusively male preserve. Someone by the name of A. M. A. Rogers was offered an Exhibition at Worcester College in 1873, but it was swiftly withdrawn when it was discovered that the initials stood for Annie Mary Anne. Five years later the first women's college, Lady Margaret Hall, was founded by Elizabeth Wordsworth, a great-niece of the poet. It has since opened its doors to men. A year later, in 1879, St Anne's College, also now open to both men and women, was established, and in 1886 the formidable Charlotte Moberley — she who, together with her colleague Eleanor Jourdain, claimed to have encountered Marie Antoinette on a visit to Versailles — became the first Principal of St Hugh's also no longer single sex. St Hilda's followed six years later. Perhaps Oxford's most famous women's college is Somerville, founded in 1879 with twelve students as an alternative to Lady Margaret Hall, for Lady Margaret Hall, which began life with nine students, insisted that entrants should be Anglicans. One of Somerville's graduates was Dorothy Sayers, who made Somerville the setting for her novel *Gaudy Night*. Fellow novelists nurtured by Somerville include Rose Macaulay, Hilda Reid, Winifred Holtby, Margaret Kennedy and Vera Brittain. Three distinguished social reformers, Margaret Fry, Eleanor Rathbone and Barbara Ward, were educated there; so was Iris Murdoch and Britain's first woman Prime Minister, Margaret Thatcher, described by her former Principal, Dame Janet Vaughan, as 'a perfectly good second-class chemist'. Mrs Thatcher's most devastating loss of face occurred however in 1985, when Convocation refused to award her an honorary doctorate, one retired don from Lady Margaret Hall having privately admitted to dusting the moths from her gown and casting a vote against the Prime Minister although she had no right to vote at all.

Somerville's most remarkable old girl is surely Dorothy Hodgkin, another chemist who in 1964 won the Nobel Prize for Chemistry, and a year later was admitted by the Queen to the Order of Merit, only the second woman admitted to the Order in sixty-three years. The scholar of French literature, Enid Starkie of Somerville, became perhaps the best-known female don in Oxford.

Women were now, rather grudgingly, allowed to sit most University examinations, but they were still denied a degree and had to make do with a diploma. Lord Curzon, when he was Chancellor, thought that women should be eligible for degrees, but hastened to explain this did not mean that they should be allowed a vote. Dr Pusey said the establishment of women's halls had been 'one of the greatest misfortunes that has happened even in our own time in Oxford' and, as in almost every sphere of life except that of child-bearing, women had − at Oxford − to fight their way step by step. Four years after degrees for women had become a *fait accompli*, in 1924 a list of rules for women was drawn up. They might not enter men's rooms, either in college or in lodgings, without permission from their Principal, nor indeed without a chaperone. They could not even go out in the evening without permission, and had to report on their return. No mixed party was to be held in a café except between the hours of 2.00 p.m. and 5.30 p.m., and only then with permission and providing at least two women attended.

One of the differences between men and women at Oxford soon became all too apparent; while many of the rich young men from Eton and Winchester were there to drink and hunt, the women were there for one purpose only: to pursue an academic career. The Rector of Exeter College, Dr Lewis Farnell, who became Vice-Chancellor, wrote in 1939, with evident distaste both for women and their desire to take sensible advantage of their time at Oxford, 'though their numbers are so small, a casual visitor to Oxford might well gain the impression that the women form an actual majority. They are perpetually awheel. They bicycle in droves from lecture to lecture, capped and gowned, handle-bars laden with note-books, and note-books crammed with notes. Relatively few men go to lectures, the usefulness of which was superseded some while ago by the invention of the printing press.' A printing press had been in existence since 1476.

Farnell had the gall, considering the conduct down the centuries of so many rakes at Oxford, to complain that few women took the least pains 'to be attractive or even mature', and one of their many crimes, it seems, was a failure to run up tailors' bills in the High Street. He did not care for their preference for cocoa over claret, and although the chances of his having deigned to enter a women's college were slim, he pretended to know that in Hall they dined on 'warm cutlets and gravy off cold plates at a long table decked with daffodils'.

It is true that women's colleges did encourage a certain amount of bluestocking earnestness, and not being ancient foundations, their architecture and furnishings often created rather an austere atmosphere. Viscountess Rhondda, whom no one could accuse of anti-liberalism (she had founded the literary and political weekly *Time & Tide*), found that Somerville smelt frowsty. 'I disliked,' she wrote in 1933, 'the ugliness of most of the public rooms, and I disliked the glass and the crockery and the way in which the tables were set. I disliked the food, and more still, the way it was served.' She disapproved as well of the dowdiness of the dons, 'and more still that of the other girls'.

But the men had had a head-start when it came to creating their own ambience, which may have been enough to cause over-reaction towards studied drabness on the part of women. J. G. Sinclair's 'essentials for "success" in Oxford' listed in 1931 '(at least) one pair of plus fours; a repertoire of pornographic stories; some skill, legendary or otherwise, at golf; a Morris car; a sneer on your face; and an exhaustless capacity for suppurating self-conceit'.

William Morris, later Lord Nuffield, had assembled the first Morris motorcar in 1913; these were later manufactured outside Oxford at Cowley, and in 1937 Nuffield went on to found a college. Although ineffably boring, Lord Nuffield brought much-needed employment to Oxford, enticing many potential scouts, as certain of the college servants were called, into his factory as a result. He earned an immaculate and well-deserved snub after dining at the University one night. Handed his hat on leaving he inquired of a college servant, 'How do you know it's mine?'

'I don't, my Lord,' the scout replied, 'but it's the one you gave me.'

Scouts in Oxford colleges should not be confused with boys who go camping; almost extinct now as a specific breed (many of their domestic duties have been taken over by women), they were college servants who made the undergraduates' beds, cleaned their rooms, laid and re-laid coal fires, sometimes accepted bribes for not reporting misconduct, and generally conducted themselves like a gentleman's gentleman or a valet. Until the Second World War virtually demolished the concept of domestic service, even the smallest colleges could muster an impressive number of servants; in 1912 Hertford had thirty-two. But between the wars the members of a wealthy college like Magdalen were looked after by as many as fifty servants, including half a dozen chefs, and this at a time when the numbers of undergraduates in any college was far fewer than today.

Scouts have not always enjoyed a good press. In a book called *Almae Matres* it was claimed that they encouraged their undergraduates in 'extravagant festivities', pilfered sugar, tea, candles, coal and wine, and acted as 'pimp, pander and hypocrite'. But something of the chores undertaken by conscientious scouts may be judged when one realises it was not until 1928 that Corpus Christi provided running water for the undergraduates on their staircases. Yet, despite the long hours and hard work, many scouts remained in service all their lives, making sure that employment was found for their sons too. Richard Cadman was a scout at Trinity for fifty years. In 1836 Charles Patey went to work at Merton when he was seven years old (Patey's Quad is named after his father, who worked there before him). In 1869 Charles became butler, and he died in harness in 1916 after serving the college for seventy-eight years.

Scouts, as servants tend to be, were on the whole rather reactionary. When Edward Smith retired from Wadham College in 1935 (undergraduates he had looked after included Lord Birkenhead and Sir John Simon) he remarked, 'The place has never been the same since we have had women and coffee shops.' The coffee shops of seventeenth-century Oxford had suddenly resurrected themselves after the Great War. 'Our cafés began to do a roaring trade between 11 and 12 in the morning,' Lewis Farnell groaned in *An Oxonian Looks Back*, 'undergraduates of both sexes sitting there together indulging themselves with pleasant conversation and unnecessary and unmanly food.' What constituted unmanly food he failed to explain.

The Second World War may have ended the availability of cheap and plentiful labour but it was really the First World War that divides the Oxford of the past from that of the present. Over 14,000 Oxford men went to that bloody conflict (Exeter College, normally occupied by 150 undergraduates, was left with seven in residence), and many of those who survived — about two-thirds of those who had volunteered — found it almost impossible to return to the idyllic scenes of their youth. Too many of their friends were dead. New College lost 263 men; Christ Church 256. The average student population of the entire University was not more than 3,000, and in four years, 2,700 Oxford men died. Harold Macmillan, who had entered Balliol two years before the war, and whose studies were thus interrupted, once said, 'To me Oxford was a city of ghosts. Of our eight scholars and Exhibitioners who came up in 1912, Humphrey Sumner and I alone were alive. It was too much.' There were still wealthy dilettanti who could afford to lounge around in the 1920s and 1930s. Peter Ralli arrived at New College with £3,000, most of which he spent in three years giving delicious dinners, and when he sat his History finals in 1922 he produced one, immortal, sentence: 'Her subjects wanted Queen Elizabeth to abolish tunnage and poundage, but the splendid creature stood firm'. But more and more upper-middle-class men had to turn to the serious business of earning a living, and notwithstanding the frivolity of Evelyn Waugh and his chums, more work began to be undertaken than ever before. The class structure broke down too. In 1920, Oxford University accepted its first government subsidy, and by 1928 half

34

its undergraduates were on scholarships. When it was alleged in an article in the *Independent* newspaper in 1990 that Worcester College 'selectively discriminated against applicants from the maintained sector', the Provost, Lord Briggs, and no fewer than twenty-seven tutorial Fellows indignantly denied the fact.

'Let us be clear,' they wrote in a letter to the editor. 'Worcester College welcomes applications from pupils at all types of school. We select our students on the basis of merit and academic potential alone. For several years the success rate for applicants from public sector schools has been approximately the same as or greater than that for those from the private sector.'

By this time, too, about one in seven of Oxford's undergraduates came from overseas. What was to stir up far greater controversy in 1990 than class or race was whether academic excellence should be the only criterion for entry to Oxford or whether academic latitude should be granted to candidates with athletic prowess.

In 1989 Manchester College became Oxford's first foundation devoted exclusively to mature students, who nevertheless still account for only 1.5 per cent of the current population of about 14,000 undergraduates, only 150 of whom, in 1990, were over the age of twenty-two. It remains a very young person's place, but another milestone was reached in 1990 when Rewley House, the home of Oxford's Department of External Studies, was granted the status of a society to expand continuing education.

The city of Oxford has produced marmalade, and the University a cut of trousers called Oxford bags, 'very wide and flapping at the ankles' as Tom Driberg (later Lord Bradwell) described them. He was at Christ Church, and in his posthumous autobiography, *Ruling Passions*, he remembered that in his first year, 'I got the widest pair I could find, at Hall Brothers in the High, and in an unusual colour − green. This was indeed "asking for it". Soon I heard that most horrifying sound, the cry of a pack baying for its victim: a dozen or twenty young men were tumbling up the stairs to my rooms, shouting my name opprobriously. Soon the offending trousers were off me: I heard next day that they had been carried round Tom Quad in triumph, cut up, and hung in strips around the junior common-room.'

While seventeenth-century Oxford undergraduates seem to have had a strong inclination to visit brothels, the Oxford of Driberg's day, between the two world wars, was without a doubt its heyday

35

for ostentatious and undisguised homosexual behaviour, not all of it conducted by men who were overtly homosexual. Many, like a future twice-married Prime Minister, Anthony Eden, resplendent today in a portrait in Christ Church Hall in his Garter robes, who almost certainly had an affair at Oxford with Edward Sackville-West, were merely denied access to young women, for those women who were being educated at Oxford were few in number and permanently chaperoned. And in any case, in those days 'nice' young women did not, on the whole, sleep with men before marriage.

Others, like Evelyn Waugh, whose first novel, *Decline and Fall*, opens with a drunken orgy at an Oxford College, 'Scone', were experimenting with a sexual side to their nature which they later – and, certainly in his case, with disastrous results – attempted to repress. 'To innocent outsiders,' Driberg commented, 'Evelyn Waugh's description in *Decline and Fall* of a bump supper and its aftermath have seemed wildly exaggerated. It was, if anything, a mild account of the night of any Bullingdon Club dinner in Christ Church.'

He may have been right. In 1927 the *Oxford Chronicle* reported: 'An orgy of wrecking and smashing indulged in by the members of the Bullingdon Club on Saturday resulted in considerable damage being done at Christ Church. It is understood that the annual dinner of the Club was held at Cowley on Saturday night, and the members and guests afterwards returned to Christ Church by motor-bus.

'In a drunken frenzy, they seized hold of hockey-sticks, copper kettles and pieces of coal, with which they proceeded to smash lamps and windows in the Peckwater Quadrangle. On two sides of the quadrangle not a single window on the ground floor remained unbroken. On the first floor many windows and electric light bulbs were smashed, and in some cases the window frames had been pulled out. Some of the windows of Christ Church Library were also broken . . .

'The scandal is that conduct which would involve townsmen in severe penalties, publicly imposed, is hushed up by college authorities when members of the University are involved, and that, however stern the disciplinary measures taken by the particular college concerned may be, the really effective penalty, public exposure and social disgrace, is escaped by the culprits.'

While the Bullingdon Club attracted mainly hearty heterosexuals, those of a different inclination flocked to a club called the Hypocrites', which met over a bicycle shop in St Aldate's, but soon after Evelyn Waugh's departure from Oxford it was closed down. Tom Driberg said the Hypocrites' Club 'had been the scene of some lively and drunken revels . . . mainly homosexual in character.' He remembered dancing with 'John F.', while 'Evelyn and another rolled on a sofa with (as one of them said later) their ''tongues licking each other's tonsils''.'

One major consequence of the opening (in the 1970s) of men's colleges to women has been that the conventionally delayed progression for so many English middle-class public schoolboys from adolescent homosexuality to adult heterosexuality, where such a progression is likely to take place anyway, has at least been offered an opportunity to be delayed for a shorter time than in the past. It has to be remembered too how profoundly ignorant many young men were about sex before the Second World War. In his autobiography, *The Marble Foot*, Peter Quennell, who was at Balliol, writes, 'When I arrived at Oxford, I still believed that an infant's route of exit must unquestionably be the navel, since that superfluous, if decorative feature seemed to serve no other purpose'.

In an interview she gave to the *Independent* in 1990, the novelist Joanna Trollope, a descendant of Anthony Trollope, who entered St Hugh's in 1962, said however that she thought she had been very lucky to be at Oxford while the colleges were still single sex. 'It was the first time of making proper female friends. When the portcullis came down and the drawbridge up at night, a world of the most marvellous privacy went on. I think a lot of men would feel exactly the same − that the real nurturing of intense friendships of your own sex is terribly difficult now.'

With people like David Cecil, J. R. R. Tolkien and Nevill Coghill lecturing, Miss Trollope found that 'Learning was a complete eye-opener. Nobody had ever asked me my opinion before about anything, and it was spellbinding to have an adult talk to you as an equal.' How the misogynists of old must have been turning in their graves at the thought of able women who did not go around smashing up the place taking an intelligent delight in all that Oxford had to offer.

There is scarcely a sport one can think of that cannot be indulged in at Oxford, but perhaps because England's oldest universities, Oxford and Cambridge, are both settled upon rivers, it is their

37

annual contest at rowing that has captured the public's imagination. But it is not everyone's desire to take part in team activities, or to compete, and in a way the river at Oxford − in theory the Thames but in part called the Isis − is symbolic of the University itself, catering for every taste and inclination. Those who do not wish to row in unison ('all rowed fast, but none so fast as stroke' was one sardonic wit's comment on the mania for rowing) can scull; others may drift in a punt through some of the most lush and bird-strewn meadows in England.

Oxford has always produced prejudice and hyperbole, sarcasm and humour. Swinburne said that no one in Oxford could ever be said to die for they had never begun to live. It was, thought John Bright, 'the home of dead languages and undying prejudices'. Ramsay MacDonald described Oxford as 'a painted lady, from whom Labour has nothing to expect', which was rubbish: one of his successors as leader of the Labour Party, Michael Foot, was President of the Oxford Union in 1933, and another Labour Prime Minister, Harold Wilson, a graduate of Jesus and a Fellow of University College, packed eight Oxford Firsts into his cabinet.

'An Ocean or Great Sea of Privilege' is how Oxford was described in a charter granted during the reign of Charles I. Privilege then referred to the ancient rights of the University over the town, to licence plays, banish people 'of vicious life', to hear court cases and to afford protection from prosecution to its own members. The University has run amok with its privileges ever since. In 1821 some students who needed a body to dissect did not hesitate to waylay a funeral procession and make off with the corpse. In modern parlance, privilege might be taken to mean that only those with a private income can afford to go to Oxford (at the turn of the century an undergraduate's weekly college bill at Balliol for food and services may only have come to £2, but that was equivalent to a working man's weekly wage), but this also is no longer true. Yet who can doubt that the thousands of undergraduates and visitors to the town, enabled as they are to enjoy so wide a variety of English domestic architecture, to wander into such a wealth of college chapels, to sit in peace and tranquillity in some of the loveliest gardens open to the public, are privileged today in the true sense of that word.

Oxford has been spared the worst vandalism wreaked by town planners on many of our once treasured cathedral cities. It is, like Cambridge, Bath and Edinburgh, essentially a place to walk round, for that is the only way to absorb the unique atmosphere of any great town designed for people to live in. And when, at night, you glance south down St Aldate's, to be struck anew by Wren's great bell tower at Christ Church stark against the midnight blue, or you turn into Broad Street to enjoy in silence the much-derided disembodied statues floating like ghostly sentinels before the Sheldonian Theatre, it is impossible not to marvel at the fact that despite commercialisation and diesel fumes so much of Oxford's 1,000 years of history remains visibly and publicly intact.

One

WOLSEY'S DREAM
AND ALICE'S TOO

Carfax Tower (open 26 March to 28 October, Monday to Saturday, 2.00 p.m. to 5.30 p.m., admission charges), Civic and Tourist Information Office (open Monday to Saturday, 9.30 a.m. to 5.00 p.m.), Town Hall, Museum of Oxford (open Tuesday to Saturday, 10.00 a.m. to 5.00 p.m., admission free), Museum of Modern Art (open Tuesday to Saturday, 10.00 a.m. to 6.00 p.m., Sunday, 2.00 p.m. to 6.00 p.m., admission charges), Café Moma (open Tuesday to Saturday, 10.00 a.m. to 5.00 p.m., Sunday, 2.00 p.m. to 5.00 p.m.), Pembroke College (open most hours), St Aldate Church, Christ Church (open 9.30 a.m. to 6.00 p.m. Hall open 9.30 a.m. to 12 noon and 2.00 p.m. to 4.30 p.m. winter, 5.30 p.m. summer. Picture Gallery open 10.30 a.m. to 1.00 p.m. and 2.00 p.m. to 4.30 p.m., admission charges, explanatory talk Thursdays, 2.15 p.m., closed Sunday mornings), Christ Church Cathedral (open during the day except for late afternoon choir practice, admission charges to cathedral and college), Bate Collection of Historical Instruments (open Monday to Friday, admission free), Folly House, Christ Church Meadow (open during daylight hours), Restaurant Elizabeth (closed Mondays).

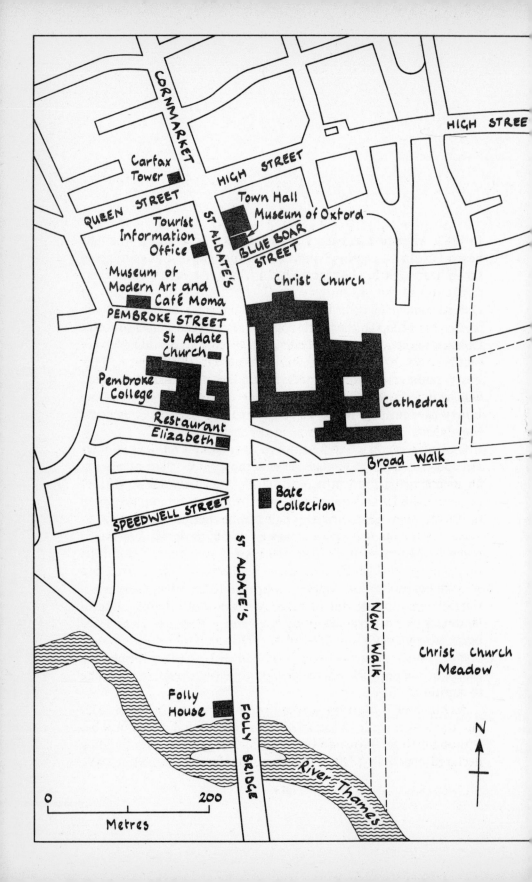

In 1883, when he was twenty-six, Elgar went to Leipzig, where he heard Haydn's *Surprise* Symphony. 'I thought it strange to go so far to hear so little', he reported to a friend. Anyone who staggers to the top of the Saxon tower at Carfax for a bird's-eye view of Oxford could likewise be forgiven for thinking it a long way to climb to see very little. To the north you can discern the chapel of Keble College; to the south, the cathedral and Wren's masterful bell tower on the street front of Christ Church stand out. But the view to the west is nothing more than a modern muddle, and up the High Street, which runs directly from Carfax to the east, queues of buses and Lowry-like scuttling figures distract from the University Church and Magdalen's massive bell tower in the distance.

Oxford was created to be enjoyed at ground level. Its buildings are constructed on a human scale, some grander than others but all meant to be lived in or enjoyed without recourse to lifts or helicopter pads, and there is little to be gained by looking down on them. They need, on the whole, to be met round corners.

But Carfax (*quatre vois* in Norman French, meaning 'four ways') really is the centre of Oxford, the Piccadilly Circus, if you like, the point from which Cornmarket – the 'Oxford Street' of Oxford – radiates north, St Aldate's south and the High Street east. Carfax is a useful point of reference, an easy meeting place, a landmark from which to begin and end a walk. It always has been. When the City of Oxford and District Tramway Company operated horse trams between 1879 and 1907, Carfax formed the centre of the network where cars could be switched from one line to another.

A church of St Martin was recorded on the site of Carfax in 1032, and the tower, made of local rubbish stone, whatever that may be, is thought to be thirteenth-century, all that remains of a building declared unsafe in 1820, rebuilt, and finally demolished in 1896.

It was in this old St Martin's Church that Shakespeare is said to have stood as godfather to the poet William Davenant, whose father John was landlord of the Crown Inn in Cornmarket, now destroyed. The church tower has become officially a Clock Tower and Civic Belfry, emblazoned with the city's rather pedestrian motto *Fortis est Veritas* (Truth is Strength), and in theory it is the solemn duty of the civic dignitaries somehow, in their finery, to negotiate three flights of spiral staircase to proclaim a new sovereign from the top of it, although proclamations at ground level are not unknown. The clock is seventeenth-century, and the two gaily painted little men on either side of the clock (they look like Roman centurions) are called quarterboys, for on the quarter they strike the bells. But these two quarterboys are replicas of the originals (now in the Museum of Oxford), and have only perched on the tower since 1898 – just in time to hear the Carfax Chimes, composed by the Victorian musical scholar Sir John Stainer, played for the first time in 1899.

Stainer devoted most of his life to Oxford. He went up to Christ Church in 1859, was appointed organist at Magdalen College a year later when he was only twenty, and at twenty-one he became organist to the University. In 1866 he founded the Oxford Philharmonic Society, and in 1889 he was appointed Professor of Music. He is buried in Holywell Cemetery.

In front of the tower – strictly speaking in Queen Street – is a bench much frequented by vagrants, as it was in 1636 when William Laud, Archbishop of Canterbury and Chancellor of the University, decreed that 'scholars (particularly the younger sort, and undergraduates) shall not idle and wander about the City, or its suburbs, nor in the streets, or public market, or Carfax (at Penniless Bench, as they commonly call it)'. And a small paved area offers liberal hospitality to religious fanatics. 'When they're singing it's quite nice,' as the lady who sells tickets to the tower will explain, 'but the ranting and raving goes right through you'.

In the seventeenth century Carfax was a site for stallholders, one of whom, Elizabeth Funker, sold apples. She also supplied favours to Richard Berry, a chaplain down the road at Christ Church. According to Anthony Wood, whose diaries shed much amusing light on seventeenth-century Oxford, 'having mind one night in the month of Jan . . . to vent or coole his passion' the Reverend Mr Berry sent his servant to Carfax to summon Elizabeth 'to come to his chamber and 12*d* in apples'. Unfortunately, the servant was only

44

a little boy, and by the time he had arrived at Carfax he had forgotten the name of the woman to whom he had been told to deliver the message. No doubt imagining one vendor of apples as good as another, the lad told some other 'huckster' to go to Christ Church. 'Well,' Anthony Wood goes on to tell us, 'she comes at a little past 6 at night up to his chamber; who against her coming (supposing her to be Eliz . . .) shut the shuttings of his windows and put out his candle. And when shee was come in, he said "Oh Betty art come? I am glad with all my hart; I have not seene thee a great while": and kissed her and groped her and felt her brests. "Come, what wilt have to supper? What joynt of meat wilt have?" and the like. "Come, I have not layd with thee a great while", and soe put his hands under her coates. But shee bid him "forbear" and told him "he was mistaken: if he would pay her for her apples, well and good; she would not play such vile actions with him." "Who", quoth he "are you not Eliz. . ." "Noe, marry, am I not." With that he thrust her downstairs and kikt her.'

St Aldate's, the street leading south from Carfax, was called Fish Street until the nineteenth century; there is no saint called Aldate, and the name may be a corruption of Old Gate, for the south gate in the old city walls was opposite Christ Church. On the south-east corner, at the commencement of the High Street, there stood between 1610 and 1771 'a very fair and beautifull conduit', which provided water pumped from a hill above North Hinksey, 'to the great content of the inhabitants of Oxon'. On one occasion, it is said, it spouted claret.

And it was on the opposite corner, now occupied by the Abbey National Building Society, that the Swyndlestock Tavern was located. Opened in 1250 and closed down in 1709, this was the tavern in which the famous three-day battle between the University and the town broke out in 1355. If you walk down St Aldate's, almost immediately on your right is the Civic and Tourist Information Office, with a counter where you can sometimes wait rather a long time to buy tickets for concerts; a little further on is the Bulldog, where mine host, Mr Mohammed Amir Kianzad, advertises Bière Anglaise Directors.

On the left-hand side of St Aldate's, opposite the Information Office, is a grandiose Town Hall, built in the most flamboyant Victorian style in 1897. In 1922 it was the scene of a spoof lecture on Freudian psychology delivered by one Dr Emil Busch of

Frankfurt, in reality a thinly disguised Balliol undergraduate, Jim Wedderburn, who succeeded two years later as the 11th Earl of Dundee. He fooled his audience so completely that some of them accompanied him to the station, still deep in discourse. This is a very public and enterprising Town Hall. It boasts a Gainsborough and the biggest mace in England; you can leave your baby in a crèche here, or attend a tea dance. At the top of the stairs is an illuminated tank of goldfish, and more serious furnishings include a royal charter of 1199. All the city archives can be seen on request.

On the southern corner of the Town Hall is the Museum of Oxford, a rather folksy labyrinth of reconstructed slum dwellings and the like, worth a visit if you have the time or inclination. But as Oxford has two unique museums on offer, the Ashmolean and the Pitt Rivers, you can afford to give a run-of-the-mill museum, like any second-rate churches, a miss.

Regain the west side of St Aldate's, and the first turning on the right is Pembroke Street. Worth a passing glance is the first house on the right in Pembroke Street, Number 45; the home of a tutor, E. P. C. Greene, MA, as a brass plate proclaims, it is adorned with his own charmingly painted crest – a griffin with what looks like an olive branch in its beak – above the door. Oxford is full of minor surprises like this; further down on the left, one of the least prosperous-looking of this mixture of seventeenth- and eighteenth-century houses sports, high up on the wall, what looks like a royal coat of arms.

There are two reasons for coming down Pembroke Street: to patronise in its converted warehouse the Museum of Modern Art and its Café Moma, should you wish either to admire modern art or to have coffee, lunch or tea, and to visit Pembroke College. If you are not going to the end of the street, to the museum, then nip down a short unnamed alley on your left to the college.

The Museum of Modern Art at 30 Pembroke Street has acquired international recognition, with exhibitions of work by artists from Japan and China, Eastern Europe and Africa. On the ground floor is a bookshop, and downstairs a café where you are given a choice of eleven brands of tea. Wine and beer are available with salads and hot self-service meals, and do not feel too disappointed if the Laranda, 'a rustic rich fruity red, with just a hint of mint', is missing from the wine list.

There is nothing to detain you to the right as you leave the

Museum of Modern Art, only the ghost of Roger Bacon, 'known as the wonderful doctor, who by the experimental method extended marvellously the realm of science'. He died in 1292 near what is now a car park, and is commemorated, if that is the right word, by a mean little alleyway, Roger Bacon Lane, that runs between a Christian bookshop and Sainsbury's. So retrace your steps east along Pembroke Street, turn down the alley behind St Aldate Church, past what is left of Beef Lane − now closed off to provide a new quadrangle for Pembroke − and you are facing the rather cramped-looking gatehouse of Pembroke College.

The ubiquitous Herberts of Wilton House in Wiltshire have paraded through English history for hundreds of years, and William Herbert, 3rd Earl of Pembroke, who lived from 1580 to 1630, was both Chancellor of Oxford University and, it was said at the time, godfather to Pembroke College. His bust can be seen at the top of the stairs leading to the Hall, and if the Hall is closed, some obliging member of the college will generally open it for you.

Pembroke are engagingly hospitable and it is one of the few colleges you can wander into at almost any hour. The Old Quadrangle, the first you enter, dates from 1627 to 1670, but it was modernised by the Victorians, and its very smallness may surprise a visitor to his first Oxford college. Pembroke is essentially a small and intimate affair, but it opens up as you enter, to your right, the Chapel Quadrangle, with its classical eighteenth-century chapel on the left. Before the college acquired its own chapel as late as 1732 the undergraduates worshipped across the cobbles in St Aldate Church. The huge Hall at right angles to the chapel is one hundred years later still, and dominates but does not overshadow the lawn and its battlemented wall. The Hall, built in fact in 1848, and the range of buildings contemporary with it along the north side of the quad, were going up at the time that Francis Jeune was Master of the college; his skittish wife had equally good sense, rebelling against the mores of Victorian Oxford by ordering her bonnets from Paris in order to keep one step ahead of fashion.

It was said that Jeune bankrupted the college for half a century in order to build the Hall, which was far larger than was required in view of the number of undergraduates in residence, and at the time of its construction it was only second in size to Christ Church. Over the High Table in place of honour hangs a painting of Queen Anne, who gave to the college a canonry of Gloucester in order

47

to pay the Master's stipend. Since 1888 the Master has lived in what were originally almshouses built by Cardinal Wolsey, and his Lodgings provide an attractive front on to St Aldate's. To Lord Nuffield, whose portrait hangs above the gallery, the college is also indebted, for it was he who released Pembroke from its links with Gloucester Cathedral by finding the Master's salary himself. The only modern painting of note is Bryan Organ's portrait of Sir Geoffrey Arthur, Master from 1975 to 1984.

Do not fail to enter the chapel; it is essential also to switch on the light by the door. The effect will be to illuminate a monument to the very best in Victorian taste and craftsmanship. The altar piece and panelling are original, but the eight statues, representing the theme of the Incarnation, and the sumptuous ceiling, amounting to a rich stage-set of gold, greens and red, were all modelled, in plaster, as late as 1884. The equally stunning windows date from the same year. It is magnificent, one of the most welcoming and beautiful of the small college chapels. Before Pius XII became Pope he was shown Pembroke's chapel. Despite its rather evangelical tradition, he exclaimed, 'It is just like one of ours!' Back home in Rome he attempted to cap his original compliment by reporting that he had seen the 'finest non-conformist chapel in England'.

But do not allow all this excellent Victoriana to let you forget that Pembroke College is an early seventeenth-century foundation. On the other hand, do not trouble to go in search of Samuel Johnson's rooms; like much of the original buildings, they have been swept away. He was only at Pembroke for a year (in 1728), gave up crossing the road to borrow books from friends in Christ Church once his shoes had worn out, and left without taking a degree. But, as was inevitable with such a physical and mental colossus, he left an indelible imprint.

Bishop Thomas Percy wrote to Johnson's biographer James Boswell to say, 'I have heard from some of his contemporaries that he was generally seen lounging at the College gate, with a circle of young students round him, whom he was encouraging with wit, and keeping from their studies'. In a life of Johnson published in 1787 by Sir John Hawkins, it was said that he used to become infuriated (not unnaturally) by interruptions to his own studies by the college custom of servants knocking at his door from time to time to make sure that he was working. He was in fact a rebellious student, which from all we know of his intemperate character comes as no surprise. 'I was mad and violent,' he admitted in later life. 'I was miserably poor, and I thought to fight my way by my literature and my wit; so I disregarded all power and authority.'

Johnson's feelings about Oxford blew with the prevailing wind. He first returned to Pembroke in 1754, and 'was highly pleased to find all the College servants which he had left there still remaining, particularly a very old butler; and expressed great satisfaction at being recognised by them, and conversed with them familiarly'. But he was less enchanted by his reception from the Master, John Ratcliffe, who incurred Johnson's displeasure by failing to order a copy of his dictionary, 'now near publication'. Worse still, Dr Ratcliffe did not even invite his distinguished visitor to dine with him. But twenty-one years later the University itself made amends, by conferring on Samuel Johnson an honorary doctorate, and it was said that after that he wore his gown 'almost ostentatiously'.

Johnson himself confessed, 'I have been in my gown ever since I came here,' and like almost all unhappy or disgruntled college students, he came to look back upon his undergraduate days through rose-tinted lenses. 'You cannot imagine with what delight he showed me every part of his old College,' Hannah More, whose *Memoirs* were published in 1834, recorded on 13 June 1782. 'He would let no one show it me but himself.' He and his friends, he told her, had been 'a nest of singing-birds'.

Dr Johnson was not the only impoverished young man to enter Pembroke. In 1823 an enterprising chap called Robert Hawker went up. But his father, an ill-paid clergyman, broke the news the following year that it would not be possible for Robert to return to college. 'Without waiting to put on his hat', Robert rushed off to propose to his godmother, a spinster of forty-one who had the good fortune to possess a private income of £200 a year. Although Robert was only twenty they married, and he returned to Oxford with his wife − and financial saviour − 'riding behind him on a pillion'.

Pembroke College educated Sir Philip Sidney and John Pym, and became the inspiration for one of the first of the Victorian 'Oxford novels', when Thackeray, in *Pendennis*, published in 1849, renamed Pembroke 'St Boniface'. When a notable Pembroke scholar, Walter Ramsden, died in 1947, his death inspired John Betjeman (who was to become Poet Laureate in 1972) to write a poem that began with the memorable lines:

> Dr Ramsden cannot read *The Times* obituary today
> He's dead.

Twelve years after the depressive but ebullient Samuel Johnson left Pembroke a student of a very different hue arrived: George Whitefield. He has left an account of his conversion to Methodism, which was by now well into its stride under the influence at Lincoln College of John Wesley. 'I had not long been at the University,' he recalled, looking back on the year 1740, 'before I found the benefit of the foundation I had laid in the country for a holy life. I was quickly solicited to join in their excess of riot with several who lay in the same room. God, in answer to prayers before put up, gave me grace to withstand them . . . when they perceived they could not prevail, they let me alone as a singular, odd fellow.'

Thus saved from undergraduate debauchery, young George Whitefield, later ordained a Methodist minister, 'began to pray and sing psalms thrice every day, besides morning and evening, and to fast every Friday, and to receive the Sacrament at a parish church near our college'. This may have been St Aldate Church, although by the time Whitefield entered Pembroke the college had its own chapel. He gave up eating fruit and powdering his hair, wore 'woolen gloves, a patched gown, and dirty shoes', and even took to lying flat on his face in the cold at night in Christ Church Meadow, only returning to Pembroke when, at five minutes past nine, the great bell in Tom Quad rang the curfew.

As you leave Pembroke College and walk into Pembroke Square you walk almost slap into St Aldate Church, Norman in origin but very heavily restored in 1862. The result, by any standards, and certainly those of Oxford, is a rather dull evangelical establishment. But a tip, worth a few pence in the poor box, is that behind the font you will find a lavatory; public lavatories in Oxford are few and far between and far from salubrious.

If you follow in Dr Johnson's footsteps by crossing St Aldate's, you will come up against the largest, one of the wealthiest, and in some ways one of the grandest colleges in Oxford: Christ Church. It surely has the most impressive street-front of them all. The college was founded twice; its chapel is a diocesan cathedral; its head of house is dean of the cathedral; its Fellows are called Students; and the daughter of one of its deans provided the inspiration for *Alice in Wonderland*. No Oxford college is entirely typical, but if one can be said to be unique it has to be Christ Church – or the 'House' as it is frequently called: *Aedes Christi*, 'The House of Christ'.

When Thomas Wolsey, Cardinal Archbishop of York, first planned a college on this site in 1523 it was known as Cardinal's College. True to his expansive nature, Wolsey had always intended a grandiose establishment, fit to attract such luminaries as William Tindall, one of the translators into English of the Bible, and John Taverner, the organist and composer. He had the foundations dug in ten days, and such was his power and authority that he suppressed twenty-two monasteries to provide funds for Cardinal's College ('neither God was served in them,' he claimed, 'nor religion kept'), cleared a number of University buildings to make space for it, and spent £8,000 in one year alone. But within six years he had fallen from grace; within seven he was dead, and all that had belonged to Wolsey reverted to the crown. Perhaps the reason Wolsey's luck ran out was because Cardinal's College was to have been the thirteenth college in Oxford.

In 1532 Henry VIII, awash with money after taking a leaf out of Wolsey's book and laying waste monasteries wholesale, refounded the college, called it Christ Church, created a diocese of Oxford (before 1542 the town of Oxford was in the diocese of Lincoln; today Oxford is the largest diocese in the Church of England and has the smallest cathedral), and combined the endowments of the college and the cathedral, which explains why – in so far as so many historical anomalies are ever truly explicable – the dean is not Dean of Oxford but Dean of Christ Church.

Tom Gate, the central tower built by Sir Christopher Wren in 1682 to house the bell called Great Tom, is courteously guarded by gentlemen in bowler hats, who direct visitors to an entrance reached by walking a few yards further down St Aldate's and turning in to the War Memorial Garden, created in 1926 by the College Steward, Major A. K. Slessor. On the left, where once stood a little street of shops, is a busy walled herbaceous border: the destruction of these shops opened up a superb view of the south range of Tom Quad and the south façade of Wolsey's Hall, one of the most impressive architectural vistas in Oxford.

Now you enter Christ Church through the Meadow Buildings on your left, the only redeeming feature of this mid-Victorian venture into fashion (Dean Liddell spent £22,000 on what he fancied was a tribute to the age of Pugin and Ruskin) being the views its rooms must command over the meadow itself. But almost at once you are safely in the cathedral cloisters, where in the eighteenth century things were done properly and people like William Pound knew their place; his memorial tells us he was 'many years one of the Porters of this College, who, by an exemplary life and Behaviour, and an honest attention to the Duties of his Station, deserved and obtained the approbation and esteem of the whole Society'.

By the entrance to the Chapter House is a sad memorial to one who had no chance to shine; Jeremy Kitchen, a chorister who died in 1985 at the age of eighteen. With its thirteenth-century glass, the Chapter House would be a restful spot in which to linger were it not now a shop, but there are many fine examples on display of seventeenth-century Communion plate, together with a Bible and Prayer Book of 1636.

You enter the cathedral from the cloisters. Part of this strangely haphazard building predates Wolsey by 300 years, and the thirteenth-century spire was the first to be built in England. Unlike most cathedrals, Christ Church has no choir screen, so that the brief vista from the west end to the east can be taken in at a glance. And as in a college chapel rather than a cathedral, seats for the congregation face inwards. The modest tomb of Robert King, Oxford's first bishop who died in 1557, can be found at the entrance to the Military Chapel. He lived in a palace in St Aldate's opposite the War Memorial Garden, but in 1635 the episcopal residence was moved to Cuddesdon. The Old Palace, a modest gabled building on the corner of St Aldate's and Rose Lane, replaced Bishop King's palace in 1628.

Near a bust of Edward Pusey — one of the cathedral's most famous canons, who died in 1882 at the age of eighty-two after a lifetime devoted to the restoration of catholic worship in the Church of England — is a memorial dedicated 'in affectionate remembrance' to Prince Leopold, Queen Victoria's youngest son, a haemophiliac who died aged thirty. He was at Christ Church from 1872 to 1875 and, like his eldest brother, the Prince of Wales, who matriculated at Christ Church on 17 October 1859, Leopold was not permitted by his anxious mother to reside in college but was compelled to live with a private tutor in St Giles'. He contrived nevertheless to fall in love with Alice Liddell, daughter of Henry Liddell, a Greek scholar and Dean of Christ Church for thirty-six years. But it was considered quite out of the question at that time for a prince to marry a commoner, and Prince Leopold had to make do with Princess Helene of Waldeck and Pyrmont. Their son, the Duke of Saxe-Coburg and Gotha, became a Nazi.

While at Christ Church the Prince of Wales lived in Frewin Hall, in New Inn Hall Street, now an extension of Brasenose College, but on the day he arrived at Christ Church, according to a letter Dean Liddell wrote to his father, the entire college lined up in Tom Quad to greet him. 'At five he came, and the bells struck up as he entered. He walked to my house between two lines of men, who capped him. I went out to meet him, and as he entered the house there was a spontaneous cheer . . . I took him up to the drawing-room, and entered his name in the buttery book. He then retired with his Tutor, Mr Fisher, and put on a nobleman's cap and gown in the gallery, and returned to receive greetings as the first Prince of Wales who had matriculated since Henry V.' This may have been a romantic flight of fancy on Liddell's part. There is a tradition that both the Black Prince and Henry V had rooms at Queen's College, but no evidence exists that either were members.

The heir to the throne – later Edward VII – stayed two years, sometimes dined in Hall, and declined to be photographed by an importunate young mathematics teacher, the Reverend Charles Dodgson, a perpetual curate who loved royalty and little girls in equal measure. It was he who was to immortalise Alice Liddell. The Prince also stood as godfather to a boy born to Mrs Liddell, hastily baptised Albert Edward Arthur in his honour, who died soon afterwards. On 12 December 1860 the Prince's parents, accompanied by Prince Alfred and Princess Alice and her fiancé, paid a visit to the college, looking in at the Hall, the cathedral and the library. In the evening they were entertained in the deanery to *tableaux vivants*.

While he was at Oxford, Edward got in some practice at playing rather pathetic practical jokes, the sort he would inflict on guests at Sandringham House in later life. One day he encouraged the Duke of Hamilton to enter a shop and ask for a pound of treacle. Because he had brought no jar with him, the Duke produced a sovereign and asked to have the treacle poured into his hat. He then placed his hat on the shop assistant's head, and ran out without waiting for his change.

Perhaps the outstanding architectural feature of this miniature cathedral is the vaulted roof above the choir, which dates from 1503. But there are some extraordinarily interesting windows too: a recently restored early fourteenth-century window depicting the martyred Archbishop of Canterbury, Thomas à Becket, in what is called the Lucy Chapel; the seventeenth-century Jonah Window at the west end of the north nave aisle; and, over the altar of the Latin Chapel in the far north-east corner, there are marvellous panels by Edward Burne-Jones, the leader of the Pre-Raphaelite painters, depicting scenes from the life of the eighth-century 'Virgin and Abbess', St Frideswide, patron saint of Oxford. Burne-Jones was an undergraduate at Exeter College.

In 1918 Sir William Walton was admitted to Christ Church when he was only sixteen. Music is one of the glories of Christ Church Cathedral, for Henry VIII decreed that 'eight young singing children' — they happen always to have been boys — should belong to the choir. By providing a clerk to teach them grammar he also laid the foundations for Christ Church Cathedral School, now with buildings in Brewer Street, a smart sprint from St Aldate's. The number of singing boys was increased in 1855 to fourteen (there are now sixteen), eight of them continuing to lodge with canons in Tom Quad, others with landladies in the town, and by 1865 they had been joined by half a dozen non-choristers. The boys were educated in rooms beneath the Hall, and claimed 'a prescriptive right to the run of Tom Quad and could be down on the grass and play round the fountain and also through every alley and staircase in the College'.

In 1875, following complaints that the boys made too much noise, they were all housed together at Number 1 Brewer Street, now the Headmaster's Lodgings, where they were mothered by a sort of landlady-cum-matron, and taught by the Cathedral Precentor. They moved to their present accommodation further down the street in 1892, and today there are some thirty boarders (including of course all sixteen cathedral choristers and those waiting to join the choir), and about sixty-five day boys. Ages range from five to thirteen.

The school also provides twenty-six boys for the Exeter and Worcester College choirs, and these youngsters undertake a quite

1 The quarterboys attached to the seventeenth century clock on the Saxon tower and civic belfry at Carfax, so called because they strike every quarter of an hour. It was from this tower, originally part of the Church of St Martin, first recorded in 1032, that in 1355 the bells summoned townspeople to join in a three-day battle with university undergraduates. A set of chimes was composed for the bells by the Victorian musical scholar Sir John Stainer.

2 Stained glass windows dating from 1884 in the seventeenth century chapel of Pembroke College. The brilliantly successful Victorian modernisation of the interior of the chapel so impressed Pope Pius XII that he exclaimed, 'It is just like one of ours!'

3 Even a small college like Pembroke could muster seventeen servants in 1890. Those who looked after the undergraduates personally, cleaning their rooms, making their beds and lighting fires, were called scouts. *Photograph by courtesy of the Master and Fellows of Pembroke College.*

4 From a balcony like this in the Meadow Buildings at Christ Church Sir Harold Acton proclaimed his own poems through a megaphone while an undergraduate at the House, as Christ Church is often called, during the early 1920s. The Buildings, with views across Christ Church Meadow, are a Victorian extension to a college originally founded by Cardinal Wolsey and re-established in 1532 by Henry VIII.

5 Tom Quad, or the Great Quadrangle, at Christ Church, with Christopher Wren's gate of 1682 in the centre of the west range. From above the gate a bell called Great Tom tolls a curfew at five minutes past nine every night. Almost all the rest of the west front was built in the early sixteenth century by Cardinal Wolsey. In the centre of the quadrangle, constructed as a fountain, is a copy of Giovanni da Bologna's Mercury.

6 Canterbury Quad at Christ Church, with its Doric archway. Above it peeps the tower of Merton College Chapel. Rooms in this eighteenth century quadrangle, built by James Wyatt, were originally intended as accommodation for Gentlemen Commoners and peers.

7 One of the most interesting paintings on exhibition in the picture gallery at Christ Church is a portrait of John Riley, who worked as a kitchen scullion in the seventeenth century. It is the earliest known portrait of any Oxford college servant. *Photograph by courtesy of the Governing Body, Christ Church, Oxford.*

8 A photograph taken in 1872 by Julia Margaret Cameron of Alice Liddell, a daughter of Henry Liddell, Dean of Christ Church from 1855 to 1891, whose controversial friendship with Lewis Carroll provided the inspiration for *Alice's Adventures in Wonderland*. Carroll, whose real name was Charles Dodgson, was a perpetual curate and a mathematics don at Christ Church. Someone else who fell seriously in love with Alice Liddell, when he was an undergraduate at Christ Church, was Prince Leopold, the youngest son of Queen Victoria. *Photograph by courtesy of the Royal Photographic Society.*

9 Folly House, also sometimes known as Isis House or Caudwell's Castle, which stands on the west side of Folly Bridge, south of St Aldate's. It was built in 1849 entirely for fun, and with its statues, wrought iron balconies and battlemented roof it is one of Oxford's most unusual nineteenth century buildings.

10 One of the nicest walks within the centre of Oxford is round Christ Church Meadow and along the north bank of the Cherwell, a tributary of the Thames. In summer, swans and punters drift idly by while harmless grass snakes doze beneath the trees.

11 The majestic sixteenth century bell tower of Magdalen College, glimpsed above the trees in the Botanic Garden. From the top of the tower on May morning the college choir serenades the town below. The ragged yew tree on the left is the oldest plant in the garden, planted by the first head gardener, Jacob Bobart, about 1650.

12 The Cloisters Quadrangle at Magdalen College is ornamented with a fascinating selection of medieval statues, including this pair, apparently dancing, said to be Jacob and the Angel.

13 Magdalen College undergraduates about to set off for a race meeting in 1912. At that time all the undergraduates would have come from public schools, equipped with a private income, and few would have needed to take a degree to further their career. *Photograph by courtesy of the President and Fellows of Magdalen College.*

14 A unique feature of Magdalen College is its Deer Park, a source of venison for the Hall since about 1710. The Park can best be viewed from Addison's Walk.

exceptional work-load: choir practice every midday and evening; some seven services a week plus additional weddings and memorial services; and music practice first thing in the morning, for every chorister has to learn to play two instruments as well as sing. All this activity is carried out on top of a normal academic and recreational curriculum and requires concentration, stamina and exceptional intelligence. The boys sacrifice some of their holidays to sing at Christmas and in Holy Week, but compensations include tours on the Continent and much fêting by local organisations during their extra weeks at school. Only two choristers have dropped out in eighteen years, and all have better voices than the lad who was interviewed around 1800 by Dean Cyril Jackson, who asked him, 'Well, boy, what do you know of music?'

'Please, sir,' replied the candidate for a place in the choir, 'I have no more ear nor a stone, and no more voice nor an ass.'

'Go your ways, boy,' Jackson told him. 'You'll make a very good chorister.'

Leave the cathedral by the west door, and here, in Tom Quad, or the Great Quadrangle as it is officially called, you are at the centre of Wolsey's uncompleted dream. All that you can see to the south, and along the front nearly up to the north-west corner (with the exception, of course, of Wren's bell tower), is Wolsey's; his plans to create cloisters were unfortunately abandoned. The north wing, like the bell tower, is late seventeenth-century, and was completed by John Fell, who combined the deanery of Christ Church (he was Dean from 1660 to 1686) with the bishopric of Oxford. It was Fell who in 1684 sullied his reputation, however, by depriving the budding philosopher John Locke, whose portrait can be seen in the Hall, of his Studentship of Christ Church.

Wolsey's Hall, immediately on the left, is approached by a grand flight of stairs designed by George III's architect James Wyatt, shielded by an earlier fan-vaulted roof, dating from about 1640 – late for fan-vaulting: this is in reality seventeenth-century Gothic Revival. In the ante-chamber leading to the Hall is a seated statue of Cyril Jackson, Dean from 1783 to 1809, who lived surrounded by footmen, and to whom even senior tutors raised their caps. The college scouts however were excused this obeisance for fear that 'the better-looking among them might be mistaken for undergraduates'. Offered the bishopric of Oxford, Dean Jackson referred the Prime Minister to his brother. 'Try Bill,' he said, 'he'll take it.' And he did. It has been told of Bishop Jackson that on one occasion he began a sermon, 'St Paul says in one of his Epistles – and I partly agree with him . . .' But this story is also attributed to Thomas Gaisford, Dean of Christ Church from 1831 to 1855.

When Henry Liddell was Dean, and an undergraduate who happened to be a peer failed to raise his cap to *him* in the street, Liddell inquired, 'How long have you been a member of the University?'

'A week, sir,' the young man replied.

'I understand,' said the Dean. 'Puppies cannot see till they are eight days old.'

Rather an unappetising account of the Hall was left by a German visitor, Zacharias von Üffenbach, in 1710. It was, he said, 'fearfully large and high but otherwise poor and ugly in appearance; it also reeks so strongly of bread and meat that one cannot remain in it, and I should find it impossible to dine and live there. The disgust was increased (for the table was already set), when we looked at the coarse and dirty and loathsome table cloths, square wooden plates and the wooden bowls into which the bones are thrown; this odious custom obtains in all the colleges.'

A decade later, in 1720, there was a fire, and the roof had to be restored. But the overall effect remains a Hall in which the most aristocratic of young Oxford students might feel at home. With examples of work by Gainsborough, Kneller, Romney, Lawrence and Millais, Christ Church possesses the finest collection of portraits in any college Hall, artistically and historically. Of especial interest is a posthumous painting to the left of the door of Charles Dodgson, alias Lewis Carroll, a lugubrious effort we owe to a painter by the unlikely name of Sir Hubert von Herkomer. On the right of the door, above Romney's portrait of John Wesley, hangs a painting of William Penn, the founder of Pennsylvania. On the same wall is an undistinguished portrait of W. H. Auden. It was scarcely to the University's credit that from 1956 to 1961 Auden was Professor of Poetry; he scraped in with 216 votes against 192 cast for Harold Nicolson, surely a ludicrous candidate for anyone to support against one of the greatest English poets of the twentieth century.

The High Table is dominated by a portrait of Henry VIII, with Wolsey on his right. Also among this important and attractive collection of paintings is a particularly striking portrait of Gladstone, who took a Double First at Christ Church in 1831.

If you walk along the east terrace, past the deanery and through an archway, you will enter Peckwater Quadrangle – and the eighteenth century. Peckwater Quad makes an exceptionally handsome classical square, with three identical wings for undergraduates and staff. It was here that Charles Dodgson (who spent forty-four years at Christ Church) had rooms; he became an undergraduate in 1854, was a mathematics lecturer from 1855 to 1881 and Senior Student from 1858 to 1898. And on the south side is a really massive freestanding Palladian library, completed in 1772, the inspiration of Henry Aldrich, Dean from 1689 to 1710.

It was in Peckwater Quad that in 1870 some undergraduates who had removed a number of statues from the library lit a bonfire round them, 'the most brutal and senseless act of Vandalism that has disgraced our time', in the opinion of *The Times*. Dodgson leapt to the defence of his well-bred Goths in a letter to the *Observer*, whose leading article had also deplored the incident; he described them as 'gentlemanly and orderly'.

Peckwater Quad leads on to James Wyatt's later and much smaller Canterbury Quadrangle, with its great Doric gateway. Building here was financed by a former scholar of Christ Church, Richard Robinson, Archbishop of Armagh. He was a generous patron of the arts but a frightful snob, who insisted that the best rooms in Canterbury Quad should always be reserved for Gentlemen Commoners and peers.

On the right of Canterbury Quad you will find the entrance to the picture gallery, opened in 1968 through the generosity of Charles Forte. Initially the entrance seems to promise descent to a forbidding concrete bunker, but the gallery is a great success and well worth a visit. There is a display of glass presented by William Hardy, at Christ Church from 1916 to 1918, and the permanent exhibition ranges from fourteenth-century Florentine 'primitive' religious paintings to the seventeenth century. Also always on display is a small selection of the 1,734 Old Master drawings bequeathed in 1765 by a wealthy connoisseur, General John Guise, among them works by Claude and Poussin. One of the most interesting is a study by Van Dyck of Prince James, later incorporated into his *Five Eldest Children of Charles I*, which hangs in the State Apartments at Windsor Castle.

But before Christ Church could come into this magnificent inheritance it had to fight a legal battle, for the General's family contested his will. The college won, and very generously handed back to the family by way of compensation a couple of paintings – one a virtually worthless portrait of the relative who had done them out of a fortune.

Do not fail to go to the end of the gallery, past a tiny portion of the deanery garden in which Alice used to play (on the window ledge stands *The Dancer* by Henri Gaudier-Brzeska), and then turn round the corner. Here is an affectionate and penetrating portrait of John Riley, a scullion who worked in the kitchens at Christ Church late in the seventeenth century, the earliest known portrait of any Oxford college servant.

Thomas De Quincey once exclaimed, possibly under the early influence of opium, 'Oxford, ancient Mother! I owe thee nothing!' But he may have been jaundiced in his view because the aristocratic Dean Jackson refused him admission to Christ Church; and after squandering his time in solitude at Worcester College, which he entered in 1803, he left without taking a degree. A twentieth-century undergraduate at the House, Edward Sackville-West, published a biography of De Quincey, *A Flame in Sunlight*, in 1936. He also left without a degree, but this was not an uncommon affectation in those days among the wealthy and privileged who had come to Oxford to broaden their cultural and social horizons rather than prepare for a career. Lord Rosebery's youthful ambition had been to win the Derby: he arrived at Christ Church with a string of horses, leaving in 1868 after a tiff with the Dean – and without a degree.

Eddy Sackville-West's schoolboy diary entry for 5 June 1919, recounting his first visit to Christ Church while still at Eton, typifies the ease with which it was still possible between the wars to enter Oxford, and the whiff of snobbery that hung about Christ Church itself. His first paper, a French translation, he found 'Childish. Took ½ an hour.' He says he was asked 'about 10 words & the examiner was out of the room most of the time. A purely nominal affair, it seems.' On being told next day by the Dean that he had passed, Eddy noted, 'All the Etonians passed except Coventry & they did *far* less than the other boys – but Etonians are always the most popular'.

Another rich, spoilt Old Etonian who shortly afterwards followed Eddy Sackville-West to Christ Church was Harold Acton, who rather unfashionably opted for rooms in the Meadow Buildings.

These he painted lemon yellow and filled with Victorian bric-à-brac, and from his balcony he took to reciting his own poems through a megaphone. He claims it was he who designed Oxford bags, the broad flapping trousers that got Tom Driberg into trouble. It is interesting to recall from *Ruling Passions* that a set of undergraduate rooms in Peckwater Quad such as Driberg inhabited during his second year consisted of a 'large panelled living-room with two small windows, a bedroom and a study', accommodation a don would be fortunate to be allocated nowadays. It was in these rooms, 'with growing awe', that Driberg and W. H. Auden together first read *The Waste Land*.

One of Driberg's most wealthy contemporaries at Christ Church was Edward James, believed by some to be an illegitimate son of another former undergraduate, Edward VII, who was in fact his godfather; James looked nothing like the King. Apparently he had 'the best set of rooms in the House,' in Canterbury Quad, which would have gratified Archbishop Robinson. At the age of thirteen, while at Eton, James became the unwitting cause of a suicide, for in 1922, when it became known that the Liberal politician Lord Harcourt − always known as Lulu − had made a pass at him, Harcourt did the decent thing and committed suicide at his London house in Brook Street, now the Savile Club. The *National Dictionary of Biography* discreetly records his death as taking place at Nuneham Courtenay. Eddy Sackville-West became a member of the Savile, and made use of the club's writing paper on which to send love letters to Benjamin Britten.

Although they flirted a lot and often wasted time, the pre-Second World War generation of aesthetes were self-evidently clever, and some worked hard at establishing youthful reputations. Harold Acton published a volume of poetry during his second term, and Eddy Sackville-West got straight down to a novel, a Gothic monstrosity called *The Ruin*, which had to await publication as his second novel because it was entirely autobiographical; into it he popped, as a kind of anti-hero, an undergraduate at New College, Jack McDougal, later Evelyn Waugh's publisher, with whom he was having a hectic and not very happy affair.

Scribbling on Gridiron Club notepaper in 1920 (the Gridiron was − and still is − a dining club much patronised by the socially and politically ambitious), Edward Sackville-West tried his hand at the clerihew. One was in honour of Keats:

John Keats
Was lost in the streets
He didn't know where to turn
So he wrote an ode to a Grecian Urn.

Unfortunately however Oxford did not inspire Keats to any serious poetic efforts, despite his belief that it was 'the finest City in the world'.

Two other members of the Gridiron, both contemporaries of Sackville-West's at Christ Church, were commemorated in this way:

David Cecil
Was like a thistle
Only more refined
In body and mind.

Henry Channon
Slept in a cannon
Francis Stoner
Was the donor.

Lord David Cecil had been a great friend of Eddy's at Eton, but at Oxford he rather kept his distance, not wishing to become too closely identified with the Bohemian set among whom Eddy moved. Henry Channon, always known as Chips, the intimate of royalty and later the Member of Parliament for Southend-on-Sea, had arrived at Christ Church in 1919 at the ripe old age of twenty-two, and retained for his four years spent there among the rich and famous the kind of immature romanticism only attainable by an Anglo-American snob. When he returned in June 1950 to dine in Hall, he wrote in his diary, 'The beauty of Christ Church filled me with its usual sad and strange nostalgia. As I wandered about the crowded quads, I thought of my old happy days, the happiest of my life, when I lived a life of pleasure and loveliness and my boon companions were Prince Paul [of Serbia], Gage [Viscount Gage], and dear, dead Ivo Grenfell. Dinner in the great hall was impressive . . . Robes, roses, choirboys in red, Burgundy, the lit pictures and cloying monastic atmosphere were all inebriating. Oxford always tears my heart.'

Christ Church has offered hospitality to some diverse characters.

In 1556 Elizabeth I attended a performance of *Palaemon and Arcyte* by Richard Edwards, when a stairway crowded with spectators collapsed, killing three people and injuring five others, 'which disaster coming to the Queen's knowledge she sent forthwith the Vicechancellor and her Chirurgeons to help them, and to have a care that they wanted nothing for their recovery. Afterwards the Actors performed their parts so well, that the Queen laughed heartily thereat, and gave the Author of the Play great thanks for his pains.'

Marshal von Blücher, whose tardy arrival on the field at Waterloo eventually enabled Wellington to win 'a damn close run thing', was a guest in 1814 and drank a bottle of brandy before breakfast. Another famous imbiber, Paul Verlaine, stayed at the House so that he could lecture in a room behind Blackwell's bookshop. But according to Sir William Rothenstein, writing in *Men and Memories*, York Powell, who had fixed up Verlaine's lodgings, 'was in terror lest the poet should get drunk while staying at Christ Church. What would the Dean, what would Dodgson, say?' To add to Powell's and Rothenstein's worries, Verlaine showed no inclination to leave, and 'needed a good deal of gentle persuasion before he was put into a train again for London'.

During the summers of 1931 and 1932 Einstein stayed at Christ Church, dividing his time between mathematics and the violin. And before the war, Lord Cherwell, at one time a Fellow of Wadham, who took his title from the tributary of the Thames that snakes by Christ Church Meadow and under Magdalen Bridge, was allocated a spacious set of rooms in Meadow Buildings. 'White paint was used throughout,' according to Sir Roy Harrod, the distinguished economist who was appointed a lecturer at Christ Church at the age of twenty-two, 'and the contents were hideous'.

Leave the Great Quadrangle down the centre path, and walk round the goldfish pond, where the statue of Mercury balances on one leg, a dismal reminder of some of the more outlandish vandalism to which undergraduates are prone. (In 1862 the deanery garden was broken into and all the plants and shrubs destroyed.) The original Mercury, his body cast in lead and his head in bronze, was erected in 1695 but desecrated in 1817 by a gang of drunken louts led by the 14th Earl of Derby; he later became one of Queen Victoria's prime ministers. What you see now is a lead copy of Giovanni da Bologna's Mercury in the Bargello in Florence, dating from 1928; he is perched on a pedestal designed by Sir Edwin Lutyens, which acts as a fountain.

It was in 1681 that Dean Fell commissioned Christopher Wren to build his triumphant tower beneath which you exit into St Aldate's, and from its belfry 101 strokes ring out at five minutes past nine every night, supposedly to summon back to college Henry VIII's original 100 students plus an additional student added by bequest in 1663. Certainly Archbishop Laud in his Statutes of 1636 'enacted that all scholars of every degree, who happen to be engaged on any occasion beyond the walls of their colleges or halls, shall retire before nine o'clock (which is usually announced by the ringing of the great bell at Christ Church College)'. But the reason Christ Church time is now five minutes later than Greenwich depends on whose information you seek. One theory has it that the University curfew was of course at nine o'clock but that the smart set from Christ Church were given an extra five minutes in which to return from hunting on Boars Hill, but how they were meant to get back from there in five minutes remains a mystery. In time-honoured if pointless tradition, however, cathedral services still start five minutes later than advertised.

Great Tom of Christ Church has a peculiarly complex history. When it was removed from the abbey at Osney to the cathedral in 1545 it was christened Mary, but in 1612 it underwent a sex change and became known as Tom. Its clapper kept wearing out and the bell needed to be recast from time to time, a task that taxed the most experienced seventeenth-century bell-founders. By the time it was hoisted into Wren's new tower it measured seven feet one inch in diameter and weighed over seven tons. (When the bell was re-hung in 1953 it weighed six tons five cwt.) It was first rung on 3 December 1683, on the death of a student. Today it tolls for an hour on the death of the sovereign and the dean.

Only a very short distance south of Christ Church, in St Aldate's, is the University's Faculty of Music; for anyone interested in musical instruments it contains, on the ground floor and to the left of the front door, an amazing collection given to the University in 1963 by Philip Bate. It includes a harpsichord on which Haydn is reputed to have played, and on loan are the horns, clarinets and flageolets depicted in Zoffany's famous painting *The Sharp Family*. Quite apart from the range and number of instruments on display, what is unique about this collection is that the instruments are lent to students and other musicians. If musical instruments and their history happen to be your forte, this is the place for you.

Before going for a refreshing walk round the meadow it is worth a few minutes diversion to continue south down St Aldate's to Folly Bridge (constructed in 1827), for here, on the west side, stands a folly indeed, one of the city's most unusual nineteenth-century houses, variously known as Folly House, Isis House and Caudwell's Castle. Built in 1849 with niches for statues, a battlemented roof and late-Regency wrought iron balconies, it has now been turned into flats, but externally it retains every vestige of its original spirit of fun.

The pub by the bridge, the Head of the River, was only converted out of a nineteenth-century warehouse in 1975 (and advertises a 'delicious range of home cooked fayre', to show how modern it is), but the spot itself is historic, for it was from Folly Bridge that on 4 July 1862, 'a cool, wet day' in reality, Charles Dodgson rowed Alice Liddell and her two sisters as far as Godstowe, a trip that took them two and a half hours. But writing in the *Theatre* twenty-five years later, Dodgson recalled 'the cloudless blue above, the watery mirror below, the boat drifting idly on its way, the tinkle of the drops that fell from the oars, as they waved so sleepily to and fro, and (the one bright gleam of life in all the slumberous scene) the three eager faces, hungry for news of fairyland, and who would not be said ''nay'' to: from whose lips "tell us a story, please" had all the stern immutability of Fate!'

They rowed as far as the Trout, a pub where, sixty years later, Evelyn Waugh and an undergraduate he loved, Richard Pates of Balliol, used to meet for breakfast, and which still beckons Oxfordians and visitors; where fat fish swim to the bank to be fed, and peacocks, not totally house-trained, strut on the roof above the patrons' heads. Here, that afternoon in 1862, in Dodgson's fertile imagination, Alice fell down a rabbit hole.

In 1864 Dodgson presented to Alice Liddell the manuscript of his masterpiece, *Alice's Adventures in Wonderland*, and in 1928, when she was seventy-six and feeling hard up, she sent it to Sotheby's, where it fetched £15,400. Six months later it was sold on to an American collector for £30,000, but through a generous philanthropic gesture it came, in 1948, to rest in the British Museum. The signed first edition presented by Dodgson to the college library, like a number of their other treasures, has been stolen. Assuming it still exists, it can never be sold on the open market, for it is the property of Christ Church. But if it was for sale, its value might be £100,000; perhaps a good deal more.

It is strange that the other children's book of incontestable genius, *The Wind in the Willows*, should have had connections with Christ Church too, for it was written by Kenneth Grahame in the form of letters to his son Alistair, killed by a train near Oxford in 1920 when he was an undergraduate at the House. The manuscript of *The Wind in the Willows* has ended up in the Bodleian.

If you now return to the Memorial Garden, or enter it over a little bridge from the car park of the Head of the River, you can enjoy a delightful walk round Christ Church Meadow, either by turning directly south and returning via the Broad Walk, or vice versa. Either route will take you past lush land, usually being grazed by contented cattle, and along the leafy north bank of the Cherwell, which first thing on a sunny morning, before anyone else is up, supplies by far the nicest walk anywhere in the city centre. Grass snakes lazily doze, and it is from the Cherwell that you will be able to enjoy the finest panorama there has ever been of the 'dreaming spires'. However, you may need to pinch yourself to make sure, unlike Alice, that you are not dreaming in order to credit that for thirty years town planners seriously desired to drive a motorway through this pristine landscape. One of those who campaigned against such an insane idea was Tom Driberg, who received an honourary MA from Christ Church in gratitude; in 1927 he had failed to gain a degree, having arrived for his Finals straight from a Ball. Not being entirely sober, he had fallen fast asleep.

The meadow, where rather expensive outdoor concerts are held in the summer, is held in trust by the Dean and Canons of Christ Church. In 1860 they instructed their 'Meadow Keepers and Constables' to prevent entry into the meadow of beggars, 'all persons in ragged or very dirty clothes', and 'persons of improper character or are not decent in appearance and behaviour'. These orders are still in force and might be thought to exclude, on one ground or another, half the modern population of Oxford. 'Indecent, rude or disorderly conduct of every description' is proscribed, and Christ Church Meadow indeed remains the epitome of respectability, especially at night, for at dusk the Dean makes sure the gates are bolted and barred.

Almost opposite the gates to the Memorial Garden is a shop

trading in knick-knacks that is said to be the Sheep Shop in *Alice Through the Looking Glass*. And next door, at 81 St Aldate's, is the Restaurant Elizabeth, which serves a table d'hôte luncheon of delectable quality at a very reasonable price. After a visit to such a treasure trove as Christ Church, a visit to the Elizabeth, which was featured in *The Good Food Guide* as long ago as 1960, may seem an appropriate and relatively inexpensive luxury in which to indulge.

Two

WILDE AFFAIRS AT MAGDALEN

Botanic Garden (open 9.00 a.m. to 5.00 p.m., greenhouses 2.00 p.m. to 4.00 p.m., admission free), Magdalen College and Deer Park (open 2.00 p.m. to 6.15 p.m.), St Cross Church and Holywell Cemetery, Wykeham Coffee House (open Monday to Saturday, 10.00 a.m. to 5.30 p.m., Sunday, 12 noon to 5.30 p.m., unlicensed), Holywell Music Room, Turf Tavern (open Monday to Saturday, 11.00 a.m. to 11.00 p.m., Sunday, 12 noon to 3.00 p.m., 7.00 p.m. to 10.30 p.m.).

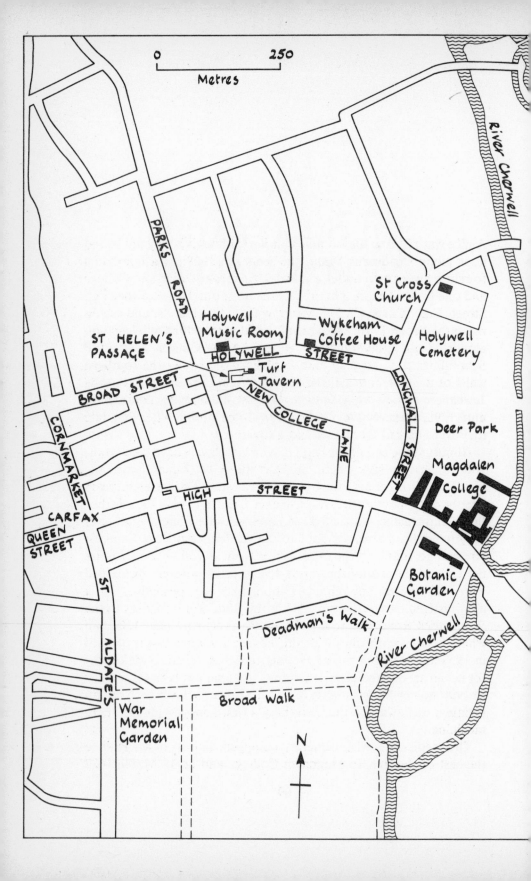

A nice way to go to the Botanic Garden, although it may not sound it, is along Deadmans Walk, the scene, in 1928, of a hoax duel fought between two undergraduates, one from University College and one from Merton. This avoids the noise and bustle of the High Street. Enter Christ Church Meadow from St Aldate's, and as you reach the Broad Walk take the left-hand path, which will lead you alongside the playing field where Christ Church Cathedral Schoolboys run and play, and round the outside of the southern walls of the city. It is called Deadmans Walk because it led to the Jewish cemetery – outside the city walls and therefore considered, until 1290, a respectable place for Jews to be buried. After that date they were barred from England altogether.

Almost at the end of the wall, in which even yew have taken root, you will pass the spot where, on 4 October 1784, James Sadler, the first English aeronaut, took off in a balloon. Twenty-eight years later he dared to cross the Irish Channel. Turn left, leave the meadow through the gates, walk up Rose Lane, and the Botanic Garden is on your right. There is a door to the garden from Rose Lane, or you can go round to the High Street front if you wish to admire the rose garden commemorating ten research workers in Oxford who 'discovered the clinical importance of penicillin,' first administered to a patient in 1941 at the Radcliffe Infirmary in the Woodstock Road. There are those, however, who have less than whole-hearted enthusiasm for this bower, for when it was planted in 1953 an ancient copse of Wellingtonia was felled to make way for it, 'an act of vandalism,' say some, 'that has not been forgotten'. In 1990, somewhat belatedly, one of the research workers, Norman Heatley, was awarded the University's first honorary doctorate in medicine.

The medieval Jewish cemetery belonged, like so much land to the east of the city, to Magdalen College, and on 12 March 1622

Henry Danvers, later created Earl of Danby, a graduate of Christ Church, gave £5,000 to the University to clear the cemetery and establish on a five-acre site the first physic garden for the growing of medicinal herbs in England. His reward was to be painted by Van Dyck. There was only one problem: the Cherwell, which you may think flows sluggishly by, is apt to flood in winter, and 4,000 cartloads of 'mucke and dunge' had to be strewn around to raise the level of the land.

The imposing arch at the entrance was designed by Charles I's favourite architect, Inigo Jones, but of far more constructive use were the walls, intended to divide the garden into compartments and to provide an environment for climbing plants; both arch and walls were in place by 1633. The first head gardener, Jacob Bobart, was appointed nine years later. Born in 1596 in Brunswick, Bobart was clearly a man of many parts, for until he became *Horti Praefectus* at the new physic garden he was landlord of the Greyhound Inn in the High Street. Before that he had been a soldier. Against the walls, Bobart planted fruit trees: selling produce from the trees to supplement his income became a very necessary expedient during the Civil War, when he received no pay at all.

Bobart was said, and surely with good reason, to have been an excellent botanist and gardener, for by 1648 he had published his first catalogue of plants grown in the garden; they numbered 1,600. Within ten years he had added another 400.

If you walk down the centre path, from the entrance along to the second pond, you will see on the right of the path a yew tree. It does not look particularly old for it has been clipped too often, but it was planted in about 1650 by Jacob Bobart, and it is the oldest plant in the garden. Touch the trunk of this tree and you are in touch indeed with the seventeenth century and the creator of the Botanic Garden.

Thomas Baskerville has left a near contemporary impression of Bobart's achievements and standing. 'Amongst ye severall famous structures & curiosities wherewith ye flourishing University of Oxford is enriched, that of ye Publick Physick Garden deserves not ye last place, being a matter of great use & ornament, prouving serviceable not only to all Physitians, Apothecaryes, and those who are most imediately concerned in the practise of Physick, but to persons of all qualities serving to help ye diseased and for ye delight & pleasure of those of perfect health, containing therein 3,000 severall sorts of plants for ye honour of our nation and Universitie & service of ye Comonwealth.'

It was Jacob Bobart who changed the face of England's streets, for in 1666 he raised a hybrid seedling which became the ancestor of the London Plane Tree. And it was from Oxford's Botanic Garden that the yellow Oxford Ragwort began its slow but steady march on London. When seeds of *Senecio squalidus* from the region of Mount Etna were sown in the eighteenth century they took root in the garden walls, and spread across the footpaths of Christ Church Meadow and along the towpaths of the river; by the middle of the nineteenth century the plant had discovered railway lines, and in 1940 it reached the capital just in time to colonise bombed sites left by the Blitz.

When Jacob Bobart died in 1679 Anthony Wood regarded him as 'the best gardener in England.' He was succeeded by his son, known as Jacob Bobart the Younger. Compared in stature to his father, he was 'but a shrimp', according to Baskerville, and in 1710 Zacharias von Üffenbach, who the same year had found the Hall at Christ Church so far below his expectations, wrote a distinctly unflattering description of the new head gardener. 'I was greatly shocked by the hideous features and generally villainous appearance of this good and honest man,' he wrote. 'His wife, a filthy old hag, was with him, and although she may be the ugliest of her sex he is certainly the more repulsive of the two. An unusually pointed and very long nose, little eyes set deep in the head, a twisted mouth almost without upper lips, a great deep scar in one cheek and the whole face and hands as black and coarse as those of the poorest gardener or farm-labourer. His clothing and especially his hat were also very bad. Such is the aspect of the Professor, who would most naturally be taken for the gardener.'

Since the Bobarts' day the University Botanic Garden has acquired over 8,000 species and variety of plants, the most comprehensive collection of plants for its size of any botanic garden in the country. Its main purpose is to provide teaching materials for the study at Oxford of botany and biology, but it is much frequented by school children, notebooks in hand, and by those who just want to escape the turmoil of the town and eat their sandwiches in peace. At least, that is the theory, but peace does not always prevail, even here. One day in July 1990, overcome, apparently, by the heat, a visitor punched a gardener in the face, and instead of punching him back or taking out a writ the aggrieved member of staff decided to punish thousands of innocent potential visitors by having the garden closed for a week.

Rather more than half the garden is given over to formal beds in which plants are grouped according to their botanical family, but the southern end of the garden is far wilder and more fun, and at its extremity is a small but very effective bog garden. The garden's Arboretum can be found, with difficulty, some three miles south of Oxford at Nuneham Courtenay, and is open from 1 May to 31 October.

From almost anywhere in the Botanic Garden you will have been aware of the massive bell tower of Magdalen College rearing over the walls, and once you emerge into the High Street you are confronted by one of the outstanding landmarks Oxford has on offer, in some ways the most impressive; it is a truly wonderful tower, built in 1509, serene, majestic, powerful, reassuring. From this tower, with its ring of ten bells, the oldest being older even than the tower itself (it was cast about 1410), the chapel choir sing at six o'clock on May morning to a breathless crowd of undergraduates below. All High Street traffic stops, and the unaccompanied strains of *Now is the month of Maying* and *Sumer is icumen in* bring thirteenth-century Oxford back to life for a few magical moments.

The college itself is big without being boastful, resplendent in historical and literary associations, and although architecturally diverse it has achieved a domestic harmony. The range stretching furthest east, along the street front, was originally the Hospital of St John the Baptist, and its gargoyles are some of the most diverse and amusing in Oxford. In the right-hand corner of the first quadrangle, St John's, is a fifteenth-century open-air pulpit, from which once a year a sermon is still preached on the theme of St John the Baptist.

Unlike Magdalene College, Cambridge, Magdalen College, Oxford is spelt without a final 'e'; both are pronounced 'maudlin'. As recently as 1724 Nicholas Hawksmoor was spelling it 'Maudlin'. The college was founded in 1458 by William of Waynflete, who became not only Bishop of Winchester but the only man ever to have been headmaster both of Winchester and Eton. Its first thirty scholars were called Demies, since scholars originally received half the salary of a Fellow. And as Waynflete intended, the choir still has sixteen boys. Until 1828 there was a grammar school incorporated with the college, part of which, dating from 1614, remains in the north-west corner of St John's Quadrangle; but Magdalen College School now resides on the far side of Magdalen Bridge, and every afternoon a troop of sixteen choristers scurry chattering across the bridge for Evensong.

You enter the chapel through what is called the Founder's Tower, and the door is on your right, just before the cloisters. Inside the ante-chapel, on the left, is a particularly fine set of misericords, seats against which weary clerics could surreptitiously lean back during a lengthy liturgy. Dating from 1480, and originally built in the late Perpendicular style, the chapel itself has been heavily restored (the reredos, depicting figures from the Old Testament, was carved during the reign of William IV), and in some ways the ante-chapel is more interesting: there are, for example, some quite unusual sepia windows from the mid-seventeenth century.

It is usually necessary to view the chapel from the ante-chapel, divided off when services are not being held by a door kept bolted. The first President, William Tybard, lies buried in front of the altar, his tomb protected by a tatty carpet. On the north choir wall is a brass plaque commemorating C. S. Lewis and, in the ante-chapel, on the east wall to the right as you enter, is a monument to Queen Victoria's grandson, Prince Christian of Schleswig-Holstein, who entered Magdalen in 1886 and was killed in the Boer War. As this is Oxford, the monument is inscribed in Latin: *In Piam Memoriam Christini Victoris Principis de Slesvico-Holstinia*.

Because of the original choral foundation, the chapel's reputation stands high. During term there is a Choral Evensong six days a week, and a Sung Eucharist on Sundays and in the evening on major feast days. As a boy, Ivor Novello sang in the choir, and the comedian Dudley Moore was organ scholar here from 1954 to 1958. The organ on which he played is Victorian, for Cromwell dined at Magdalen one night and then removed the original organ, parts of which ended up in Tewkesbury Abbey.

The cloisters, begun in 1470, afford exciting views from the north aisle of the Hall, chapel and bell tower, and offer also a wide selection of enterprising medieval statues. Lions and eagles mingle with schoolmasters, physicians, a hippopotamus carrying its young, a pair of boxers, another couple apparently dancing who turn out to be Jacob and the Angel, and various animals representing human foibles: a hyena (fraud), a panther (treachery), a griffin

73

(covetousness), a dog (flattery) and a dragon (envy). With all these moral sentinels looking down, the choir sometimes sing out here, in the Cloister Quadrangle, to a privately invited audience.

If you are lucky enough to hear the choir, spare a thought for 'a poor boy at Malmesbury' who was captured in the sixteenth century by John Sheppard, the *informator choristarum*, and brought to Oxford in chains 'probably with the view of pressing him into the service of the choir'. Sheppard was 'fined a week's commons, on the ground that he had brought a stranger into College without leave'.

The conduct of Magdalen's chaplains sometimes left a good deal to be desired too, although it does not seem to have prevented their preferment. The Reverend Tom Goddard, appointed chaplain to the House of Commons in 1705, was known at Magdalen as Honest Tom Goddard 'because of his being a true friend to the pot and the pipe'. He was described as a good-natured rake, of whom it was observed that 'the very first time he read prayers after his being made chaplain, he read the Evening for the Morning Service, having drunk to that excess the night before that his head was giddy when he should perform his duty the day after'.

Up a treacherously steep staircase leading off the cloisters, but not open to the public, is what is called the Old Library. (The new library is the nineteenth-century building visible from the High Street on the corner of Longwall Street.) Its treasures include a ring given by Oscar Wilde to W. W. Ward, the corrected typescript of *Lady Windermere's Fan*, and a wig worn by probably the college's most renowned President, Martin Routh.

Dr Routh, who was a Demy in 1771 at the age of eighteen, became President of Magdalen in 1793; he was still President in 1854, sixty-one years later, when he died at the age of ninety-nine. Stories about Routh abound. He always fasted on the anniversary of Charles I's execution, and detested the House of Commons. Told that one of the Fellows had committed suicide, Routh said to the excited messenger, 'Pray, do not tell me who, sir. Allow me to guess'. When Anglicans in America found their ties with the diocese of London severed by the American War of Independence, and the Archbishop of Canterbury declined to consecrate bishops for them on the grounds that the Church of England was Established and could not provide bishops to serve in another State, Dr Routh, who was only twenty-eight at the time, advised the Americans to seek help from the Episcopal Church in Scotland. Thus, in 1784 in Aberdeen, Samuel Seabury was consecrated Bishop of Connecticut and, thanks to Routh's youthful advice, the Protestant Episcopal Church in the United States of America came into being.

Routh was in fact an eminent theologian, and was known as the Venerable Routh by the time he was forty, about the age at which he decided to enter old age anyway. The Crimean War was being fought when he died, yet it was felt by all who knew him that he had never parted from the eighteenth century, perhaps because he could remember Dr Johnson. He even had an aunt who knew another lady who had seen Charles II exercising his spaniels in Oxford, and for Magdalen undergraduates born as Queen Victoria was about to mount the throne, who knew Routh in his very last years and perhaps lived themselves until the commencement of the twentieth century, this fact became a truly astonishing, if slightly tenuous, historical link. Routh became such a famous spectacle in extreme old age — 'a mysterious dream of the past' as the historian J. R. Green described him — that on Sunday mornings crowds would wait to see him shuffle in his buckled shoes, and wearing a wig, from his Lodgings to the chapel. When he was sixty-five, perhaps in a moment of absent-mindedness, he married a woman of thirty, who herself aged prematurely, and even sprouted a moustache. His death, even at ninety-nine, seemed so uncalled for, leaving 'a vast void, strange and unaccountable', that one wag — his brother-in-law — suggested he had simply expired 'through chagrin at the fall of Russian securities'.

But perhaps there are later generations who more readily associate Magdalen College with Oscar Wilde. After becoming an undergraduate in 1874 at the age of twenty (he had already spent three years at Trinity College, Dublin, where he waltzed off with a galaxy of academic prizes, so that he arrived at Oxford as a very mature student), he won the Newdigate Poetry Prize and took a Double First. He was not just brilliant, he was also exceedingly clever. 'Never,' his biographer Hesketh Pearson was to write, 'did Oxford University turn out a less typical Oxonian than Oscar Wilde; and yet it will be seen that the man who graduated there remained in one important respect a typical undergraduate all his life'.

Wilde spent four years at Magdalen, and loved every aspect of Oxford — 'the most beautiful thing in England' he called it — apart from the professors. 'One cannot live in Oxford because of the dons,' he used to say.

'How do you find Mr Wilde's work?' the President, Frederick Bulley, asked his tutor, a man more interested in sport than teaching history.

'Mr Wilde absents himself without apology from my lectures,' the tutor replied. 'His work is most unsatisfactory.'

'That is hardly the way to treat a gentleman, Mr Wilde,' said the President.

'But, Mr President,' Wilde replied, 'he is not a gentleman.' Dr Bulley told him to leave the Hall, which no doubt he was only too pleased to do.

Wilde was once rusticated for returning to college late from a holiday in Greece, and he must have been loved by those fellow, but younger and less bold, undergraduates on whose behalf he played the role of a calm and infuriating rebel. Due one day to read in chapel from the Book of Deuteronomy, he decided the Song of Solomon was more his cup of tea, and read a long lesson from that instead. When he arrived late for a Divinity examination, William Spooner, the Warden of New College and himself an eccentric, told him to copy out the twenty-seventh chapter of the Acts of the Apostles. After some time Wilde was told he might desist. But he kept on writing, and eventually Spooner said, 'Didn't you hear us tell you, Mr Wilde, that you needn't copy out any more?'

'Oh, yes, I heard you,' Wilde replied, 'but I was so interested in what I was copying that I could not leave off. It was all about a man named Paul, who went on a voyage and was caught in a terrible storm, and I was afraid that he would be drowned. But, do you know, Mr Spooner, he was saved. And when I found that he was saved, I thought of coming to tell you.'

One of Oscar Wilde's rooms, on the kitchen staircase and overlooking the Cherwell, has in recent years been utilised as a bar, another to store furniture. By this failure to preserve as any sort of reliquary the rooms of a man who for a century has given more pleasure to the world than all the college dons put together, Magdalen does as little justice to itself as it does to the greatest theatrical genius since Sheridan. When Wilde was in residence his rooms resounded to good-humoured parties where punch was drunk and music enjoyed. Walter Parratt, organist at Magdalen from 1872 to 1882 and later Master of the King's Music, used to accompany the singers. It was after one party in these rooms that another undergraduate asked Wilde what his real ambition was, and received the starkly prophetic reply, 'Somehow or other I'll be famous, and if not famous I'll be notorious'. Being Wilde, he succeeded, of course, in being both.

It was a casual remark by Wilde to the effect that he wished that he could live up to his blue china (he possessed at that time two blue vases) that resulted in a sermon being preached in the University Church by the vicar denouncing him as a heathen, and it may also have been this occasion that led to an abortive raid on his rooms by four sporting drunks from the junior common room. The first got booted out. The second made his exit doubled up from a punch. The third – like the first – went flying down the stairs, and the fourth, a particularly hefty number, was carried in Wilde's arms to his own rooms, where Wilde proceeded to bury him beneath a pile of his own expensive furniture.

The Hall, reached up a flight of steps on the south of Cloister Quadrangle, was begun in 1474. There is a splendid Jacobean screen under the gallery, erected in 1605 in honour of a visit paid by James I and his heir, Prince Henry, a portrait of Wolsey, for he was a Fellow of Magdalen, and a fairly rare one of Elizabeth I, rare because it depicts her in raddled middle-age. It was a Magdalen graduate and President, Owen Oglethorpe, who, having been nominated Bishop of Carlisle in 1555 by the Catholic Mary I, four years later crowned Elizabeth. He died a few months later, his conscience in something of a turmoil.

James I was foolish but educated, and once declared, 'Were I not a king I would be an Oxford man'. He was greatly addicted to drink and, according to Anthony Wood, writing in 1606, the year after the King's visit to Magdalen, 'That damnd sin of drunkenness was considered. For whereas in the days of Queen Elizabeth it was little or nothing practiced (sack being then rather taken for a cordial than a usual liquor, sold also for the purpose in Apothecaries' shops), and a heinous crime it was to be overtaken with drink, or smoake tobacco, it now became in a manner common. The Court that was here last year left such impressions of debauchery upon the Students, that by a little practice they improved themselves so much, that they became more excellent than their masters, and that also without scandal, because it became a laudable fashion.'

If you leave the cloisters by any northern exit you will emerge

77

facing what is called The New Building, a splendid Georgian block that went up in 1733 but was much derided by James Wyatt, who dreamt up plans, fortunately frustrated through lack of funds, to 'Gothicize' it. Its proximity to the fifteenth-century cloisters may come as a surprise but a pleasant one, and the sudden transition is softened by a lawn and formal herbaceous border.

The historian Edward Gibbon lived in The New Building when he came to Magdalen in 1752 at the age of fifteen, and it was here that Charles Reade, while a Fellow of the college, wrote his best remembered novel, *The Cloister and the Hearth*. A gate to a bridge over the Cherwell leads to a walk named after the poet and essayist Joseph Addison, who was educated at Queen's College but was appointed a Demy at Magdalen in 1689. In about twenty minutes, Addison's Walk takes you past Magdalen Grove (on your left if you head north) and the Deer Park (where on summer nights Shakespeare is performed), first stocked in about 1710. Herds of deer require to be culled, so that the menu at Magdalen has frequently featured venison, a fact well known to Keats when writing his *Nonsense Verses on Oxford*:

> There are plenty of trees,
> And plenty of ease,
> And plenty of fat deer for Parsons;
> And when it is venison,
> Short is the benison –
> Then each on a leg or thigh fastens.

It was because William of Waynflete established his college outside the city walls that Magdalen managed to acquire land that gives the impression of commencing in the High Street and rolling away for ever into the country, a luxury not even Christ Church, with its lovely meadow, quite enjoys. But the setting has often belied the atmosphere within. Only half a century after its foundation, one member of staff was found to be 'unchaste with the wife of a tailor'; another had apparently baptised a cat and practised witchcraft; a chap called Gregory 'climbed the great gate by the tower, and brought a Stranger into College'; and – horror of horrors – the inspectors discovered that Kendell 'wears a gown not sewn together in front'.

Over the centuries, plenty of nonconformists have found their way to Magdalen, and one who arrived in 1912 was the Prince of Wales. A visit to France having whetted his appetite for travel (so he later told us in his memoirs after he had abdicated and been created Duke of Windsor), 'Oxford in consequence loomed as a dreary chore to be finished with the least possible effort and as quickly as possible'.

Fortunately for princes they do not need degrees, and fortunately for us King Edward VIII only reigned for 325 days. He was so ignorant and unlettered he was even spared having to pass Responsions, the University entrance examination. Unlike his grandfather, Edward VII, he was permitted to live in college, in rooms in the cloisters, but these he occupied attended by his private tutor from boyhood, a valet and an equerry.

In the Duke of Windsor's time there was a steward, Richard Gunstone, whose party trick consisted of inserting a banana into the neck of a bottle filled with burning paper 'and watching the vacuum suck it down with a thud', which astonishing feat of physics he one day performed for the benefit of George V. 'By God,' the King exclaimed (like his son, he was a man of limited vocabulary and simple tastes), 'that is one of the darnedest tricks I have ever seen.' Mr Gunstone retired in 1914 after thirty-four years with the college, and could recall an undergraduate risking his life by climbing to the top of the tower to tie his pocket handkerchief to a pinnacle.

A decade later Magdalen College received two more failures, but failures of a kind very different from the Prince of Wales: men who messed up their undergraduate lives but went on to enhance the world of literature. In 1925 John Betjeman went into residence only, eventually, to be rusticated; and two years later Alan Pryce-Jones arrived: his Oxford career was even more disastrous than Betjeman's, for he lasted just two terms, but he ended up as editor of *The Times Literary Supplement*.

One of the questions set for the general paper of Magdalen's entrance examination in 1925 was, 'Can "skyscrapers" or railway stations be made beautiful? If so, how?' This must have been right up John Betjeman's street. Other questions invited candidates to say which they found finer, the Greek language and literature or Latin; to offer their views on co-education; and to say what kind of services should be rewarded in the Birthday Honours list.

Both Betjeman and Pryce-Jones had rooms in The New Building, and both had to endure the unbelievable snobbery of the President, Sir Herbert Warren, who was born as the Crimean War was breaking out, and elected President in 1885 when he was only thirty-one. (His one virtue, in Betjeman's eyes, may have been that he had known Tennyson.) He would actually introduce people to his wife by saying, 'Meet Lady Warren, the daughter of Sir Benjamin Brodie, Bart.' But he was capable of meeting other people's absurdities head-on. An Indian prince informed the President that in his own country he was styled 'the son of God'.

'You will find, Your Highness,' said Warren, 'that we have the sons of many famous fathers here.'

Warren's declared intent was to sweep away the aestheticism of Oscar Wilde and fill Magdalen with hearties, a good enough reason for civilised people like Betjeman and Pryce-Jones to dislike him. But the man John Betjeman really came to hate was C. S. Lewis, his tutor in English Language and Literature, at that time an atheist, later a proselytising Christian philosopher. They wasted no time getting off on the wrong foot, for Betjeman produced for Lewis's consideration an essay suggesting that Lord Alfred Douglas was a greater poet than Shakespeare, an amusing conceit quite beyond the comprehension of Lewis's pedantic outlook. Things did not improve when Betjeman turned up for a tutorial wearing carpet slippers.

Heartiness at Magdalen was carried to such extremes under Warren that drunkenness on the premises became *de rigueur*. A contemporary of John Betjeman, Martyn Skinner, told Betjeman's biographer, Bevis Hillier, that 'one man got so tight that he smashed up his own rooms without realising they were his'.

In 1906 Magdalen had appointed as Dean of Divinity a cleric called J. M. Thompson, who five years later published a book with the innocent sounding title *Miracles in the New Testament*. It set out, however, to disprove the miracles, and the Bishop of Winchester, Magdalen's Visitor, withdrew Thompson's licence to officiate as a priest in the college. Thompson taught John Betjeman history, and often entertained him to tea on Sundays, Betjeman leaving the house when he heard the bells of St Barnabas in the north-west suburb of Jericho summoning him to Evensong:

Good Lord, as the angelus floats down the road,
Byzantine St Barnabas, be Thine Abode.

80

Like many of his generation, Betjeman experimented with homosexuality while at Oxford, and was discovered in bed with Auden, whose scout had to be bribed £5 to keep quiet. In 1979 Betjeman, by then a Knight Bachelor and Poet Laureate, got all mention of the incident removed from the English edition – but not the American – of Charles Osborne's superb biography of Auden. There is no fun, of course, to be had from deriding perfectly 'normal' homosexuals, but in 1928 the undergraduate magazine *Isis* published 'A Lofty Ideal', a brilliantly funny portrait by Alec Clifton-Taylor of an aesthete whose ambition it was to win a Blue – not for rowing or rugger but for playing bézique.

He came up to Oxford an infant adult,
He was pledged to the latest aesthetical cult,
His waistcoat was seen
To be soft apple-green
And he painted his finger-nails ultramarine.
His pyjamas were purple with bobbles of black,
And some verses by the Sitwells were seen on his back:
But the charms of the aesthetes, the charms of his clique,
Were small when compared to the charms of bézique!

Isis has not always hit the nail on the head. Reviewing *Oxford Poetry* in 1926 it noted: 'Through about seventy lines Mr Auden continues to show his inability to appreciate the meaning of words.' Unfortunately, also, the magazine tends to lurch from one financial crisis to another. On one occasion it was bailed out by Elizabeth Taylor (the actress, not the novelist), whose husband, Richard Burton, read English for six months at Exeter College during the war. In recent years it has been edited by the satirist Miles Kington and the playwright Dennis Potter and, in 1990, by George Bridges, a great-grandson of the Poet Laureate Robert Bridges.

One of John Betjeman's most distinguished contemporaries was Henry Green, who arrived at Magdalen in 1925 and published his first novel, *Blindness*, the very next year. Like Betjeman, he loathed C. S. Lewis, and anxious to gain material for another novel, he soon quit Oxford to work in his father's factory in Birmingham. But he stayed long enough to encounter a drunken hearty in the cloisters who, imagining the tin of Eno's Fruit Salts Green was carrying to be some sort of alcohol, grabbed the can and swallowed the lot.

81

On returning from Addison's Walk one should pay one's respects, on the lawn of The New Building, to a great plane tree planted in 1801, a scion of the hybrid plane first raised in the Botanic Garden across the road. And just before you leave Magdalen you can go into the Chaplain's Quadrangle, immediately to the left of the Lodge, where there is a skeletal sculpture by David Wynne of Jesus, seemingly fending off Mary Magdalene after the Resurrection, when she recognises him and he says to her, 'Touch me not; for I am not yet ascended to my Father'.

On your left as you leave the college is Magdalen Bridge, built in 1773 to replace an eleventh-century stone bridge; the parapets were rebuilt in 1882, but by 1990 they had so completely collapsed again that at enormous cost a major work of reconstruction was put in hand. The result is a triumph.

If you are thinking of taking a picnic into the Botanic Garden and want wine or beer, there is a large branch of Bottoms Up at the east end of Magdalen Bridge, and there is a reliable delicatessen called Parmenters at 58 High Street, two doors up from Longwall Street. And it is up Longwall Street, the first turn right to the west of Magdalen College, that you now want to walk, with the wall enclosing Magdalen Grove on your right and a row of houses on the left which, though not in a good state of repair, have at least not yet been knocked down to make way for something similar to New College's 1961 Sacher Building. Substantial remains of the medieval city wall run behind these houses, and you can see them quite well through a gap on the right of the hideous Sacher Building.

Round the bend on your left (just before Longwall Street becomes St Cross Road), at what is now 21 Longwall Street but used to be 100a, is the site of the garage in which, in 1912, the twenty-five-year-old William Morris built his prototype of the 'bullnose' Oxford Morris car and laid the foundations for a fortune.

A fascinating diversion well worth making will take you a short way up St Cross Road to the Church of St Cross, with its thirteenth-century tower. Inside it is much restored, but retains a splendid painted ceiling in the nave and a large niche in the north chancel arch for a relic of the True Cross, empty alas. On the right, entered by a wooden gate just before the iron gates to the churchyard, is Holywell Cemetery, listed in the Domesday Book as meadow. A variety of wildlife have still failed to realise that the University has encroached on their domain (the church now serves as a chapel for the nearby St Catherine's College, built in 1964), and foxes and pheasants, toads and dragonfly happily cohabit with the dead.

And very distinguished dead they are too. Almost immediately on your right as you enter is a tombstone 'To the beautiful memory of Kenneth Grahame, who passed the River on the 6th July 1932 leaving childhood and literature through him the more blest for all time'. Sir John Stainer has a large celtic cross (as well as a memorial window in the Lady Chapel), and a plain and otherwise unadorned headstone simply reads, 'Kenneth Tynan, 1927–1980'. Sir Maurice Bowra, the fashionable Warden of Wadham, Greek scholar and one time Vice-Chancellor, is buried near him. Walter Pater and Charles Williams represent art criticism and poetry. The theologian Austin Farrer, Warden of Keble College from 1960 to 1968, lies here, alongside a former archbishop of Cape Town – alongside, too, publishers and nannies, army officers and mountaineers, librarians, curators, drapers, doctors, zoologists and astronomers, all of whose neatly regimented graves are marched across by cow parsley and blackberry in a sort of carefully contrived wilderness.

Return to Longwall Street and take the left-hand fork into Holywell Street, one of the best preserved of the domestic city thoroughfares, with an interesting mixture of seventeenth- and eighteenth-century houses. The Victorian front of New College closes in rather, but at least with one end of the street blocked off to traffic it is relatively quiet. Opposite the college, at Number 15, is the Wykeham Coffee House, with a small garden at the rear, and for those not in need of alcohol it is a useful place for meals. It provides cream teas, ploughman's lunches and a selection of sandwiches and salads.

Further along on the right is the Holywell Music Room, an elegant Georgian building (it was opened in 1748), designed by the Reverend Thomas Camplin when he was Vice-Principal of St Edmund Hall. The room can claim to have been the first public concert hall in England. It is owned by Wadham College, just round the corner, and it was to Wadham that George IV presented the chandeliers hung in Westminster Hall for his coronation banquet which now hang in the Music Room. Haydn conducted a rehearsal here, and the price of a ticket today includes coffee before or after the concert at either the King's Arms (on the corner of Holywell Street and Parks Road), or the Turf Tavern (to be found on a minor excursion down Bath Place, opposite the Music Room).

A prank was once played at the Music Room by Tom Driberg, an episode which found its way into the *Sunday Times*, as no doubt he intended it should. Advertising a programme in homage to Beethoven, Driberg composed some risqué poems which were set to 'music' – the score included a part for typewriters – by another conspirator, Archie Gwynne Brown, and the climax to the performance was a disconcerting flushing of a lavatory off-stage.

Unless you are wealthy and wish to stay in the most expensive guest house in Oxford, scurry past the Bath Place Hotel and Restaurant and take the left-hand snicket to the Turf, a seventeenth-century inn once called the Spotted Cow, so snugly hidden away that only tourists, students and Dylan Thomas have ever been able to find it. The cellar is thirteenth-century, and the space where you can now eat and drink out of doors is said to have been the scene of the last cock fight to take place in England. The landlord makes no bones about charging high prices; no doubt the place would be overcrowded if he did not. The Turf is quite special, it is open virtually all day, and you do not have to drink: in deference to intelligent continental habits they serve coffee and tea as well.

Three

KEEPING THE BOOKS DRY AT WADHAM

Wadham College (open 1.00 p.m. to 4.30 p.m.), University Museum (open Monday to Saturday, 12 noon to 5.00 p.m., admission free), Pitt Rivers Museum (open Monday to Saturday, 2.00 p.m. to 4.00 p.m., admission free), University Park (open until half an hour before sunset), Parsons Pleasure (open 1 May to 30 September, admission free), Keble College (open 10.00 a.m. to 7.00 p.m. summer, 10.00 a.m. to sunset winter), Eagle and Child (meals, 12 noon to 2.00 p.m., 6.00 p.m. to 8.00 p.m.).

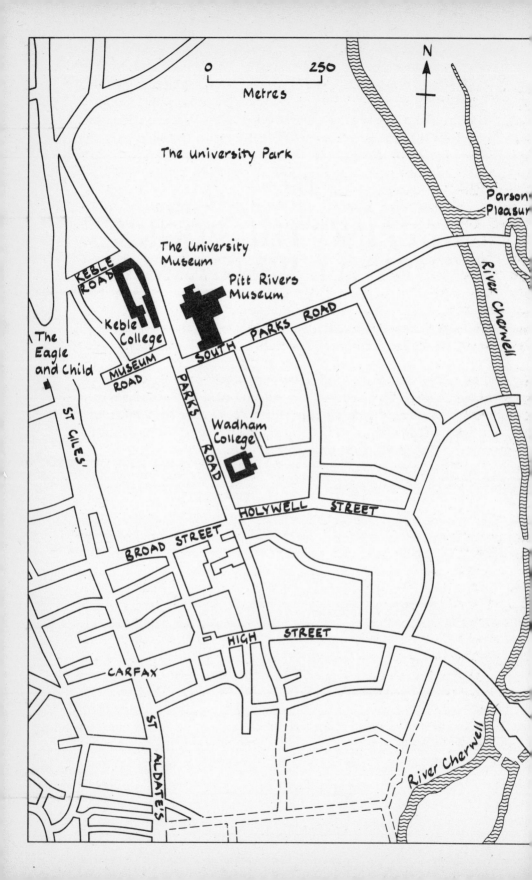

15 A witty memorial by John Doubleday, half chair and half man, to Sir Maurice Bowra, Warden of Wadham College from 1938 to 1970. It stands in the college garden. Bowra was such an hospitable host to undergraduates and academics from far afield that he once remarked, 'I'm a man more dined against than dining'.

16 A portrait of John Keble, painted when he was eighty-four. With John Newman and Edward Pusey, Keble is generally regarded as one of the founders of the Oxford Movement, and in his memory Keble College was established in 1870. John Keble entered Corpus Christi College at the age of fourteen and took a Double First in classics and mathematics, was elected a Fellow of Oriel College and became Professor of Poetry. *The painting hangs in the Hall at Keble, and is reproduced by courtesy of the Warden and Fellows of Keble College.*

17 The Eagle and Child in St Giles', an Oxford public house with strong literary connections. Its regular patrons once included C.S. Lewis, Charles Williams, J.R.R. Tolkien and Lord David Cecil.

18 The north-east corner of Canterbury Quad at St John's College, built by Archbishop William Laud, who was President of St John's from 1611 to 1621. He celebrated the completion of the quadrangle in 1636, by which time he was Chancellor of the University, by giving a dinner attended by Charles I, Queen Henrietta-Maria and the King's nephew, Prince Rupert of the Rhine.

19 A group of inventive gargoyles to be seen in the seventeenth century Canterbury Quad at St John's. These often very amusing adornments, in which stonemasons took great pride, are a feature of all the older colleges and city churches.

20 The garden at St John's is one of the largest and most restful in Oxford, and affords a superb view of the east front of Canterbury Quad.

21 The oldest structure in Oxford, the Saxon tower of St Michael's Church. It was from the top of this tower that in 1555 Thomas Cranmer, Archbishop of Canterbury, was forced to watch the Bishops of London and Worcester, Nicholas Ridley and Hugh Latimer, being burnt at the stake at a spot now in the middle of Broad Street.

22 Oxford's High Street is full of pleasant surprises, including this alert dog advertising his master's business.

23 Oxford's Covered Market, opened in 1774, caters for almost every need. The atmosphere is congenial and the standard of produce high.

24 The front door of the Principal's Lodgings at Jesus College, in the First Quadrangle, with its attractive shell-hood. Jesus is the only college in Oxford to have been founded during the reign of Elizabeth I, by the Queen herself, in 1571.

25 The early eighteenth century spire of a former High Street church, St Anne's, forms a stunning climax to Turl Street. The redundant church is now the library of Lincoln College, and is open at certain hours to the public. It retains a richly ornamented plasterwork ceiling and altar rails and pews from the eighteenth century.

26 The elaborately pinnacled fourteenth century spire of the University Church of St Mary the Virgin. It was in this building that Thomas Cranmer was condemned for heresy and John Keble launched the Oxford Movement. A portion of Nicholas Stone's once controversial seventeenth century Virgin Porch can be seen in the foregound.

Just as Pembroke College speaks of Dr Johnson, Christ Church of Lewis Carroll and Magdalen of Oscar Wilde, it is difficult not to feel that in modern times Wadham College has become indissolubly linked with the name of one of its most civilised, if slightly outré, dons, Maurice Bowra, elected Warden in 1938 when he was only forty.

From the crossroads at Holywell Street, walk north up Parks Road, past a handsome seventeenth-century house without a front door (an explanation for this will become apparent), and immediately on your right is the unrelieved symmetry of Wadham's severe but satisfying front, dating from 1610 – early, you may think, yet it was to be 260 years before another college was built in Oxford. When Wadham went up, in the space of three years, thirteenth-century foundations like Merton must have looked with disdain upon this Stuart parvenu.

It was money bequeathed for the purpose in 1609 by a wealthy Devonian, Nicholas Wadham, a man of 'great length in his extraction, breadth in his estate, and depth in his liberality', whose 'hospitable house was an inn at all times, a court at Christmas', that initially led to Wadham's existence. But had his seventy-five-year-old widow Dorothy not been a tough old bird (she lived to be eighty-four, an incredible age in the seventeenth century), fighting off his family and petitioning James I for a charter, her husband's wishes might never have come to fruition. She drew up the statutes, and not only appointed the first Warden, Robert Wight, who took up his appointment in 1613 and became bishop both of Lichfield and Coventry, but without even visiting Oxford found a cook, and told her architect, William Arnold (she chose him because she knew his work at Montacute House in Somerset), to build the library over the kitchen so as to keep the books dry.

The cook was a man, for Mrs Wadham had no doubt heard that

where women were concerned, Oxford undergraduates were not always to be trusted. In fact, she laid down that no woman was to be employed in the college save a laundress — and she was to be 'of such age, condition, and reputation as to be above suspicion'. Ironically, three and a half centuries later Wadham became one of the first Oxford colleges to admit women as undergraduates.

You enter the college through the centre of the front range, and here in the Front Quadrangle (gravelled until 1809), all again is symmetry. It has been faulted for that, but the proportions seem harmonious enough. Entry to the Hall in the east range, beneath statues of Nicholas and Dorothy Wadham and James I, is again positioned dead centre.

Its hammerbeam roof is the Hall's most remarkable architectural feature, but it possesses too some fine Tudor portraits, and a much later one of Lord Lovelace, who allegedly freed England 'from popery and slavery when he held Oxford for William of Orange'. Henry Lamb's portrait of Maurice Bowra hangs to the right of the High Table, and almost opposite him is a painting of the great seventeenth-century architect Sir Christopher Wren, who became a Fellow Commoner at Wadham in 1646.

There is also a painting of a nineteenth-century architect, Sir Thomas Jackson, a scholar of Wadham in 1854 and elected a Fellow in 1882. Many regard Jackson as a great architect too. He it was who in 1882 designed the Examination Schools in the High Street — perhaps the most artificial building in Oxford, desperately pretending to be Elizabethan; indeed, Jackson had in mind as his model Kirby Hall in Northamptonshire, Sir Christopher Hatton's unique sixteenth-century mansion.

During the First World War Jackson's Schools became the Third Southern General Hospital, and part of the flooring was removed to provide access to the subterranean warren of rooms below street level. Down a chute inserted through this hole in the floor the bodies of soldiers who had died from their wounds were dispatched, to be washed by orderlies in a zinc bath which remains there still. Then they were laid out in a temporary mortuary next door. Hundreds traverse the pavement in front of the Examination Schools every day, unaware of past tragedies enacted beneath their feet.

Sir Maurice Bowra had been an undergraduate at New College, where he took a Double First. In 1922, at the age of twenty-four, he immediately became a Fellow and Tutor at Wadham, and from

1938 to 1970 he served as an amusing and much loved Warden. If on leaving the Hall you turn right and walk into the garden, you will there encounter a strange reincarnation of Bowra in the form of John Doubleday's statue, half man and half chair. But do not be tempted to sit on it; Bowra would only pinch your bottom.

Maurice Bowra became one of the best-known dons of his time, for he did not confine his interests and friendships to his own college. It was Eddy Sackville-West, younger by three years, who introduced him to the writings of Proust and, in person, to David Cecil, then an undergraduate at Christ Church. Bowra was generous with hospitality and kindness, to the extent that he once remarked, 'I'm a man more dined against than dining'. In a book commemorating Bowra, Anthony Powell remembered the 'good college food, lots to drink, almost invariably champagne', and it was at Maurice Bowra's table, for example, that even in wartime literati like Rosamond Lehmann and Enid Starkie would meet. He also did not take himself too seriously. More interested in young men than young ladies, Bowra once excused his affection for a rather plain woman with the self-deprecating quip, 'Buggers can't be choosers'.

When Bowra died in 1971 *The Times* said that Oxford had lost 'the most remarkable figure of his time in the university', for he had a genius for communication, and 'generations of undergraduates and young dons have felt that they owed to him their first real grasp of the infinite variety of civilisation'. *The Times* even thought that this influence could be detected in the work of major twentieth-century thinkers like Isaiah Berlin and A. J. Ayer, and the paper recorded how his 'boundless hospitality' had made Wadham 'the most familiar of all Oxford colleges to many Londoners'. Bowra's wit and flamboyance may sometimes have disguised the fact that he was enormously learned and well-read. He took Anatole France as an early model, and his own extensive literary output reflected in particular his great knowledge and love of Greek poetry.

Kenneth Clark, appointed Director of the National Gallery in 1934 at the age of thirty-one, said that without question Maurice Bowra had been the strongest influence in his life, and John Betjeman, one of many undergraduates who drifted over to Wadham from other colleges, was to write

certain then,
As now, that Maurice Bowra's company
Taught me far more than all my tutors did.

Perhaps the key to Bowra's success as a don was his ability to appear safe to the Establishment, yet anti-Establishment to undergraduates. He was also quite fearless, and rather short in stature. One of his acts of kindness involved speaking in court on behalf of a Wadham undergraduate who had been caught *in flagrante* with a mechanic on the bank of the canal.

'Stand up, Mr Bowra,' said the judge.

'I am standing up,' Bowra replied.

One of Maurice Bowra's most interesting predecessors was John Wilkins, later Bishop of Chester who, says John Aubrey, 'after the Visitation at Oxon by the Parliament, had gott to be Warden of Wadham College'. He had married the sister of Oliver Cromwell, was Warden from 1648 to 1659, and managed to ingratiate himself with Charles II by founding the Royal Society whose early hair-brained experiments included transferring blood from a sheep to a man. Wilkins's portrait hangs in the Hall next to that of Christopher Wren.

In the garden you can still relax beneath the enormous beech that Francis Kilvert returned to admire in 1874. 'All was usual,' he recorded in his almost illegible but now famous diary, 'the copper beech still spread a purple gloom in the corner, the three glorious limes swept their luxuriant foliage flat upon the sward, the great poplars towered over the steeple, the laburnum showers its golden rain by the quiet cloisters and the wisteria still hung its blue flower clusters upon the garden wall. The fabric of the college was unchanged, the grey chapel walls still rose fair and peaceful from the green turf.' All that marred this return visit after an absence of a decade was that 'One or two of the College servants remembered my face still, almost all had forgotten my name'. Let us hope that twentieth-century Wadham college servants have not forgotten the names of Michael Foot, Leader of the Labour Party from 1980 to 1983, or Cecil Day-Lewis, Poet Laureate, from 1968 to 1972.

You will find the ancient door to the chapel on Staircase Three, between the garden and the Front Quad. You first enter a cool, paved ante-chapel, much studded with Jacobean monuments. The most impressive, on the north wall, is of an ill-fated young baronet,

90

Sir John Portman, who died in 1624 at the age of nineteen, while an undergraduate.

Behind the screen dividing the chapel from the ante-chapel, lovely with elaborate filigree carving, stand what were originally boxed-in seats for servants, used now for storage.

The stone reredos only dates from 1834, but the marvellous Biblical window above the altar, the work of a Dutchman, Bernard van Linge, was made in 1622 — at a cost of £113.

In the nineteenth century the chapel played a prominent part in opposing the liturgical effects of the Oxford Movement: a Victorian Warden, Benjamin Symonds, who held sway from 1831 to 1871, was an evangelical who had the dubious distinction of failing the future Cardinal Newman. He was even instrumental in having Dr Pusey suspended from preaching in the University Church for two years. His oddest quirk was to scoop up the collection and take it away in his pocket.

On leaving the chapel, cross the Front Quad and through Staircase Four, in the Back Quadrangle, you will find a surprise. To the left is the first modern extension, much of its 1951 Cotswold stone now mercifully obscured by climbing plants, and to the right is the back of the house — first seen in Parks Road — without a door on to the street; it was built, in fact, as college rooms in 1693. In front, across the grass (and this is the surprise), is what appears to be merely a wall. But at either end steps lead up to a terrace, and here a most enterprising piece of design took place between 1970 and 1975, when new rooms were incorporated with the backs of the seventeenth-century houses in Holywell Street, and a well was provided to light Blackwell's Music Shop down below.

Back in Parks Road, turn right, and on your left you will pass the gardens of Trinity, on your right a charming pair of semi-detached cottages, their walls in summer a confusion of climbing hydrangea, sweet peas, clematis and roses. Cross over South Parks Road, averting your eyes from the Radcliffe Science Laboratory, and on your right, set well back from the road, stands one of the most original museums in the world.

To appreciate the genesis of the University Museum, with its solitary conifer on the lawn, which must be the tallest tree in Oxford, it is necessary to recall that before accepted patterns of theological and scientific thought were overthrown by the publication in 1859 of Darwin's *The Origin of Species by Means of Natural Selection*, a watershed in thought which coincided with the Victorian rebellion in the arts led by John Ruskin and the Pre-Raphaelites, the study of science at Oxford was as dormant as the dodo. The building of this museum, quite apart from its design, was the occasion of one of Oxford's famous battles (the Vice-Chancellor believed that 'Science tended to Infidelity'), and during this battle a number of minor skirmishes were to show up the puerile thinking which academics so often bring to administration. Convocation, for example, permitted the installation of gas pipes for lighting, but voted against the purchase of gas burners.

Fortunately, the Reader in Anatomy, John Acland (he later became Regius Professor of Medicine), believed it was the business of a university to study the universe; equally fortunately, he was a friend of Ruskin's. What they combined to achieve was a museum of natural history with laboratories and lecture rooms all under one roof. And what a roof! Decorated cast-iron columns, like palm trees at Kew, soar up to a sky of glass through which, in exceptional gales, great chunks of masonry have been known to hurtle down on to vulnerable Iquanodon bernissartensis in the central court below. With a gallery built around this court, supported on columns carved out of Porphyritic Granite from Cornwall, Carboniferous Limestone from Limerick, the whole concept, a 'fabric *really* and *obviously useful*', as Ruskin, an educationalist and moralist as well as an artist, described it himself, was something entirely new in the way of showing off and explaining the past.

But Ruskin's over-zealous emphasis on a muscular application to life has not survived. 'You have no business to read in the long vacation,' he told the undergraduates in 1878. 'Come *here* to make scholars of yourselves, and go to the mountains or the sea to make men of yourselves. Give at least a month in each year to rough sailors' work and sea fishing. Don't lounge or flirt on the beach, but make yourselves good seamen. Then, on the mountains, go and help the shepherd at his work, the woodmen at theirs, and learn to know the hills by night and day. If you are staying in level country, learn to plough, and whatever else that is useful. Then here in Oxford, read to the utmost of your power, and practise singing, fencing, wrestling and riding.'

Ruskin was not content to advise undergraduates to patronise working men by interfering with their labours. He even attempted to erect one of the pillars, bedecked with flora and fauna, himself, but he did the job so ineptly that it had to be taken down and built again. He extended his paternalism to the army of builders, many of them Irish, employed to put his Venetian Gothic into effect under the direction of the Dublin architect Benjamin Woodward. Work began in 1855 and was completed four years later, and not only was a room provided in which the workmen could eat, they were bombarded with books, and subjected, first thing in the morning, to prayers. The result of their labours did not meet with universal approval. 'Perfectly indecent,' was Tennyson's verdict on the University Museum in 1860.

A truly extraordinary experience can be undertaken by walking to the east end of the central court, for there you will find the entrance to the Pitt Rivers Museum of Ethnology and Prehistory. It would seem that Lieutenant General Augustus Lane Fox Pitt Rivers of the Grenadier Guards spent several lifetimes collecting artefacts from every part of the world and from every age up to his own; by 1883 he had amassed 14,000 objects. These he presented to Oxford University. No one knows how many objects the museum contains today; the figure is vaguely placed at between 500,000 and one million, and when it comes to describing them collectively, words fail. Unique, fascinating, spell-binding, overwhelming. No one could ever absorb and study the whole of this collection. It is caught in a kind of time-warp. Glass cases are jammed full of curiosities, and beneath the cases lie tier upon tier of drawers jammed full too. Some of these objects are large and easy to assimilate, like an Egyptian mummy dating from about 720 BC, its case lifted so that the mummy itself is clearly visible, a macabre gift from the Prince of Wales. How did he acquire it? Perhaps he opened a bridge across the Nile. Others are tiny but comprehensive. You could study the history of tobacco smoking and its substitutes by spending an afternoon standing over one small display case alone. Items relating to magic and witchcraft are evidently not deemed sufficient; charms and sympathetic magic are covered too. Brooches and pins, skulls and clay pipes, devices for carrying babies and children's toys from Mandalay, surgical instruments from Algeria, a butterfly kite from China, pottery from the Cameroons, Neolithic flint axes, Mogul armour, all are here, in staggering abundance and variety. Funerary practices jostle for space with modes of transport, Aboriginal paintings with puppets, snowshoes with weights and measures. There are objects here you will see nowhere else. It is a museum which draws its devotees back time and again, and when you have recovered from your first attack of claustrophobia you will quite understand why.

The centre of Oxford lacks its own municipal open spaces, and nothing could better illustrate the grip the University still exercises over citizens' pleasures and pastimes than its continued ownership and policing of the University Park which, if you now feel like a stroll, you will find a little way further up Parks Road on your right. Some thirty acres of the Parks — and pedants insist you either call them the Parks or the University Park — were recorded in 1086, when the land was owned by the Norman sheriff who built the now derelict castle. By the time Merton College sold the Parks to the University in 1865, they covered nearly 100 acres. You may not ride a bicycle, although many people do, or play a wireless, or any games unless you have permission; and, as is the case with so much open land in Oxford owned by the University, you are shut out of it at night.

The Parks are so named because during the Civil War the area was used as a park in which to train Royalist troops, many recruited from the University. In 1642 Anthony Wood recorded soldiers being drilled in 'the New Park' where they were divided 'into four Squadrons, of which two were Musquiteers, the third Pikes, and the fourth Hallbeards. After they had been reasonably instructed in the words of command, and in their postures, they were put into Battle-array, and skirmished together in a very decent manner.' Many of the elms were cut down at this time to help build defences; Charles I dutifully replanted, but his own elms have vanished too, victims of Dutch elm disease.

Much of the grass is left to grow, producing crops of interesting insects, and the elegant concrete footbridge that crosses the Cherwell on the eastern border (built in 1923 as part of a plan to relieve unemployment and described by John Betjeman as humping itself like a Magpie Moth Caterpillar) leads, if you turn left, to walks by the river or across clover-laden meadows. If you turn right over the bridge and follow the river you will come, clearly visible on the opposite bank, upon the last bastion of male privilege in Oxford, Parsons Pleasure, a rather squalid nudist bathing area generally frequented by dons of a certain age and corpulency.

Whatever pleasures may in all innocence have been experienced here, by parsons or others, Parsons Pleasure's most exuberant hour arrived not in fact but in fiction, when in Robert Robinson's hilarious whodunit, *Landscape with Dead Dons*, a man who had already committed two murders attempts a third, and at a word of command from a police officer the entire naked contingent of Parsons Pleasure proceed to give chase. Two High Churchmen emerging from Keble decide they are Baptists. An eminent scientist standing outside the Pitt Rivers Museum attributes the vision to 'some trick of the dying sun'. Past the cricketers, 'turned to stone', down Broad Street, on along George Street, into Gloucester Green and along Beaumont Street the denuded crocodile runs, until eventually the murderer is felled on the steps of the Martyr's Memorial by a telescope hurled at his legs by a lady called Mrs Spectre, who just happens to be walking down the steps of the Ashmolean as this bizarre spectacle is passing.

You can scarcely miss Keble College in Parks Road, across the road in fact from the University Museum and the University Park. For a modern college – at least, it was modern in 1870 – it occupies a really generous stretch of land, with the Warden's spacious Lodgings – 'a lordly pleasure house' it was dubbed in 1877 – at the far south end, and Butterfield's impressive chapel exuding Victorian self-assurance at the north.

John Keble, regarded as a saint by many High Church Anglicans, was born in 1792, and spent four years at Oxford as an undergraduate. To begin to grasp the significance of those years it is necessary to realise that he entered Corpus Christi College at the age of fourteen, and that four years later he took a Double First in classics and mathematics. He was only the second person since Robert Peel to achieve that particular distinction. It comes as no surprise that such a brilliant young man was immediately elected to a Fellowship at Oriel. By 1822, having by then been ordained, and having decided also – which was rare at the time – to take his pastoral responsibilities seriously, he was being spoken of as 'the first man in Oxford'.

The novelist Charlotte M. Yonge described John Keble as 'beamy', and indeed, judging from a striking portrait painted when he was eighty-four, his face was that of a person it would be hard not to love. As a young man he was on intimate terms of friendship with two other Oriel Fellows, Edward Pusey and John Newman, but before ever it seemed likely that he – or they – would embark upon a catholic crusade for the Church of England, he was elected,

95

in 1831, Professor of Poetry. This was on the strength of a volume of his own poems called *The Christian Year*, poor stuff which went into an almost unbelievable ninety editions in his lifetime.

It was, however, Keble's return to Oxford to take up the Chair of Poetry after a period in a Hampshire parish that led to his preaching a sermon in the University Church in 1833 which Newman came to regard as the starting point of the Oxford Movement.

But later on, following Newman's conversion to Rome in 1845, Keble failed to play an active public role in the Oxford Movement, leaving the more aggressive Canon Pusey to pursue the cause at Oxford while he himself retreated once more to the life of a country parson. His influence upon men of his time seems to have been almost entirely through the manifest goodness that radiated from his nature, and very soon after his death in 1866 there was talk of founding a new college in Oxford in his memory. Contrary to popular belief, Keble College was not primarily intended as some sort of seminary for the Anglo-Catholic priesthood but as an austerely run secular college where impecunious scholars might live economically, taking all their meals in Hall, for example, and living in only one room. But undergraduates were encouraged to contemplate ordination. Cyril Garbett, the authoritarian Archbishop of York, was an undergraduate at Keble.

The inmates were faced with indifferent food, were never served wine, suffered the indignity of uncurtained windows, were forbidden a sofa (clearly the first Warden, a young Christ Church tutor called Edward Talbot, had heard what sofas and curtains could lead to) and had to return to college by nine. On Wednesday evenings they compensated for the spartan routine by smuggling in a prize-fighter.

Money having poured in, a four and a half acre site was purchased for £7,047 from St John's College, who still own vast tracts of St Giles'. William Butterfield, whose All Saints Church in London's Margaret Street had become a mecca for Anglo-Catholics, was hired as architect and, in 1870, on the anniversary of Keble's birthday, the Archbishop of Canterbury laid the foundation stone — which someone promptly managed to lose.

Edward Pusey and a fellow canon of Christ Church, another Tractarian called Henry Liddon, after whom the central quadrangle is named, were instrumental in the appointment of Butterfield as architect, and their choice ensured that Keble's chapel would be equipped with all the trappings necessary for High Church worship.

But the most controversial aspect of Butterfield's work is not the chapel itself but the architectural style he adopted for the entire ensemble of chapel, Hall and rooms. The college is all of a piece, and either you love it or you hate it.

John Betjeman loved it, and excused Butterfield's idiosyncratic use of bricks of different colours to produce patterns when he wrote, 'As brick cannot be carved, he decorated its surfaces with bands of coloured bricks to emphasise the lines of construction. Broad, plain bands at the bottom where the walls had to support much weight, more elaborate pattern towards the gables and roofs.'

An unjaundiced examination of Keble College reveals the tricks Butterfield very properly got up to to relieve the monotony of his building materials. Some windows can be seen to be flush with the wall while others are set back. Some windows are single, some in pairs, others tripartite. And the skyline varies all the time. Butterfield even placed a chimney stack on the roof of the chapel.

The college is signposted like an amusement park and, like Pembroke and Christ Church, it is open virtually all day. Unlike almost any other college, it advertises its lavatories. On the left of the central Liddon Quadrangle, sunk by Butterfield to give an increased sense of height to his buildings, and on which, when the grass is not waterlogged, undergraduates play croquet, is a steep flight of steps leading to the Hall and library. But the Hall, the longest in Oxford, finished in 1878, always seems to be locked, which is a pity, for it is here that George Richmond's fine portrait of Keble hangs. The library has amassed in a short space of time some remarkable treasures: not only John Keble's books and manuscripts, but also the most important collection of medieval manuscripts outside the Bodleian, including a thirteenth-century Lectionary and two fifteenth-century Books of Hours.

In the north-east corner of the Liddon Quad is a rather dull garden, and in the same corner you enter the chapel through a tiny cloister. The first thing one notices is that Butterfield insisted on designing the chapel as though it was a parish church, with pews for the congregation facing east. By the time this vast edifice was being built (between 1873 and 1876), funds from the original donations had run out, and one wealthy man, William Gibbs, paid for it. The chapel is overwhelmingly decorated with mosaics illustrating events from the Old and New Testaments and, above the glittering altar, Christ, in mosaic, rises in majesty.

By suspending the organ above the south transept, a side chapel was able to be added in 1892, where the Sacrament is reserved and William Holman Hunt's *The Light of the World* is displayed. It may seem rather unfair to mention the Pre-Raphaelite first, but this is the painting most people come to see; however, on the north wall of the side chapel there is also a ravishing sixteenth-century painting, *The Dead Christ Mourned by his Mother*.

It took Holman Hunt eight years to perfect his whimsical allegory, intended to depict the following words of Our Lord: 'Behold I stand at the door and knock. If any man hear my voice and open the door I shall come in to him and will sup with him and he with me.' After it had been exhibited at the Royal Academy in 1854 it was purchased for 400 guineas by Thomas Combe, Superintendent of the Oxford University Press. When Combe died in 1872 his widow gave the painting to Keble on condition it was hung in the chapel, but the obdurate Butterfield turned his nose up at it and it was found a place in the library, being moved to its present position once the side chapel had been built – still against Butterfield's wishes.

There is a time-switch on the south wall so that you can illuminate this strange and at one time highly controversial work. Thomas Carlyle called it 'empty make-believe' and 'a mere papistical phantasy'; when it was exhibited, the *Athenaeum* told its readers the face expressed 'such a strange mingling of disgust, fear, and imbecility, that we turn from it to relieve the sight'. It is criticism of this inspired order that tends, in the long run, to give paintings a good name, but there may have been some excuse for caustic comments about the figure and the face of Christ; as a model, Holman Hunt inexplicably failed to use a man but called upon the services of Christina Rossetti, and when she was not available, of Lizzie Siddal, Dante Gabriel Rossetti's mistress and model and eventually his wife.

In recent years Keble has attracted some distinguished Wardens. From 1939 to 1955 Harry Carpenter, later Bishop of Oxford, held the post. He was succeeded by Eric Abbott, who became Dean of Westminster, and from 1960 until his death in 1968, the Warden was Austin Farrer, another revered modern churchman. During the decade 1969 to 1979, Professor Dennis Nineham, one of Oxford's most distinguished twentieth-century theologians, was Warden. The appointment in 1980 of a layman as Warden, and the admission a year before of women, might have surprised the founders of Keble

College, but in a way it emphasises the fact that this originally Tractarian-inspired institution has now taken its place in the mainstream of Oxford colleges.

If you turn right out of Keble and take the first right-hand turn up Museum Road, continuing along an obvious passageway, you will come to a giant horse chestnut leaning across the roof of what must once have been an enchanting pub, the Lamb and Flag, but unless you are addicted to a permanent diet of gaming machines and mindless music, the ambiance to which a former Saturday night haunt of Louis MacNeice and Enid Starkie has now been debased, you will not lunch here. You will (with caution) cross St Giles' and head for the Eagle and Child.

But before crossing the road walk a few paces north to admire Number 16 St Giles', built in 1702. This is where the circuit judge used to lodge. It was also the town house of Sarah, Duchess of Marlborough. St Giles' itself, that stretch of thoroughfare from the Martyrs' Memorial to the war memorial where the road forks off to Woodstock and Banbury, used to be the market place outside the north gate of the city, and for two unbearable days in September it is given over to a fake re-enactment of a nineteenth-century street fair. The stench and noise are best avoided.

Normally, however, St Giles' – and particularly the west side – offers one of the most pleasing mixtures in Oxford of seventeenth-to nineteenth-century domestic architecture, and a Queen Anne House almost opposite the Judge's Lodgings, Number 41, with its handsome portico, is where Enid Starkie, Somerville's colourful undergraduate and don, lived from 1932 to 1963. Someone described her as 'a voluble, flamboyant hummingbird', and without her excitable and exciting presence no Oxford party, in her time, was complete. She was a friend of André Gide and Jean Cocteau; when her biographer and former pupil Joanna Richardson pounced on her papers, she was a bit miffed to find she had not been privy to Starkie's own homosexual life-style. Starkie's house is now the Theological Faculty's Centre and Library, which is fortuitous, for Enid Starkie was a lapsed Catholic.

At the Eagle and Child you will find cosy inglenooks in which to drink Burton's beer and eat well-above-average pub food. It seems unlikely that, in addition to other well-authenticated poetic patrons, Louis MacNeice did not drift over here from the Lamb and Flag. In his autobiography, *With an Eye to the Future*, Osbert Lancaster, who arrived at Lincoln College in 1926, described MacNeice's appearance as 'at that time of his life uncompromisingly and defiantly poetic; the curly black hair, the carelessly draped scarf above the brown velvet jacket, the walking stick, all combined with an habitual air of bored and slightly arrogant detachment to arouse intense astonishment without immediately inspiring sympathy'.

Rest assured anyway that at the Eagle and Child you repose where once C. S. Lewis, Charles Williams, J. R. R. Tolkien and Lord David Cecil took their ease. At the rear of the pub is a No Smoking area and a small garden, and for a modest fee the management will permit you to pay by cheque. Like the Turf Tavern, this is one of the last surviving pubs from Oxford's past.

Four

A CHURCHILL
APPREHENDED AT
THE RANDOLPH

Pusey House (weekdays, Holy Communion 8.00 a.m., Sundays, High Mass 11.00 a.m.), St John's College (open 1.00 p.m. to 5.00 p.m.), Ashmolean Museum (open Tuesday to Saturday, 10.00 a.m. to 4.00 p.m., Sunday, 2.00 p.m. to 4.00 p.m., admission free), Randolph Hotel, St Mary Magdalen, St Michael's Church (Saxon Tower open 10.00 a.m. to 4.00 p.m. winter, 10.00 a.m. to 5.00 p.m. summer, admission charges), St Michael's Street (Oxford Union), New Inn Hall Street (St Peter's College), New Road Baptist Church Coffee House (open Monday to Friday, 10.00 a.m. to 2.00 p.m.).

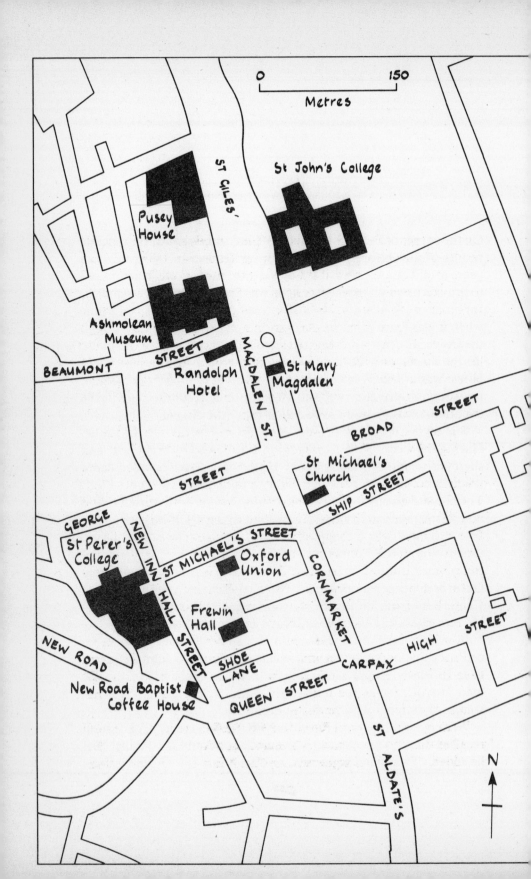

On the corner of Pusey Street and St Giles' stands one of the tangible results of the Oxford Movement, Pusey House. In 1884, only two years after Canon Edward Pusey's death, money was being raised to provide premises in which to house his library (hastily reassembled, for much of it had already been dispersed), and to establish, at a time when it was feared that secularisation was about to sweep through the University, 'a house of sacred learning'. At the heart of this house lies the chapel, provided with a high and low altar. And because Pusey House was originally intended to serve as a sort of University mission, no women, until they were admitted to men's colleges late in the twentieth century, were expected to enter the chapel.

But anyone may walk in today, and services are open to the public. During the week, Holy Communion is followed by breakfast, and sherry is served on Sunday after High Mass. How civilised can a religious community be? Pusey House is altogether a law unto itself. The chapter consists of a Principal and two 'priest librarians' who administer a research library now containing 100,000 books. The first Principal was a remarkable man, Charles Gore, who found time to found the Community of the Resurrection at Mirfield and to become bishop successively of Worcester, Birmingham and then Oxford. One of his disciples, Michael Ramsey, Archbishop of Canterbury from 1961 to 1974, worshipped at Pusey House during his retirement (he died at St John's Home in Oxford).

In a glass case in the cloisters you can see homely mementoes of Pusey, including his cup and saucer, and in 1946 John Betjeman gave to Pusey House a painting (also in the cloisters) of the old man at work in his room at Christ Church, the floor somewhat studiously strewn with books and papers.

Writing about Edward Pusey in 1900, the Reverend W. Tuckwell recalled that 'no sermons attracted undergraduates as did his'. Yet he added, 'Two things impressed me when I first saw Dr Pusey close:

his exceeding slovenliness of person: buttonless boots, necktie limp, unbrushed coat collar, grey hair . . . and the almost artificial sweetness of his smile, contrasting as it did with the sombre gloom of his face when in repose'.

Sightseeing in any coherent way in the region of St Giles' involves rather a lot of crossing of the road. You now want to dodge through the traffic to the east side to visit St John's College, founded in 1555, the year that Latimer and Ridley were burned just round the corner in Broad Street. Dodge too the public lavatories in the middle of St Giles', from which trails of blood and broken glass not infrequently lead, and make safer use of lavatories either in the Ashmolean Museum or the Randolph Hotel.

St John's was founded by a wealthy Roman Catholic businessman, Sir Thomas White, in gratitude for the restoration of Catholicism under Mary I, and one of its first Fellows was a Jesuit convert, Edmund Campion, who was to be hanged, drawn and quartered at Tyburn when the religious tide turned once again under Elizabeth I — even though on her visit to Oxford in 1566 it was Campion who had welcomed the Queen on behalf of the University. He is commemorated by Campion Hall in Brewer Street, the Oxford House of the Society of Jesus.

Architecturally, St John's owes a great debt to William Laud, who was President from 1611 to 1621, Bishop of London and Archbishop of Canterbury. The beautifully preserved fifteenth-century Front Quadrangle, still only two storeys high, is older than the college itself, for St John's was founded on the site of a Cistercian monastery; but all save the sixteenth-century south range of Canterbury Quadrangle into which the Front Quad leads was built by Laud. The south range contains the library, constructed out of a thousand wagon-loads of stone and timber salvaged from Henry I's Beaumont Palace which had stood not far away and much of the inspiration for Canterbury Quad seems to have been drawn from the fifteenth-century Foundling Hospital in Florence.

It is not until you have entered the quad and looked back that you fully realise how grand and dignified it is, with matching blocked-off arcades on the east and west supporting ornate, heavily decorated statues of Charles I and his wife. Laud, described by one contemporary as 'low of stature, little in bulk, cheerful in countenance' and by another as 'civil and moderate', celebrated the opening of his new quad in 1636, the year in which, as

Chancellor, he codified the University statutes, by spending £2,666 1s 7d on a dinner. It was attended by the King and Queen and the King's seventeen-year-old nephew, Prince Rupert, Count Palatinate of the Rhine, who was to fight – in such an undisciplined manner – during the Civil War. Seven stags were consumed along with five oxen, two lambs and a calf, and Laud was able to congratulate himself afterwards 'that all things were in very good order and that no man went out at the Gates, courtier or other, but content, which was a happiness quite beyond expectation'.

From Canterbury Quad you enter the garden, one of the most restful in Oxford, and far larger than at first appears, for beyond the lawn are groves of trees; it seems almost impossible to believe when in the garden of St John's that one is not staying at a country house. The traffic seems to have stopped, and no building other than the sublime east front of Canterbury Quad, which needs to be viewed in repose from the far end of the lawn, is visible. Two eighteenth-century landscapers of genius, Humphrey Repton and 'Capability' Brown, were largely responsible for the present effect.

On your way back through the Front Quad you will find the chapel on the right, one of whose nineteenth-century custodians, a Fellow by the name of the Reverend Edward Free, made so free of drink and 'profanity, impropriety and gross immorality' that he was deprived of his country living.

After his beheading on Tower Hill in 1645, Archbishop Laud was buried at All Hallows, Barking, but eighteen years later – on 24 July 1663 – he was reburied in the vault of St John's. The imposing tomb in the small side chapel, which could be mistaken for Laud's, commemorates another President, Thomas Baylie. In the library, however, are the cap Laud wore and the stick he carried to the block. Interestingly enough, buried with Laud in the vault is another Archbishop of Canterbury, William Juxon, who as Bishop of London attended Charles I on the scaffold. Juxon was President of St John's from 1621 to 1633.

Opposite St John's, with its entrance in Beaumont Street, is the Ashmolean Museum, a handsome neo-classical building dating from 1845. If it puts you in mind of Greece this is because it was based on the Temple of Apollo at Bassae. And if the name 'Ashmolean' rings a faint bell and you cannot quite think why, it was the Oxford antiquary Elias Ashmole, a graduate of Brasenose (he studied mathematics, chemistry and astrology), who published in 1676 what

105

has become a standard work, *The Institution, Laws and Customs of the Most Noble Order of the Garter*. Ashmole inherited a rare and diverse collection of anthropological and historical interest, and this he gave to the University. Thus in 1683 the Ashmolean, the oldest public museum in England, was opened.

The collection, originally housed in Broad Street, has been much added to, and the whole complex includes a wing in St Giles' called the Taylorian Institute, devoted to the teaching of modern languages – the gift in 1788 of Sir Robert Taylor. One of the oddest acquisitions was recorded in a Bath newspaper: 'We understand that *A Pair of Stays*, such as are generally worn by the *University Dandies*, has been deposited among the curiosities of the Ashmolean Museum, Oxford, for the purpose of transmitting to posterity an idea of the extreme heights of effeminacy and absurdity to which a compliance with the whims of fashion has been able to reduce the sons of Englishmen in the year 1818'. These 'whims of fashion' were of course being set by none other than the Prince Regent.

Ashmole's original gift included a vest from Babylon, a dodo from Mauritius 'not able to flie being so big', a specimen of blood said to have rained on the Isle of Wight, a Turkish toothbrush, a bracelet made from the 'thighes of Indian flies' and 'diverse sorts of Egges from Turkie; one given for a Dragons egge'.

There is a strange connection between the Ashmolean Museum and Jean-Paul Marat, who (as everyone knows thanks to the painter David) was knifed to death in his bath. On a visit to the museum in 1776 (it was then still in Broad Street), Marat stole three or four links from a gold chain which had once belonged to Ashmole and is exhibited today in the Founder's Gallery on the first floor. Marat, like any respectable revolutionary, needed the gold links to pay his landlord in Liverpool. (This, at any rate, is the story.) Above the truncated chain hangs a portrait of Ashmole wearing the chain, and to those with perfect eyesight the difference in length between the chain round Ashmole's neck and the one tampered with by Marat is perfectly apparent. The real mystery is why Marat did not pocket the entire chain and have done with it. As it was, he was sentenced to five years hard labour, but swiftly escaped to Paris. The frame in which Ashmole's portrait hangs was carved by Grinling Gibbons.

It would be foolhardy to attempt to cover the Ashmolean in one visit. It is best perhaps to wander round fairly swiftly so as to absorb a general impression of the wealth and comprehensiveness of its

106

collections, or else to make a beeline for whatever subject particularly interests you. In a special place of honour is the Alfred Jewel, in the opinion of the museum 'the most precious surviving example of late Saxon craftsmanship'. It is inscribed *Aelfred Mec Heht Gewyrcen* – Alfred Ordered Me to be Made. Found in Somerset in 1693, it has been in the museum since 1718. Among the English china is the most comprehensive collection in the world of First Period coloured Worcester porcelain, donated by his parents in memory of William Marshall, an undergraduate of Trinity, killed in Holland in 1944.

If you do not care for Roman sculpture there is Egyptian; if the Pre-Raphaelites do not appeal, French Impressionists may. Drawings by Michelangelo and Raphael (the Raphael drawings constitute the most important collection in the world, and together with the Michelangelo drawings they once belonged to George IV's portraitist Thomas Lawrence); coins and violins; glass by Whistler; Chippendale furniture; portraits by Gainsborough and Reynolds – the quality of every item is breathtaking. The Ashmolean is surely one of the greatest provincial museums in the world, a staggering place in which to reel from one masterpiece of human experience and endeavour to another.

So you may leave the Ashmolean feeling a bit weak at the knees, and in order to recuperate you need only step across the road to Oxford's one stab at a grand and comfortable hotel, the Randolph. Rooms and meals in the restaurant are expensive, and for ordinary mortals there exists, down steps round the corner in Magdalen Street, a very adequate café, where between 10.00 a.m. and 6.00 p.m. coffee, meals and drinks can also be obtained. In 1990 a three-course luncheon in the dining-room of the Randolph cost £15, and afternoon tea, served in the lounge between 2.30 p.m. and 6.00 p.m., £6.50.

There is something of the atmosphere of a country house hotel at the Randolph, with a portrait in the dining-room by Kneller of the 8th Earl of Pembroke in Garter robes, a spacious staircase and daily papers strewn about. And there is a real sense of being in the centre of Oxford, with the Ashmolean framed in the windows. Because of the proximity of the Spencer-Churchill family at Woodstock, there is a popular fallacy that the Randolph Hotel has connections with Lord Randolph Churchill, a younger son of the 7th Duke of Marlborough and father of the Prime Minister, Winston Churchill. In fact the hotel, built in 1864 without much consideration for the previously unspoilt Georgian street in which it stands, was named in honour of Dr Francis Randolph, who gave £1,000 in the eighteenth century to build an extension to the Ashmolean.

Nevertheless, when he was an undergraduate at Merton, Randolph Churchill did leave his mark on the hotel, dining there in 1870 with the Falstaff Club: it seems that he and his friends lived up to the Rabelaisian knight's reputation for disorderly conduct. Lord Randolph, who managed to cut his hand on a glass and 'amused his companions by pouring bottles of claret over the table', ended up under arrest, charged with being 'drunk and riotous' and with assaulting a policeman, who presumably had been called by the management. On the first charge he was acquitted, but for shoving the policeman in the back and knocking off his helmet he was fined ten shillings. He later became Chancellor of the Exchequer.

The Randolph Hotel has witnessed some quixotic encounters in its time. In 1941 the young painter and writer Denton Welch produced a rather frightful painting based on a photograph of the eccentric composer and writer Lord Berners, a photograph taken of him as 'a little boy dressed in shaggy goat-skin with a macaw perched on his shoulder'. It had appeared in Berners's autobiography, *First Childhood*. Having failed to sell the painting for £40 at the Leicester Galleries in London, Welch took a room at the Randolph so as to try and effect a sale to Berners himself who lived seventeen miles away at Faringdon.

In an account entitled 'A Morning with the Versatile Peer, Lord Berners, in the "Ancient Seat of Learning" ', published posthumously in *Time and Tide*, Denton Welch wrote: 'He came in with a bouncing step and sank down on the bed in front of the conversation piece I had made. I thought, as he sat there, that he bore a very faint resemblance to Humpty Dumpty.' But Berners made no offer to buy the picture, and they walked down the Gothic staircase to the hall.

' "Isn't it an extraordinary hotel?" Lord Berners said. "John Betjeman loves it."

' "Yes, I imagine he would," was all I could find for an answer.

'We walked about downstairs looking in all the rooms. He wanted to show me one in particular, which he remembered. Rather undressed waiters told us where the bar was and looked at us curiously, wondering why we were loose in the rooms which were closed for cleaning.

108

'I thought that Lord Berners felt annoyed with them for not recognising him as anyone in particular.'

If you turn right out of the Randolph and right into Magdalen Street you are back again – or you will be if you cross the road and enter the Church of St Mary Magdalen – in the world of the Oxford Movement. In this church, much used for private devotion, there is a powerful sense of prayer that only the most insensitive could fail to detect; it lingers with the musty mixture of worn hassock and last Sunday's incense so evocative of High Church worship. There are four altars, three in the body of the church, one, where the Sacrament is reserved, in a chapel, and there is no messing about at St Mary's: Mass on Sunday at 8.00 a.m., 10.30 a.m. and 5.30 p.m., the evening Mass being followed by Choral Evensong and Benediction. Candles burn before a statue of the Virgin Mary.

What is interesting about St Mary Magdalen – apart from the fact that the building is wider than it is long – is that although it could not be higher liturgically, there is no sense of the frippery so often attached to Anglo-Catholicism. A kind of uncluttered aestheticism permeates the atmosphere. Among the petitions on the lectern someone once left a note that read: 'I thank you, God, for the chance you've given me to see these beautiful places. Help me to stand what I don't like, too.'

Another place not so beautiful – apart from the thirteenth-century glass in the east window – but nevertheless well worth seeing is the Church of St Michael, just south of the crossroads, on the corner of Cornmarket Street (sometimes referred to as The Corn) and Ship Street. Here is a Saxon tower even older than the clock-tower at Carfax, in fact the oldest building in Oxford. Here too, straddling Cornmarket and somewhere between the church and what is now the entrance to St Michael's Street, stood the north gate of the city and, above the gate, the ghastly Bocardo prison, in which Cranmer, Latimer and Ridley were incarcerated.

The prison was known as the Bocardo by 1391, but no one knows why, and it was demolished in 1771. Prisoners used to lower a rosewood collecting box on a string suspended from a window in the hope that passers-by would help pay off their debts. The box can be seen among other treasures in the tower.

At one time St Michael's served as a chapel for Exeter College, round the corner in Turl Street, and on the north wall of the church is an engraved tablet depicting a young man 'of great learning and piety', Walter Dotyn, scholar and Fellow of Exeter, who died in 1603 at the age of twenty. Another paragon of the college, Thomas Grooke of Cornwall, also 'a young man of great learning and piety', died five years later when he was only nineteen, and he is recalled on a wall of the side chapel.

The climb to the top of the tower is the easiest such climb in Oxford, and on the way up there is a display of seventeenth-century patens and chalices, eighteenth-century pewter, letters from John Wesley to his mother and brother, and a book recording gifts and legacies received between 1586 and 1727. Here, too, is preserved the door of Cranmer's cell, taken from the Bocardo prison, nothing less than a sacred relic. A peal of six bells, the two oldest cast in 1668, can be inspected at close quarters, and at the top of the tower you stand where Cranmer was forced to stand to watch Latimer and Ridley burn between the city wall and Balliol College.

Cornmarket Street was originally called Northgate, but its name was changed when the gate was demolished. There was, needless to say, a street market for the sale of corn, and in the sixteenth century a building was constructed to protect the sacks of corn from the rain, but 'this covering or roof . . . was by the souldery in Oxon pulled downe Anno 1644 and the lead thereof converted into bullets and the timber into militarie engines'. Apart from the shop on the corner of Ship Street, which is fifteenth-century, property in the Corn has been systematically destroyed. For centuries there was a coaching inn called the Star Hotel, renamed the Clarendon, a favourite hotel with undergraduates between the wars, but that was demolished to make way for a branch of Woolworth's; the Clarendon is now a shopping centre, and what became of Woolworth's? So avoid the mêlée and cut down St Michael's Street. Number 20, on the right, now inhabited by solicitors, comes as something of a surprise; it was built by Vanbrugh, better remembered perhaps for his work at Blenheim Palace. And on the left is the hideous Victorian headquarters of the Oxford Union, that rather pompous debating chamber where once a week budding politicians like to show off their knowledge of standing orders.

The Oxford Union Society was founded in 1823. Its first meeting took place in private rooms at Christ Church, and it was five years before it found rooms to rent in the High Street. Today it possesses the largest undergraduate lending library in Oxford, employs a staff of thirty and encourages its President to raise and spend as much as

110

£75,000 a year, flying in star speakers from the USA. Gladstone has generally been regarded as the best speaker the Union has ever produced, but while staying in Oxford in 1890 he proposed holding the attention of the House by talking about the connection between Homer and recent Assyriological studies. Although there is much pushing and shoving among ambitious undergraduates for the presidency, the only debate the public even vaguely remembers is the one held in 1933 when it was proposed that 'This House will in no circumstances fight for its King and Country'. Quintin Hogg, a former President and future Lord Chancellor, and Professor C. E. M. Joad, who became a national figure of fun on the BBC's Brains Trust, were guest speakers, and the motion was carried by 275 votes to 153.

It seemed like an event of little significance within the University, where ideas tend to be aired more objectively than in certain parts of Fleet Street, but the *Daily Express*, ever in the vanguard of truth and enlightenment, declared that those who had voted for the motion were communists, practical jokers and 'sexually indeterminate'. Their actions had, the paper thundered, been 'contemptible and indecent'. A letter to the *Oxford Mail* from a boy of thirteen, Cyril Hay, was more charitable. He recalled that he had recently attended an undergraduate party, where he had drunk a 'cocqtail' which he thought was rather nice, and where he had met 'a lot of people from a place called the Union [who] were saying that they would not fight if there was another war. I thought that this was very bad.' Another letter to *Isis*, however, explained that the Union consisted chiefly 'of aliens and perverts', and the writer suggested that its members' names should be published, as the police would find them useful.

The now defunct *Morning Post* used to report Union debates, and when he was an undergraduate at Hertford College, Evelyn Waugh got in some early journalistic practice by covering debates for both the undergraduate magazines, the *Isis* and the *Cherwell*. On one occasion John Sutro of Trinity College, who became a film-maker, was incoherent through drink and eventually collapsed on the grass outside. The *Morning Post* ignored the event, so Waugh thought he had achieved a scoop by publishing an account of Sutro's inebriated performance in the *Cherwell*. But when it was discovered that Sutro's parents were avid readers, a special edition with the incident censored had to be rushed out.

William Morris and Edward Burne-Jones, who both entered Exeter College in 1853, volunteered to decorate the debating chamber in St Michael's Street. Aided by Dante Gabriel Rossetti, Ruskin and Swinburne, they splashed about without preparing the walls, so that shortly after they had produced, by all accounts, a lovely re-enactment of the Arthurian legend, their collective Pre-Raphaelite efforts faded away.

The tall spire that confronts you at the end of St Michael's Street is of some historical relevance, for it belongs to the Wesley Memorial Church, built in 1878 to celebrate the admission of Non-Conformists to the University. On the site of the building opposite the Methodist church, on the corner of St Michael's Street and New Inn Hall Street, where you should turn left, once stood Mackworth Hall, in which in 1863 one of Oxford's better known schools, St Edward's, was founded. It moved to the northern suburb of Summertown ten years later. Kenneth Grahame was educated there. On the right, despite its Georgian façade, is a poor, unlovely college, St Peter's, founded in 1928 and scarcely worth going into. Its first Master was a muscular Christian called Christopher Chavasse, who ran in the 400 metres at the 1908 Olympic Games, won a Military Cross and the Croix de Guerre, lost a leg in a boating accident and became an evangelical and rather reactionary Bishop of Rochester.

On the left-hand side of the street you will pass Frewin Hall, the extension to Brasenose College, where Richard Frewin, Camden Professor of Ancient History, lived in the eighteenth century, and a century later Edward VII took up residence when an undergraduate. It is always closed. Just past Frewin Hall is an easily identified house, also owned by Brasenose, which was the first Methodist Meeting House in Oxford. In 1783 John Wesley preached here. Number 18 New Inn Hall Street used to stand on the corner of what is now Shoe Lane. Here was the home of the poet Gerard Manley Hopkins. Brasenose have knocked that down. Then comes a depressing area called Bonn Square, the favourite haunt of bottle-swilling down-and-outs, and to your left, once again, is your central reference point, Carfax.

However, Bonn Square is not entirely given over to squalor. If you fancy coffee, tea or lunch there is an unexpectedly agreeable coffee house upstairs in the New Road Baptist Church (replete with seventeenth-century gallery for the Sunday congregation); self-service, soup, fresh sandwiches and salads, small, quiet, inexpensive and civilised. Worth knowing about.

Five

FROM WESLEY'S ROOMS TO NEWMAN'S PULPIT

Covered Market (open Monday to Saturday, 7.00 a.m. to 5.00 p.m.), Jesus College (open 2.00 p.m. to 4.30 p.m.), Exeter College (open 2.00 p.m. to 5.00 p.m.), Lincoln College (open Monday to Saturday, 2.00 p.m. to 5.00 p.m., Sunday, 11.00 a.m. to 5.00 p.m.), Lincoln College Library (open Tuesday and Thursday, 2.00 p.m. to 4.00 p.m.), the Mitre (meals, 12 noon to 2.30 p.m., 6.00 p.m. to 11.00 p.m.), St Mary the Virgin (Tower open May to September, 9.00 a.m. to 7.00 p.m., October to April, 9.30 a.m. to dusk, admission charge), Convocation Coffee House (open Monday to Saturday, 9.00 a.m. to 7.00 p.m., Sunday 12 noon to 5.00 p.m., lunch 12 noon to 2.00 p.m., tea 2.00 p.m. to 6.00 p.m.), All Souls College (quadrangles open only, times vary), Betjeman & Barton's Tea Room (open Monday to Saturday, 10.00 a.m. to 4.30 p.m., Sunday, 11.00 a.m. to 4.00 p.m.).

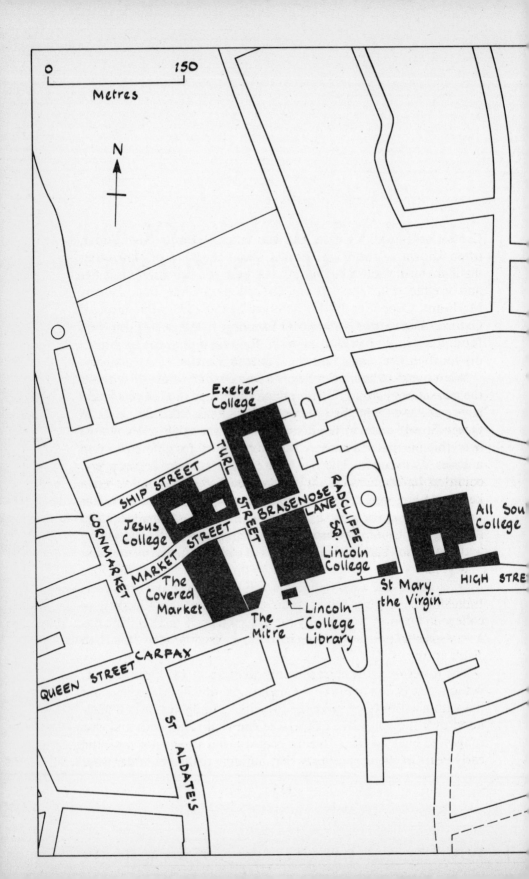

Cross Carfax walking east, and you enter Oxford's High Street, often known as the High. Forget about the kind of shops that disfigure most provincial high streets; here you can buy college ties and birettas, prints, pottery and Oxford marmalade, first made by Mr Frank Cooper at 83 High Street in the 1870s. But most of Oxford's High Street is given over to college fronts, and if you want food you will do better to take the first opening (Avenue No. 2) on your left that leads into the Covered Market.

What people who live in the centre of Oxford would do without the market it is hard to say. Before it was opened in 1774 you would have purchased your fish in the open air in St Aldate's, meat in Queen Street, cattle at Carfax and pigs in the High. Now almost everything is under one roof, the shops and cafés all mixed up in a series of avenues. There are three florists, two fishmongers, countless butchers, two bakeries, two delicatessen; you can get a key cut, have your shoes repaired, buy seed for your budgerigar or health food for yourself. You will find home-made quiche (although Sainsbury's is better, to be honest), pullovers, stationery and a sandwich bar, fresh pasta, rolls of cloth, fruit and a letterbox.

If you leave the Covered Market by one of the exits leading into Market Street and turn right, this will take you into Turl Street. Immediately on your left is Jesus College, the only Elizabethan college in Oxford, founded by the Queen herself in 1571. She has a very splendid portrait hanging in solitary splendour above the High Table in the Hall.

The tower over the entrance only went up in 1854, but it leads without distraction to the First Quadrangle, which is charming, and has within its confined space the Principal's Lodgings (with a shell-hood over the door), the chapel and the Hall. The south and east ranges go back to the sixteenth century, but it was not until the early years of the next century that building really got under way.

115

The chapel, entered in the centre of the north range, dates from 1621. Immediately on your right in the ante-chapel is a sightless bust of T. E. Lawrence, known to his family as Thomas Edward and to posterity as Aircraftman Shaw and Lawrence of Arabia. This mysterious masochist was at Jesus from 1907 to 1910, when he took a First Class Honours Degree in Modern History and then embarked upon a tangled career that has intrigued his numerous biographers ever since. The screen against which Eric Kennington's bust of Lawrence stands, dividing the ante-chapel from the chapel, is late seventeenth-century. If, however, the overall impression left by the chapel is rather disappointing, you have the Victorians to thank; they 'redesigned' the interior in 1864.

You reach the Inner Quadrangle through the west wing of the First Quad, and the door to the Hall is on your right. All but the ceiling, added in 1741, is again very early seventeenth-century, and the Hall contains perhaps one of the most notable portraits owned by any college, Sir Thomas Lawrence's painting of the Regency architect John Nash. But not all the paintings here are very pleasing; Lord Wilson's portrait (he was an Exhibitioner from 1934 to 1937 and took a First) is pretty pathetic, and the one of Lawrence dressed up in his Arabian gear is merely a copy of Augustus John's in the Tate. There is, however (hung far too high), a Van Dyck of Charles I.

Work on the Inner Quad, which has ended up looking more severe than the First Quad, was begun around 1635, but had to be suspended when the Civil War broke out. The college provided billeting for Royalist troops, and it was not until after the Restoration that building was resumed; part of the west wing dates from 1679 but part is as late as 1713, when the original architectural design was adhered to.

Apparently Jesus College once had on its staff 'the finest judge of wine in Oxford', a senior Fellow called Tom Davis. The Reverend W. Tuckwell could recall when, between 3.00 p.m. and 4.00 p.m., 'he walked alone in all weathers twice round Christchurch meadow'. This may have been in order to clear his head, for in his reminiscences Tuckwell wrote, 'Joyous was the Common Room steward who could call in his judgement to aid in the purchase of pipe or butt. He refused all the most valuable College livings in turn, because the underground cellars of their parsonages were inadequate; lived and died in his own rooms, consuming meditatively, like Mr Tulkinghorn, a daily cob-webbed bottle of his own precious port'.

116

The college had a memorable Principal, too, in Joseph Hoare, who lived nearly as long as Dr Routh of Magdalen. Hoare held office for forty-four years, and by the time he was ninety he was stone deaf. He had a cat called Tom, upon whose paw old Dr Hoare managed by mistake to plonk the leg of his chair. Tom took umbrage, and as cats in such circumstances are prone to do, he gave his master a bite.

> Poor Dr Hoare! He is no more!
> Bid Cambria's harp-strings mourn.
> The Head of a House died the death of a mouse,
> And Tom must be hanged in return.

Opposite Jesus is Exeter College. A first glance at the ivy-covered three-storey east range (with its very nasty chimneys) will be unlikely to prepare you for the full impact of the Front Quadrangle. Its proportions are all hopelessly out of balance because the massive chapel built on the north between 1856 and 1859 by Sir George Gilbert Scott was originally designed to stand in the Fellows' Garden, and is far too large for its present site. The vaulted ceiling of the gatehouse by which you enter is early eighteenth-century, and this too tells a tale, for the medieval entrance was the tower you can see in the north-east corner – Palmer's Tower, built in 1432.

The rest of the Front Quad (with the exception of the chapel, of course, and including the Hall on the south, which unfortunately is always closed) was built between 1618 and 1710. Yet Exeter, originally known as Stapeldon Hall, is one of the oldest colleges in Oxford, founded by Walter de Stapeldon in 1314; it is now called Exeter because Stapeldon became Bishop of Exeter under his neurotic patron Edward II. And like Edward, Stapeldon lost his head – but on the block.

Stapeldon's death hardly amounted to martyrdom; he had merely got mixed up with a repressive regime. But in 1581 a Catholic Fellow of the college, Ralph Sherwin, was executed by Elizabeth I, and in 1970 he was declared by Paul VI to be a saint.

You will need no directions to find the chapel. It shouts at you to enter. But hold your breath. Scott decided to celebrate his commission to replace a modest seventeenth-century chapel, regarded by the start of the nineteenth century as too small for an expanding college, in a style 'generally considered to be the period of highest perfection attained by Gothic architecture', and in doing so he conceived an apse based upon the Sainte-Chapelle in Paris. But the comparison should not be taken too far. The result is a sort of exhausting Victorian Byzantine, and although there is certainly craftsmanship to admire − the decorated organ pipes, the enamelled gates in the screen − the general impression is oppressive and far too busy.

Fortunately some of the furnishings were salvaged from the old chapel. The brass lectern, for example, was made in 1637. Admirers of the Pre-Raphaelite Movement will approve the tapestry on the south wall depicting the Adoration of the Magi, designed by Burne-Jones and executed by William Morris, 'a rather rough unpolished youth' according to his Exeter tutor. Other post-Scott additions include fourteenth-century panels by Luca di Tommé above the Rector's and Sub-Rector's stalls, representing St Peter and St Paul, and four fourteenth-century Italian paintings on wood panels.

In 1956 Scott's chapel achieved unexpected notoriety when it became the setting for the murder of the Rector, although in Robert Robinson's *Landscape With Dead Dons* the victim became the Master and Exeter College became 'Warlock'. Robinson was an undergraduate at Exeter, and he published his detective novel soon after coming down. Having been stabbed in the back with one of his own dessert-knives, the Master is discovered propped up among the statues on the chapel roof. 'I think the college which I called Warlock was a sort of surreal version of Exeter as it might have been if reconstructed by a mad architect,' Robinson has explained. 'The actual spaces − quadrangle, garden, hall − developed in my mind from those of Exeter, and propping the corpse on the chapel roof came to me because there is or there was a sort of gully you can walk round up there (but I borrowed the statues from Trinity).'

Robert Robinson also borrowed a 'blurry imago' of his tutor Nevill Coghill for the character of a don called Christelow − Christelow was actually the name of an undergraduate who had rooms on the same staircase as his. In fact, Robinson admits he 'lifted two or three of the names from fellow Exonians − Coggins and Diamantis, and the yellow kilt I gave to the American under-graduate Orson Dogg I got from my old friend Homer K. Nicholson who came from the Deep South and who was an unforgettable Roderigo in the 1950 OUDS production of *Othello*. Funny thing, it never occurred to me they might feel I'd taken a liberty!'

27 The fifteenth century chancel of St Mary the Virgin, with its plain Perpendicular stalls carved in 1453 and Victorian reredos, commemorating the Oxford Movement. The second statue from the left represents Frideswide, the patron saint of Oxford.

28 A rare mixture of architectural styles keeps interest in the High alive. Passing through Oxford in the seventeenth century, Celia Fiennes found the High Street 'a very Noble one, soe large and of a Greate Length'. It remains so today.

29 The Front Quadrangle of
St Edmund Hall, the last
surviving medieval hall in Oxford.
Today it enjoys the status of a
college. On the east side stands
the seventeenth century chapel,
with glass by William Morris and
Burne-Jones and a modern altar-
piece by Ceri Richards.

30 The Muniment Tower in the
Front Quadrangle of New
College. Its steps lead to the Hall,
a room with magnificent linenfold
panelling. It was in this Hall in
about 1488 that the first lecture
on Greek was delivered in
Oxford.

31 A sculpture by Barbara Hepworth at New College makes a startling contrast with the medieval city walls skirting most of the college garden.

32 *(overleaf)* Framed beneath the twentieth century bridge connecting the Old and New Buildings of Hertford College is, to the left, the sixteenth century Schools Quadrangle, part of the Bodleian Library, in the centre Christopher Wren's Sheldonian Theatre and on the right Nicholas Hawksmoor's Classical Clarendon Building, once the home of the Oxford University Press.

33 Sir Thomas Jackson's clever corkscrew staircase in the Entrance Quadrangle of Hertford College, 'a respectable but rather dreary little college' in the opinion of one of its most distinguished twentieth century graduates, Evelyn Waugh. The staircase leads to the Hall.

34 A great pile of steps, pillars and carvings, somewhat obscured by the Sheldonian Theatre, which must have been the original front door of the seventeenth century house in which the Ashmolean Collection was first displayed. Today the building, with an entrance in Broad Street, contains the Museum of the History of Science, an amazing demonstration of human ingenuity.

35 In the centre, Benjamin Jowett, appointed Master of Balliol College in 1870 and one of the best-known men in Victorian Oxford. His house was said to be 'the meeting point of the University and the outer world'. 'Never regret, never explain, never apologise' has become one of his most famous sayings. *Photograph by courtesy of Oxfordshire County Council, Department of Leisure and Arts.*

36 The first two storeys of the Old Quadrangle of Brasenose College, founded in 1509, are a very fine example of early Tudor domestic architecture. The dormer windows were added in the seventeenth century when a third floor became necessary to accommodate a growing student population, and the sundial was placed in position in 1719.

Professor Nevill Coghill and Robert Robinson are not the only distinguished graduates produced by Exeter this century, and the roll call is remarkably varied. Liaquat Ali Khan, the Prime Minister of Pakistan 1947–51, Roger Bannister, Alan Bennett, 'Tubby' Clayton, the founder of Toc H, Professor Frederick Soddy, who won the Nobel Prize for Chemistry, and Geoffrey Fisher, Archbishop of Canterbury from 1945 to 1961, were all at Exeter. So was a rather more influential Christian, the socialist and theologian F. D. Maurice, who defected to Cambridge to become Professor of Moral Philosophy; in the opinion of Fisher's successor at Canterbury, Michael Ramsey, Maurice was 'one of the greatest figures in the history of Christianity in our land'.

R. D. Blackmore, who wrote *Lorna Doone*, was a scholar at Exeter, but the college believes that all its undergraduates have been eclipsed by J. R. R. Tolkien, who learnt Gothic and Anglo-Saxon at school, arrived at Oxford in 1911, and took a First in English four years later. His trilogy, *The Lord of the Rings*, which some people find unreadable, has become cult reading for others.

Gilbert Scott had a rare old time at Exeter. Not content with creating the chapel, in 1857 he built new Lodgings for the Rector, in the Margary Quadrangle, which is reached by squeezing between the east end of the chapel and Palmer's Tower. And on the north side of the Fellows' Garden, which you can locate easily enough by going through Staircase Five in the Front Quad, he provided a Gothic but sedate and restful library. It does not interfere with the early seventeenth-century building at right angles to it known as Peryam's Mansion. The library's most precious possession is an illuminated fourteenth-century Psalter, once owned by Elizabeth I.

One of the strange features of this garden, in which incidentally you may not smoke, is the way it benefits from the proximity of buildings the college does not own, which serve to enhance the setting to a very considerable extent. In a kind of continuation of Scott's library, the southern walls of the University's Convocation House, Divinity School and Bodleian Library form a northern boundary for Exeter. And if you climb the steps to the terrace you can look over into Brasenose Lane, where Dr Johnson was observed to straddle his ample legs across the open drain, still clearly visible, that ran down the centre.

A very remarkable man became Rector of Exeter in the seventeenth century, from 1612, in fact, until 1642. He was a former college servant, John Prideaux, who arrived in Oxford from Devon about 1594 'in very poor habit and sordid (no better than leather Breeches) to seek his fortune', and so improved his education while 'doing servile offices in the kitchen' that he rose not only to be Rector but Regius Professor of Divinity, a canon of Christ Church, Vice-Chancellor (twice), chaplain to Charles I and eventually Bishop of Worcester. Not all the students who studied under him were to side with the King, however. Sir John Eliot urged the impeachment of Charles's reckless friend the Duke of Buckingham, and was left by Charles to rot in the Tower of London; another Member of Parliament and former undergraduate of Exeter, William Strode, was one of the five whom Charles attempted to arrest; and a third, John Blackmore, actually signed the King's death warrant. Thus to a marked degree Exeter was at variance with other colleges, most of whose members supported the King during the Civil War.

The sobriety of so much of Exeter's Victorian architecture should not blind us to more riotous times. According to Anthony Wood, writing in 1655, Exeter College was 'now much debauched by a drunken Governor', by whom he meant the Rector. He thought him 'good-natured, generous, and a good scholar', but he had 'forgot the way of a college life and the decorum of a scholar.' He was 'much given to bibbing; and when there is a music meeting in one of the Fellow's chambers he will sit there, smoke and drink till he is drunk, and has to be led to his lodgings by the junior Fellows'.

Worse was to befall in the early years of the eighteenth century when, according to Thomas Hearne, who kept a diary as amusing but far more malicious than Anthony Wood's, someone called Geffery Ammon 'happened to kill a gentleman (either a servitour or battler) of Exeter College, by throwing a bottle at him, which struck his temples. The gentleman immediately went to the bog-house, where he died.' It seems there had been a quarrel over the cost of a bill, and when Ammon was tried at the Assize he was found guilty of manslaughter.

Hearne also recorded on 6 December 1717 that the Rector, Matthew Hole, 'now very near, if not quite, fourscore Years of Age, courts a young Girl, living at the Turl-Gate, in Oxford, with her Father, named Brickland, and a seller of Cheney-Ware. She is handsome, but an Ideot.'

Turn left out of Exeter, re-cross Market Street and on your left is Turl Street's third college, Lincoln, the cradle of Methodism; on

120

the south wall of the Front Quadrangle you can see a modern bronze bust of John Wesley, elected a Fellow of Lincoln in 1726. The college was founded by the Bishop of Lincoln, Richard Fleming, in 1427, as a 'little college of true students of theology who would defend the mysteries of Scripture against those ignorant laymen who profaned with swinish snouts its most holy pearls', and it remains a small college today, its fifteenth-century origins quite unspoilt.

The Front Quadrangle was three-quarters finished by 1460. The Hall, in the north-east corner, small, compact and welcoming, dates from about 1437. It retains its fifteenth-century roof, and fine seventeenth-century panelling enhances the room. Immediately on the left as you enter is a rather dingy portrait attributed to Sir Peter Lely of the seventeenth-century playwright William Davenant, an undergraduate who became Poet Laureate, and on the left above the High Table is a copy, and not a very good one, of Romney's portrait of Wesley.

At the south end of the east wing is a passageway leading to the Grove: what is left in fact of a secluded garden, much built on at the end of the nineteenth century by the ubiquitous T. G. Jackson. The seventeenth-century chapel is reached by returning to the Front Quad and walking through another passageway in the centre of the south range. It was in the Chapel Quadrangle, on the first floor of Staircase Five in the west wing, built in 1608, that John Wesley lived. The room where he gave tutorials is on the first floor of Staircase Two in the Front Quad, and although it remains a tutor's room, a condition of its use is that the tutor vacates it every afternoon so that visitors may borrow a key from the porter's lodge and see it. In 1926, to commemorate the two-hundredth anniversary of Wesley's election to a Fellowship, Methodists in America paid for lovely fifteenth-century linenfold panelling to be installed, and at the same time the room was supplied with eighteenth-century furniture.

The chapel was consecrated in 1631, and the east window, altar, credence table and pulpit are all contemporary, but the ceiling, embossed with the coats of arms of benefactors, was not inserted until 1686. It had to be restored in 1957, and by 1990 the tiled floor had undergone such extensive wear and tear that it was necessary to close the chapel, other than for services, in order to attend to the damage.

It was one of Lincoln's Rectors, Hugh Weston, appointed Dean of Westminster by Mary I, who was chairman of the Commissioners appointed in 1554 to dispute with Cranmer, Latimer and Ridley. Another sixteenth-century Rector of Lincoln, John Underhill, became Bishop of Oxford; so, too, did Nathaniel Crewe, elected Rector in 1668. In 1737 a Fellow of Lincoln, John Potter, was appointed Archbishop of Canterbury.

But apart from Wesley, perhaps Lincoln's most influential scholar was John Radcliffe, a Fellow from 1670 until 1675, whose name fairly adorns the city. He only resigned his Fellowship because, being a wealthy doctor of medicine (physician to Queen Anne in fact), he had no desire to take holy orders, at that time compulsory for a Fellow, and when he died in 1714 his estate provided funds to build first a quadrangle at University College; then the Radcliffe Camera (which dominates Radcliffe Square); the Radcliffe Infirmary – Oxford's best-known hospital – in the Woodstock Road; and the Observatory that stands in the hospital grounds.

Although Lincoln had refused to budge on the question of ordination in 1675, in 1882 it became the first Oxford college to admit a Jewish Fellow, the philosopher Samuel Alexander.

In 1616 Lincoln provided the University with its Senior Proctor for that year. He was a Fellow called Robert Sanderson, who seems to have regarded good example as more beneficial than punishment. 'If,' we are told, 'in his night-walk he met with irregular Scholars absent from their Colleges at University hours, or disorderly or drunk, or in scandalous company, he did not use his power of punishing to an extremity; but did usually take their names, and a promise to appear before him unsent for next morning: and when they did, convinced them, with such obligingness, and reason added to it, that they parted from him with such resolutions, as the man after God's own heart was possessed with.'

Soft heartedness again prevailed when in 1625 the college had occasion to expel a Fellow by the name of Matthias Watson, who had followed a 'notorious lewd and deboscht course of lyfe'. They agreed 'to buy him a new sute of apparell and to hire a messenger and horse to carrie him downe to his freinds and to supply him with sufficient money for his expenses by the waye'.

Across the road from Exeter is the Turl Bar, should you be in need of refreshment, said by those who frequent it to be all right. On your left is a building that has to rate as one of Oxford's most monstrous fakes, the Rector's Lodgings. It also has to be said it is a very clever fake, no more Georgian than the bus station. It was built in 1930. Next door to the Lodgings, on the eastern corner of Turl Street and the High, stands one of the city's most stylish buildings, once the Church of All Saints, now the library of Lincoln College which, uniquely among working college libraries, is open to the public two afternoons a week.

In 1971 the Church Commissioners declared All Saints redundant, and four years later John Radcliffe's estate was again put to good use, meeting the cost of remodelling the interior so as to house books. The spire of the medieval church had collapsed in 1699, and the stupendous spire that now enriches the High and forms a stunning climax to Turl Street was influenced by Hawksmoor. If you have a chance, return at night when it is floodlit.

Inside, although the nave floor has been raised four feet six inches to create space for books beneath, you can still appreciate the sense of height and space achieved under the inspiration of Christ Church's Dean, Henry Aldrich. The plasterwork ceiling is richly ornamented, and eighteenth-century altar rails and pews, adapted to modern needs, ensure that undergraduates study in luxury. There is a fine seventeenth-century effigy, and a lovely seventeenth-century copy of Andrea del Sarto's *Caritas*. Its frame once adorned the altar at Magdalen, and has been most brilliantly reconstructed from broken fragments. Ironmongers were clearly appreciated in Oxford in the eighteenth century; two, John Smith and Thomas Fowler, are commemorated on the west wall.

On the west corner of Turl Street and the High stands the Mitre, since the late fifteenth century the property of Lincoln College, and one of the twentieth century's tragedies where Oxford is concerned. For hundreds of years a repository of all that county town hostelries used to be, since 1969 its rabbit warren of upstairs rooms has been turned into accommodation for undergraduates and staff and the restaurants are now leased to Bernie Inns. Their food is produced to a rigid formula, but at least it is dependable and reasonably priced.

One's heart bleeds for the poor old place nonetheless. 'St Thomas day at 3 in the morning, died suddenly Mris Lasenby the hostess of the Miter, having about 3 hours before been most strangely affrighted by 3 rude persons . . . These having been drinking at the Meermaid tavern newly opened after it had been shut a quarter of an yeare, came drunk to the Miter; were let in by a boy then up. They came as they pretended to eat somthing. The boy said they were all in bed. They enquired where the Mris (Lazenby) lyed. The boy shew'd the window (which is a lower window). They thereupon awak'd her and desired to have some meat dressed. She said 'twas late and would or could not rise. Whereupon they call her strange names, as "popish bitch", "old popish wore"; and told her "shee deserved to have her throat cut". Whereupon being extremely frightened, shee fell into fits and died at 3 in the morn.'

This was Anthony Wood – not too certain as to the spelling of the landlady's name – reporting in 1683, and he tells us too that thirty-four years earlier 'Kinaston, a merchant of London, with a long beard and haire over-grown, was at the Miter-Inn; and faigning himself a Patriarch, and that he came to Oxford for a modell of the last reformation, divers royallists repaired to him, and were blest by him, viz. John Ball, Gilbert Ironside, and Henry Langley – all of Wadham Coll: Bernard Rawlins a glasier was also there, and crav'd his blessing on his knees, which he obtained. John Harmar also, the Greek Professor of the University, appeared very formally, and made a Greek harangue before him. Whereupon some of the company, who knew the design to be waggish, fell a laughing and betray'd the matter. It was a piece of waggery to impose upon the royallists and such that had a mind to be blest by a patriarch instead of an archbishop or bishop; and it made great sport for a time, and those that were blest were asham'd of it, they being more than I have before set downe.'

A pun on the Mitre gave rise in the early nineteenth century to a snappy popular song:

> From the box of the Royal Defiance,
>   Jack Adams, who coaches so well,
> Dropped me down in that region of Science
>   In front of the Mitre Hotel.

> 'Sure never man's prospects were brighter,'
>   Cried I, as I dropped from my perch,
> 'So quickly arrived at the Mitre,
>   'I am sure to get on in the Church.'

If you walk east along the north side of the High Street, past the Victorian south range of Brasenose, you will very soon come upon the University Church of St Mary the Virgin. Above the twisted barley-sugar columns of Nicholas Stone's Baroque south door stands the Virgin herself with the infant Christ in her arms. The Virgin Porch was added in 1637, and its 'scandalous statue' was seized upon as a heaven-sent opportunity to charge Archbishop Laud with popery. Stone was an appropriately named master mason. It may be thought that on the whole St Mary's repays closer examination from without than from within. Its richly pinnacled spire, erected about 1320, rises from a contrastingly plain and solid thirteenth-century tower, open to the public, and the sheer sweep alongside the pavement of glass, and more pinnacles jutting above the roof of the nave, is a stimulating, indeed awe-inspiring, sight.

The arches that support the nave are late fifteenth-century: it was in this nave that Cranmer was harangued for heresy, and from the pulpit that the Oxford Movement was launched. But the finest portion of the church is not revealed until you walk beneath the organ loft. Here are wonderful plain Perpendicular chancel stalls carved in 1453. And somewhere beneath the floor may be buried the body of Amy Robsart, the wife of Elizabeth's favourite, Robert Dudley (who also happened to be Chancellor of the University). She died at Cumnor Place in 1560, having supposedly fallen down stairs, but the priest who conducted her funeral service at St Mary's let slip that she had been 'pitifully murdered', and most modern historians tend to agree with him.

Above the altar is a painting by the sixteenth-century Venetian, Francesco Bassano, of the angel appearing to the shepherds. The reredos is Victorian, the second statue from the left representing Oxford's patron saint, Frideswide.

In the centre of the nave, directly beneath the gallery and the Victorian west window, is the Vice-Chancellor's seat, made in 1828. Until 1646 it was in the Lady Chapel in the north aisle — which contains the tomb of a fourteenth-century Rector, Adam de Brome, founder and first Provost of Oriel College — that the Chancellor's court used to meet.

It was also in the echoing fourteenth-century vaults of St Mary that the University Convocation sat, and here, entered by the north porch, you can now enjoy morning coffee, lunch or a cream tea. Half-way up the stairs leading to the tower you will find the room that housed the University library until 1488, and it was here in 1942 that the first meeting of Oxfam was held. The room is now available for making brass rubbings.

'Of all human things,' Cardinal Newman once said, 'Oxford is nearest my heart,' and it was at St Mary's that John Newman, before his conversion to Rome, was for fifteen years parish priest. Thirty years after Newman's departure, J. C. Shairp recalled, in *Studies in Poetry and Philosophy*, 'those wonderful afternoon sermons. Sunday after Sunday, month by month, year by year, they went on, each continuing and deepening the impression the last had made.' He thought 'the tone of voice in which they were spoken, once you grew accustomed to it, sounded like a fine strain of unearthly music. Through the stillness of that high Gothic building the words fell on the ear like the measured drippings of water in some vast dim cave.'

But not everyone was enamoured of Newman or his sermons. A low church don, H. B. Bulteel, who eventually founded his own evangelical sect in St Ebbe's which became known as Bulteelism, coined the following disparaging verse:

There's Newman wise and simple,
How saintly is his smile!
Alas beneath each dimple
Lurk treachery and guile.

For some 400 years, before Oxford built its seventeenth-century Convocation House and Bodleian Library, St Mary's was the very hub of the University, and it still attracts outstanding preachers. But they do not all set out to reform the morals of undergraduates as did the Bishop of London in 1905. When not fulminating to schoolboys about the evils of masturbation, as John Betjeman recalled in his autobiographical poem *Summoned by Bells*, Dr Winnington-Ingram was hot on the scent of drink. 'I am certain,' he informed his Edwardian congregation at St Mary's, 'from the evidence before me that in certain colleges today there is a wave of drunkenness. I have had instances brought to my knowledge, which I am perfectly certain are true ones, where men have called on Freshmen within a day or two of their coming to Oxford, demanding drinks from them, and if they have not been given they have not only broken up the furniture of the room, but have ill-treated the men themselves. I find at what you even call "quiet colleges" you are too much accustomed today to what was certainly a rare sight when I was here twenty-five years ago, two or three drunken men coming out of what you have, I cannot help thinking misguidedly, called "drunks". It is a new name, and when I see the result of this in London, when I tell you that I have at this moment at least twenty University men hopeless drunkards on my hands, and one of the worst is a 'Varsity cox, you will see that this thing, which you apparently look on with so light a heart, meant deadly ruin to numbers in the days to come. I ask you if it is likely the mustard seed of faith will grow if you take a light view of such a sin as this.'

A little further east, on the other side of Catte Street, you will find one of Oxford's true anomalies, All Souls College, a college without any undergraduates. It was founded in 1438 by the Archbishop of Canterbury, Henry Chichele, to commemorate the dead of the 100 Years War (an unknown archer who fought at Agincourt is depicted on the chapel's reredos), but the fact that only Fellows and post-graduate research workers lurk within its superior portals has not prevented disturbances from breaking out.

'On the thirtieth of January last,' Thomas Hearne noted in his diary on 1 March 1707, 'was an abominable riot committed at All Souls college. Mr Dalton, MA and Mr Talbot, son of the bishop of Oxon, BA both fellows, had a dinner drest, at twelve o'clock, part of which was woodcocks, whose heads they cut off, in contempt of the memory of the blessed martyr. At this dinner were present, two of the pro-Proctors of Oriel coll., Mr Ibbetson, and Mr Rogers, to their shame be it spoken, both low-church men. 'Tis to be noted that this Dalton, an empty fellow, is one of those whom the archbishop of Canterbury, Dr Tenison, put into the society upon the devolution to him of that power, when Dr Finch, the late warden, died. He was for having calves-heads, but the cook refused to dress them.'

So, a disagreement over what to eat at dinner constitutes a riot at All Souls. Much wining and dining continues in this hallowed if rather empty place today, and at least one riot in modern times – or minor uprising, at any rate – can be blamed upon T. E. Lawrence, who was said by Robert Graves, in *Goodbye to All That*, to have engineered a strike by college servants for better pay and hours. Lawrence also cooked up schemes to cultivate mushrooms on the college turf and to drive the deer from Magdalen Grove into the grounds of All Souls, but nothing came of either of these semi-inspired ideas.

The Hall and chapel are never open, but the quadrangles are well worth a visit. The small square Front Quadrangle should come as no surprise in view of the restrained High Street front, particularly notable, since 1940, for a carving above the gate tower of the Last Judgement by W. C. H. King, but some people find it claustrophobic. It dates precisely from the year of the college's foundation, and the whole of the north side is taken up with the chapel, a chapel without an organ, for it was ripped out in 1549 by Edward VI's Visitors and never replaced.

The contrast between the Front Quad and Hawksmoor's eighteenth-century North Quadrangle, entered from the right of the chapel, is certainly a surprise. Much renovation has been necessary in recent years, to Hawksmoor's gatehouse and cupola in the North Quad, and to the Warden's Palladian Lodgings in the High. On the north side is the library, built between 1715 and 1740, 200 feet long, with a lovely sundial high on the wall, a sundial designed by Christopher Wren when he was the college bursar. It is truthful as well as extraordinarily accurate: '*Pereunt et imputantur*: They pass and are charged for', it says.

The massive twin towers on the east wing can afford to dominate because there is no competition from the single-storey cloister range opposite. In the cloister is a memorial tablet to Herberti (sic) Hensley Henson, the twentieth-century Bishop of Durham who favoured disestablishment, and indeed to be commemorated here at all you need to have been rather grand: a Master of the Rolls, an editor of *The Times*. For by its very nature, with its non-resident, non-academic Fellows, All Souls is more of a club than a university college, and a very wealthy club at that. Some might even describe it as a talk-shop, or a comfortable hotel.

Since February 1990 there has been a Betjeman & Barton tea room serving coffee, teas and lunches at 90 High Street, opposite Queen's College; Arthur Betjeman, who opened his first tea room in Paris in 1919, was a cousin of the Poet Laureate. One of the University's earliest dons, Hugo le Lyur, taught pupils in the house in 1270. By 1547 it was a tailor's shop. Here you can actually order a boiled egg and, with it, cinnamon toast. But beware; in summer it seems very hot, for the tea room is downstairs, and inquire the price of tea or coffee if you want to purchase some to take home. Mr Betjeman's products do not come cheap.

128

Six

IN TIPSY SEARCH OF
WAUGH AND GREENE

The Queen's College (open 2.00 p.m. to 5.00 p.m.), St Edmund Hall (quadrangles open only, all day), New College (open term-time, 2.00 p.m. to 5.00 p.m., out of term, 11.00 a.m. to 5.00 p.m., admission charge for non-residents of Oxford), Hertford College (open all day), Museum of the History of Science (open Monday to Friday, 10.30 a.m. to 1.00 p.m., 2.30 p.m. to 4.00 p.m., admission free), Trinity College (open 2.00 p.m. to 5.00 p.m.), Balliol College (quadrangles open 10.30 a.m. to 6.30 p.m.; Hall 10.30 a.m. to 11.30 a.m., 2.30 p.m. to 4.00 p.m.; chapel, 2.00 p.m. to 4.00 p.m.).

129

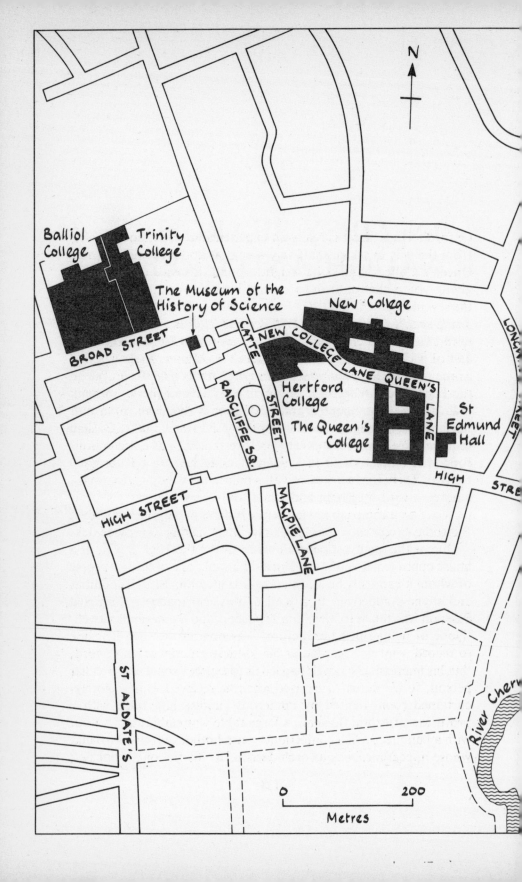

Oxford's High Street is really an experience in itself, and benefits from the way in which, half-way along, at about the point where Queen's College chucks its weight around, it bends to the south, giving you a chance to draw second breath. Towards the end of the seventeenth century Celia Fiennes, whose *Through England on a side saddle in the time of William and Mary* was not published until 1888, found 'The high Streete . . . a very Noble one, soe large and of a Greate Length', which indeed it is. Five colleges as well as the nineteenth-century Examination Schools have frontages on the High Street. There are gaily painted picture galleries, a bank that claims to be haunted and passageways that lead to an old-fashioned ironmonger's and a wildly expensive restaurant which shall remain nameless — '*not* a very good restaurant', as a pretentious food writer described it in 1990 after boasting of a bill for £100 for two. There is a hairdresser with a pole in the window, tea rooms, a hotel, a wine merchant and school outfitters, and every shop is perfectly accustomed to serving future bishops and cabinet ministers. But today credit card companies save them having to provide tick.

One of the strangest people ever to live in the High Street, in a house opposite All Souls, was Ronald Firbank, one of the few people of whom it can truly be said that he invented himself. His oddities and shyness added up to a kind of physical madness. Siegfried Sassoon was taken to meet him by Osbert and Sacheverell Sitwell. 'None of us had met him before,' Sassoon wrote when he came to record what he regarded as his 'oddest experience' in Oxford, 'but his impressionist novels had led us to expect a somewhat peculiar person, so we weren't surprised when he received us in a closely-curtained room lighted by numerous candles and filled with a profusion of exotic flowers. A large table was elaborately set out with a banquet of rich confectionery and hothouse fruits. Firbank, whose appearance was as orchidaceous as his fictional fantasies, behaved so strangely that all attempts at ordinary conversation became almost farcical. His murmured remarks were almost inaudible, and he was too nervous to sit still for more than half a minute at a time. The only coherent information he gave me was when I heavily inquired where his wonderful fruit came from. "Blenheim," he exclaimed with an hysterical giggle, and then darted away to put a picture-frame straight, leaving me wondering how peaches were grown at Blenheim in mid-winter. The Sitwells were more successful in mitigating his helpless discomposure, but even Osbert's suavely reassuring manner failed to elicit anything except the disconnected utterances which were his method of evading direct explanations. For instance, when Sacheverell spoke appreciatively of his latest novel, *Caprice*, he turned his head away and remarked, in a choking voice, "I can't bear calceolarias! Can you? . . ." '

The first book to be printed in Oxford was printed in the High Street by Theodore Rood in 1478. From 1655 to 1668 Robert Boyle lived and experimented scientifically in a house opposite Queen's College or, more properly, The Queen's College. The college stands on the north side of the High, on the corner of Queen's Lane, and was not, as one might imagine, founded by some consort to a king, or even by a queen regnant, but by one Robert de Eglesfield, chaplain to Queen Philippa, the wife of Edward III. But Eglesfield decided to give Queen Philippa the credit, probably after her husband had endowed the college with property in Southampton, and queens consort have been patrons up to the present time. Elizabeth I formerly permitted use of the word 'Queen's', much as Elizabeth II from time to time permits a charity or regiment to call itself 'Royal', and the wives of Charles I, George II and George III proved generous benefactors.

Another female benefactor was Lady Elizabeth Hastings, who endowed Exhibitions for boys from the north but stipulated that the names of the candidates should be drawn out of a hat or, more precisely, an 'urn or vase', a somewhat haphazard if democratic method of selecting undergraduates which remained in force until 1859. Lady Elizabeth thought such a method 'left something to Providence' and she was right.

Queen's is a very good example of an Oxford college that demands a huge leap of the imagination − from the medieval England of jousts and tournaments to the elegant reign of Charles II (rebuilding began in 1672), for not a stone of the original buildings remains.

The High Street front of 1734, with its empty niches, cupola and severe, regimented form, looks at its best against the night sky and seems terrifyingly intimidating by day; but at least it prepares one for the imposing, self-assured symmetrical layout of the eighteenth-century Palladian Front Quadrangle, thought by some to be the finest example of classical architecture in Oxford.

Around three sides is a colonnade, but the north range, built in 1714, is divided exactly in two, with the Hall on the left and the chapel on the right. Massive columns support a clocktower in the centre and a marble statue of George II's wife, Queen Caroline. This was to have been six feet high, and the price agreed was £120, but when the sculptor turned in a piece a few inches higher he was given an extra five guineas. A tunnel has a door on the right leading to the chapel, a building wider than most chapels, with a painted ceiling. One cannot help feeling that Robert Eglesfield would have approved of the somewhat overpowering atmosphere. He insisted that the first undergraduates should be examined every day before dinner, he forbad bows and arrows and dogs, and insisted that the boys' heads be regularly washed, employing a college barber for the purpose.

To reach the Hall you continue through the tunnel into the North Quadrangle, where first of all, on the west, a late seventeenth-century library is waiting to be admired. It is said by those who have been privileged to enter it to have woodwork and plaster as fine as anything to be found in Oxford. The mystery however is not why visitors are kept out, but who built it. Either Wren or Hawksmoor seem obvious candidates, but not a shred of evidence exists.

Entrance into the west colonnade will take you to the door (on your left) to the Hall, a magnificent high-domed room with a gold and turquoise-blue gilded ceiling and a marble fireplace; as with the chapel, everything about the Hall is on a scale commensurate with the rest of the college. To the right of the vast doors is a portrait by Kneller of Joseph Addison, a commoner at Queen's in 1687, who so enjoyed his outings round Addison's Walk at Magdalen.

Eglesfield insisted that the Provost and Fellows be summoned to dinner by trumpets, as they still are. And for many years an annual feast took place at which a boar's head was carried in on a silver salver, accompanied by the regulation trumpets, to commemorate the unlikely story that a student was attacked at

133

Shotover Hill by a boar and got the better of the animal by stuffing a volume of Aristotle down its throat.

A far more engaging undergraduate must have been the political philosopher Jeremy Bentham, whose adult recollections of his 'chamber' at Queen's being 'a very gloomy one' may have been occasioned by the fact that the poor lad arrived at Oxford in 1760 at the age of twelve. He happened also to be small for his age, and exceedingly timid. 'The fear of ghosts', he later wrote, referring to himself in the third person, 'and of the visitations of spiritual beings was strong upon him; and the darkness of the chamber and its neighbourhood added to his alarm.'

Being a 'dutiful and affectionate Son', Jeremy wrote letters home, in one of which he recounted meeting a don who, 'seeing that I had pumps on, gave me a long harangue upon the dangers of wearing them in this weather, and he told me I should get cold if I did not get shoes. When I went away he made me a present of some Reflexions on Logick, written by himself.'

Jeremy Bentham's regime at Queen's was formidable. 'You may think me idle,' he told his parents, 'but I fancy when you understand how much business I do you will alter your opinion.' His morning was taken up with prayers in chapel and lectures in Logic, then 'we must have our hair dressed and clean ourselves and at half an hour after 12 dine.' Geography lessons took place at four o'clock on Thursday, exercise was on Saturday morning and the classics were taught at night.

He showed great grit when 'The Tooth which had several bits of it broke out and was as I complained to you so extremely sore being very troublesome I with my fingers pulled it out having plucked up a good courage: besides there were two other Teeth one of which had a young one growing by the Side of it: I pulled them both out myself: however my Face swelled: before I pulled the Teeth out one or two of them aked very bad, so that with that and the Swelled face, which succeeded to the aking: I was forced to keep up in my rooms: when Mr Jefferson asked me what was the matter with me, and I told him, he told me aeger was the Latin for idle . . . I told him I thought 'twas very hard that I could never be believed by him when I said anything.'

Bentham remembered the 'formal dressing' of his hair as 'a grievous annoyance'. He wrote: 'Mine was turned up in the shape of a kidney: a quince or a club was against the Statutes; a kidney was in accordance with the Statutes. I had a fellow-student whose passion it was to dress hair, and he used to employ a part of his mornings in shaping my kidney properly'.

It was during his first year at Queen's, when he was still only twelve, that Bentham produced an ode on the death of George II. Apparently Dr Johnson admired the verse, but in later life Bentham wrote it off as 'a mediocre performance on a trumpery subject, written by a miserable child'.

Between the library and the western arcade, in the north-west corner of the North Quad, is a high-walled lane that leads to the Nuns' Garden, an oasis in which to recover from so much commanding eighteenth-century architecture. The nuns in question were supposedly followers of St Frideswide, who are said to have sought refuge here at the Reformation.

Another small and unexpected pleasure can be obtained on leaving The Queen's College by turning left into Queen's Lane and entering the second door on the right. This is St Edmund Hall, often affectionately known as Teddy Hall. It is the last surviving medieval hall in Oxford − those halls in which students lived before the establishment of residential colleges as we know them today. At one time there were at least 120 halls, no fewer than twenty-seven of them located in the High Street, so many must have been little more than lodging houses. St Edmund Hall now of course enjoys the status of a college, and is 'Open during the hours of daylight'. There is not a lot to see, for the original Hall, on the west side of the Front Quadrangle, and the late seventeenth-century chapel on the east, containing glass by William Morris and Burne-Jones, and an enterprising altar-piece by Ceri Richards which was acquired in 1958, are always closed. But with its wisteria and window-boxes, the Quad is an enchantingly higgledy-piggledy courtyard, such as you might encounter in a Cotswold village.

If you walk through Staircase One immediately on your left you will find yourself in the churchyard of St Peter-in-the-East, now a redundant church and transformed into the hall's library. In 1922 Billy Clonmore, who later took holy orders and succeeded as the 8th Earl of Wicklow, gave a supper party on the roof. Beside the footpath is the grave of James Sadler, the aeronaut who took off in a balloon from the city walls in 1784; he died forty-four years later at the age of seventy-five. On the north wall of the church is a wonderful Norman window, and with access from the south side is a Norman crypt, which you can enter if you borrow the key from the porter's lodge; spooky but worth it. It still contains a font.

One of St Edmund Hall's seventeenth-century Principals, Stephen Penton, had a lively sense of humour, and in 1688, five years after retiring, he published anonymously some advice from an Oxford don to the father of a prospective undergraduate. It included the following: 'Whatever letters of *complaints* he writes home I desire you to send me a copy; for ill-natured, untoward boys, when they find discipline sit hard upon them, they then will learn to lie, complain, and rail against the university, the college, and the tutor, and with a *whining* letter, make the mother, *make the father*, believe all that he can invent, when all this while his main design is to leave the university and go home again to spanning farthings'.

Thomas Hearne, who was a graduate of St Edmund Hall, and ended his days there, noted on Ash Wednesday 1723 that, 'It hath been an old Custom in Oxford for the Scholars of all Houses, on Shrovetuesday, to go to dinner at 10 Clock (at wch time the little Bell call'd Pan-cake Bell rings, or, at least, should ring, at St Marie's) and at four in the Afternoon, and it was always follow'd in Edmund Hall as long as I have been in Oxford, 'till Yesterday, when they went to dinner at 12 and Supper at six, nor were ther any Fritters at Dinner, as ther us'd always to be. When laudable old Customs alter, 'tis a Sign Learning dwindles.'

Hearne became one of nature's naturally irascible curmudgeons, and today he would have been bankrupted for libel. A fellow academic at St Edmund, Dr Kennett, he called a 'giddy-headed and scandalous Divine': Balliol's Dr Baron he thought 'a poor snivelling Fellow, and in many respects a Knave'. He said that his fellow diarist, the antiquarian Anthony Wood, was regarded in Oxford 'as a most egregious, illiterate, dull Blockhead, and a conceited, impudent Coxcombe'. Dr De Laune of St John's College he accused of embezzlement, and Dr Tyndal of All Souls of being 'a noted Debauchee & a man of very pernicious Principles, sly and cunning'. No one worth their salt escaped the whiplash of his tongue, or at any rate his pen. Handel and his band were 'a lowsy crew of foreign fidlers' and the great Renaissance architect and man of letters John Vanbrugh was simply 'a Blockhead'. Hearne is buried in the churchyard, now in effect the Hall's garden, and had the sense to compose his own epitaph before anyone else could do so:

Here lieth the body of Thomas Hearne MA
Who studied and preserved Antiquities.

Follow on along Queen's Lane and it will lead to New College, a college it is virtually impossible to see from without, with its entrance tucked away at the end of a short cul-de-sac. It was founded in 1379, two years after the death of Edward III, by one of the King's most prominent patrons of education, William of Wykeham, whose desire was to produce 'men of great learning, faithful to the church of God and to the king and realm'. It was he who also established Winchester College, served for five years as Surveyor of the King's Works at Windsor, and became Lord Chancellor and Bishop of Winchester.

Over the front gate are three much restored medieval statues; in the centre is the Virgin Mary, to whom William of Wykeham, on her right, had an especial devotion, and on the left is the archangel Gabriel. The Front Quadrangle of New College is important because it was the first to be designed so as to contain the basic elements of a college – a chapel, Hall, library, chambers for Fellows and scholars and lodgings for a Master. The foundation's official title is the St Mary College of Winchester in Oxford, and it may have been dubbed New College almost from the start in order to differentiate it from an earlier foundation, Oriel, also dedicated to St Mary.

Wykeham's original plan was that boys from his school in Winchester should automatically proceed to his own college in Oxford, and it was 1857 before Fellowships or scholarships were open to anyone other than a Wykehamist. A boy who died in 1676 while still at Winchester has recorded on his tomb that 'he was first in this school and, as we hope, is not last in Heaven, whither he went instead of to Oxford'.

The Front Quad is very properly dominated on the north side by the chapel, and in the north-east corner by the Muniment Tower, with its steep steps leading to the Hall; but the overall effect is not quite as it should be, for an extra storey was added to the original east, south and west wings in the seventeenth century, and now they have a rather stark battlemented roof-line.

You find the entrance to the chapel by entering a vaulted passage in the north-east corner, and a door on the right leads into the ante-chapel, in many ways so much better preserved than the chapel itself. A great modern work embellishes the ante-chapel: a statue of Lazarus by Sir Jacob Epstein, acquired in 1951, silent, mysterious

137

and ghostly when first encountered as you open the door, and deeply impressive when seen again as you turn back from the altar steps.

The central west window of the ante-chapel is the work − unique for him in this genre − of the painter Sir Joshua Reynolds. It was inserted in 1785 and has been much criticised, not always fairly. Reynolds at first removed the tracery of the central portion so that his Nativity scene could be displayed on one large panel, but the tracery had to be replaced in 1848 after a gale had caused one of the panels to bulge, and the effect of his design is now a bit chopped up and so less effective than he intended. But there is not much dispute that the saints and patriarchs depicted in olive-green, pale blue, pink and purple in the remaining windows, which date from around 1386 and are therefore entirely contemporary with the chapel (built between 1380 and 1386), adorn some of the most beautiful medieval glass in England. They are the superb work of a man who came to be known as Thomas Glazier but whose real name was probably Dedyngton. Thomas *the* Glazier he certainly was.

The north aisle of the ante-chapel contains an exceptionally important and now rather vulnerable collection of brasses, including a large effigy of Thomas Cranley, Warden of New College from 1389 to 1396 and later Archbishop of Dublin. Also worth noting, on the east wall, is a tribute to the sensitivity and courage of the chapel authorities in 1919, for they erected a memorial to three college men killed in the Great War who happened to be Germans: Prince Frederick of Waldeck-Prymont, William von Sell and Ernest von Speyer, 'who coming from a foreign land entered into the inheritance of this place and returning fought and died for their country'.

Just as the fourteenth-century windows in the ante-chapel are unsurpassed for their time, so the glass in the chapel is considered perhaps the most important example of eighteenth-century glass in the country. But there is not much else here to admire in the way of architecture. Between 1877 and 1881 George Gilbert Scott could not keep his busy hands to himself, so that the impressive reredos, like the one at Magdalen, is not original, and the roof and screen are the work of Scott as well.

There are however two incomparable works of art. On the north wall hangs El Greco's *St James*, presented to the college in 1961, and a little further along, in a case on the north wall of the sanctuary, is one of the most interesting medieval relics to have survived anywhere, William of Wykeham's crozier, bequeathed by him to the college he founded. The painting opposite the El Greco is a late sixteenth-century impression of the Founder.

No more evocative cloisters exist in any college than those built for New College; if one cannot conjure up the past while walking round here, guarded by mummified statues of the fourteenth century removed from the University Church during restoration work, then one might as well give up an unequal struggle. John Galsworthy, Richard Crossman and Hugh Gaitskell, who was quite well off (like many intellectual socialists) but lived on two shillings a day and a diet of fish and chips, have commemorative tablets. So has Anthony Colegate, an Exhibitioner who died in 1970 at the age of twenty-two, and Philip Edwards, a Commoner, who died in 1968 when he was only twenty. Another sad early death recorded in these silent cloisters is that of Robert Harvey, a scholar who died in 1932 aged twenty; apparently he 'served God by giving to men a rare and eager affection'.

A seventeenth-century organist at New College, William Meredith, acquired an agreeable epitaph when he died in 1637:

> Here lies one blown out of breath,
> Who lived a merry life and dy'd a merry death.

Judging by James Woodforde's diary entry for 5 December 1774, life at New College continued to be merry well into the next century. 'I dined & spent the Afternoon at the Wardens,' he wrote. 'We had a most elegant Dinner indeed. The first Course was Cod & Oysters, Ham & Fowls, boiled Beef, Rabbits smothered with Onions, Harrico of Mutton, Pork Griskins, Veal Collops, New-Coll: Puddings, Mince Pies, Roots &c—The second Course was a very fine rost Turkey, Haunch of Venison, a brace of Woodcocks, some Snipes, Veal Olive, Trifle, Jelly, Blomonge, stewed Pippins, Quinces preserved &c.' This positively indecent spread was accompanied by 'Madeira, Old Hocke, and Port Wines'.

One of the most famous of the college's modern Wardens, whose linguistic contortions gave a new word to the English language, was William Spooner. He held office from 1903 to 1924, and as his portrait in the Hall clearly reveals, he was an albino. He spent a total of sixty-two years at New College and, largely at the behest of his wife, lived on a princely scale. She furnished no fewer than sixteen bedrooms, and was waited on by eleven indoor servants.

In the Barn, which can be seen just before the gates to the college are reached, Spooner kept four horses.

Many of his own Spoonerisms may have sounded funnier when uttered than when read, and a good many Spoonerisms are, alas, certainly posthumous. 'You have tasted a whole worm. You have hissed my mystery lectures. You will leave by the town drain' are examples of his comical turn of phrase, the result in part of a slight speech impediment. The following exchange, however, was pure eccentricity:

'Do come to dinner tonight to meet our new Fellow, Casson.'

'But Warden, I *am* Casson.'

'Never mind, come all the same.'

A far funnier man than Spooner was the Reverend Sydney Smith, one of the great original wits, who was a Fellow of New College from 1789 to 1800. He complained that his living in Yorkshire was so far out of the way 'it was actually twelve miles from a lemon'. Advised by his doctor to walk on an empty stomach, he asked, 'Whose?'

The Hall is immensely high and impressive. It has a Victorian roof and Victorian windows, but magnificent linenfold panelling said to have been paid for by a former Fellow of the college, William Warham, Archbishop of Canterbury in the sixteenth century and a friend and patron of Erasmus. Another of its claims to fame is that it was here that the first lecture on Greek was given in Oxford, in about 1488. Above the buttery door is a pair of medieval carvings of choristers, not singing but serving food and drink, all part of the boys' duties before college scouts were invented.

An archway on the east side of the Front Quad leads to the Garden Quadrangle and the garden, of which the college is inordinately proud. Its finest features are Thomas Robinson's wrought-iron screen of 1711 and the defensive old city walls, complete with two bastions, which form two of the garden's boundaries. From here you gain an unsurpassed impression of Oxford's walls, set off by a haphazard herbaceous border and a sunken lawn. Beneath a lamp on the east wall someone has inserted a delightfully ugly little face, and through a gap in this wall can be glimpsed a sculpture by Barbara Hepworth.

New College Lane will take you on round a bend to Catte Street; just before it does so you pass beneath Thomas Jackson's once controversial twentieth-century Venetian fake, the bridge linking the Old Buildings of Hertford College to the New. But first, on your right, is Number 6 New College Lane. This is the house where Edmund Halley, after whom the best known comet in the heavens is named, lived and had his observatory. He was an undergraduate at Queen's and, from 1703 to 1742, Savilian Professor of Geometry.

'Hertford was a respectable but rather dreary little college,' Evelyn Waugh remembered in his autobiography, *A Little Learning*. He got a scholarship there in 1922, read Modern History, spent much of his time the worse for drink and left with a Third Class degree. He also absorbed material for two of his immensely successful novels, *Decline and Fall* and *Brideshead Revisited*. There have been innumerable candidates put forward as the originals of characters in these books; most recently Duncan Fallowell in an article in the *Sunday Telegraph* has settled upon Alastair Graham (whose brief sojourn at Brasenose was also largely spent with a tankard in his hand) as the prototype for Lord Sebastian Flyte. One of Graham's most serious competitors has always been Hugh Lygon, a younger son of Earl Beauchamp, who was an undergraduate at Pembroke.

As you stand outside Hertford in Catte Street, Jackson's stylish frontage (and clever corkscrew staircase inside) are on your right, and the New Buildings are on the left of the bridge. But with the west front of Hawksmoor's contribution to All Souls to the south, and the University's Bodleian Library, one of the greatest seventeenth-century buildings in England, a few feet in front, Hertford has rather a lot to live up to.

The college started life as Hart Hall in about 1284 (the charter of Elias de Hertford is undated), and only became Hertford College in 1740. By 1814 it was reduced to one member. John Donne, regarded (in 1619) by Ben Jonson as 'the first poet in the world', was at Hertford. So, in the eighteenth century, was a future Prime Minister, Henry Pelham. Pelham's high-principled Principal, Henry Newton, laid down that 'At the tolling of the Second Bell, all the Members of the Society, clean, dressed, shall forthwith repair to the Chapel before Prayers begin, and behave themselves decently there.' They were also 'to go to Bed at a seasonable Hour' and to live 'always Temperately'. In 1764 Charles James Fox entered Hertford College, and once walked from Oxford to Holland House in London, only breaking the fifty-six-mile journey to lunch at an inn on bread and porter, leaving behind his gold watch against eventual payment.

There is no garden at Hertford, which tends to emphasise the rather claustrophobic muddle of the Old Buildings. These include the original Elizabethan Hall in the north-east corner of the Entrance Quadrangle, a mixture of seventeenth- and eighteenth-century buildings opposite the lodge, a chapel dating from 1716, now the library, Jackson's Hall (reached up the corkscrew staircase) and his chapel, not built until 1908, which stands in the south-east corner.

Evelyn Waugh declined to enter the chapel, not because he did not care for Jackson's architecture but because on 18 June 1921, after enjoying religion at Lancing, he wrote in his diary, 'In the last few weeks I have ceased to be a Christian'. He thoroughly approved, however, of the kitchen – or at any rate of the excellent food that came out of it – and when asked by what he described as 'a tipsy white colonial' who had invaded his room in belligerent mood what he did for the college, he replied that he drank for it.

Waugh thought that in his day a government department might have condemned Hertford for use as a penal institution 'on the grounds of danger from fire and lack of hygiene'. He called it 'the period between the hip-bath and the bath-room proper' and claimed 'there were some privies hidden behind the chapel'. He greatly disliked the senior history tutor, who was also Dean of the college and eventually Principal, C. R. M. F. Cruttwell, whose appearance he described as 'not prepossessing'. Waugh said that as Dean, Cruttwell 'seemed often to fancy himself in command of a recalcitrant platoon. He had binges like a subaltern on leave, got grossly drunk when he dined out and was sometimes to be seen as St Mary's struck midnight, feeling his way blindly round the railings of the Radcliffe Camera [he must have meant the Sheldonian Theatre] believing them to be those of the college.'

Another author, Eric Whelpton, also at Hertford, agreed that Cruttwell was eccentric but said, 'He was constantly denigrated by that frightful little sod Evelyn Waugh. I wrote a letter defending Cruttwell [this was presumably in 1964, the year Waugh's autobiography was published] and attacking Waugh in *The Times*. I am told that Waugh was very much upset and that I probably hastened his death.'

For all his blinkered prejudice against individuals, which matured with age as disillusion and self-disgust set in, Evelyn Waugh has left a nostalgic impression of the Oxford of his day, inhabited as it was by so many brilliant men (Waugh himself became perhaps the finest prose stylist of his generation):

'In the quiet streets predatory shopkeepers waited on the university and tempted the young into debts that were seldom repudiated. At Canterbury Gate and in the Broad hansom-cabs and open victorias were for hire. Bicycles and clergymen abounded and clergymen on bicycles were, with the cattle coming to market, the only hazards of traffic. I doubt if there were thirty cars in the university owned by dons or undergraduates. Telephones were never used. Correspondence was on crested cards delivered by college messengers on bicycles.

'It was a male community. Undergraduates lived in purdah. Except during Eights Week girls were very rarely to be seen in the men's colleges. The proctors retained, and in my day on one occasion at least asserted, their right to expel beyond the university limits, independent women who were thought to be a temptation. The late train from Paddington was by tradition known as "the fornicator", but it was not much frequented for that purpose. Most men were well content to live in a society as confined as it had been before the coming of the railway and to indulge in light flirtations during the vacation and deep friendships during the term.'

You may leave Hertford College tempted to explore the environs of the Bodleian, but for the time being leave this wonderful place on your left and walk down Broad Street, so named for obvious reasons, although it once served as a horse market and used to be called Horsemonger Street. Like so many of Oxford's main thoroughfares, the Broad is a delightful mixture of architectural periods. One does not much associate the Broad with permanent residents, but for many years Yeats lived here. Three colleges, if you include the north range of Exeter, jostle for contention with a pretty cottage terrace between the group of shops on the north side, which includes Blackwell's prosperous bookshop, and the entrance to Trinity, and there is an excellent commercial development on the south where you can buy paintbrushes and yet more books.

A very handsome house certainly not to be overlooked on the outside, and looked over if its contents are your cup of tea, is the Museum of the History of Science, immediately to the right of the Sheldonian Theatre on the south side of the street. This is the building in which the Ashmolean Collection was originally housed before being moved to Beaumont Street, and a fine example of seventeenth-century domestic architecture it is too.

The contents include early astronomical and mathematical instruments, microscopes, including a silver microscope made by

George Adams for George III, mouth-watering pocket-watches, clocks, early X-ray apparatus, and surgical and dental instruments. No mere catalogue of the contents of this amazing place could begin to convey the scope of its possessions. To have so much historical evidence of the ingenuity of man contained and so well displayed under one roof seems little short of miraculous.

On the north side of Broad Street you will find the entrance to Trinity College, with its Front Quadrangle laid out to lawn, as an estate agent might say; its grass and established trees make it quite unlike any college quad elsewhere. Established in 1554 by a typical Tudor time-server, a civil servant called Sir Thomas Pope, one of whose duties was to guard Princess Elizabeth at Hatfield House, Trinity has the first non-Gothic chapel to be built in Oxford, a building many people come to visit as if on a pilgrimage.

Yet it is for its secular beauty that this late seventeenth-century chapel in the north-west corner of the Front Quad (its door is round the back in the Chapel Quadrangle) is admired. The altar-piece is simply an inlaid panel, surrounded by carved wooden flowers and fruit. One might be in the Waterloo Chamber at Windsor, for these great swags are the work of Charles II's protegé, Grinling Gibbons. Urns and vases contribute to a decorative effect of which one never tires, for it is ornate without being vulgar, even though pouting putti take the place of angels. Painted panels and stucco decorate the ceiling, and the whole effect is stunning.

If for a moment you fancy yourself out of doors, do not be surprised. The faint whiff of apple, peach, cherry and pear is supplied by the unusual choice of woods. An even odder surprise can be had by creeping along the pews on the north and peeping in at what looks like a bookcase; here repose the founder and his wife.

The Chapel Quad is sometimes also called the Durham Quadrangle, for it contains parts of the medieval college used by the Benedictine monks of Durham, whose priory was dissolved at the Reformation. On the east is the old library, where Dr Johnson liked to read, and on the west stands the Hall, with strangely painted walls meant, presumably, in imitation of marble, and portraits of Henry Ireton, William Pitt, Randall Davidson (Archbishop of Canterbury from 1903 to 1928), Cardinal Newman (who also has a bust on a plinth in the garden), and Frederick North, Earl of Guilford, his name misspelt Guildford.

Wren had a major hand in the Garden Quadrangle, so called

144

because it leads through eighteenth-century wrought-iron gates to a spacious if unadventurous garden of herbaceous borders and a rather ragged copse. In 1668 Wren built on the north side, but only the first two storeys are his. The west range was added in 1682 and the south in 1728, and the result is less characteristic of the best Restoration architecture than it should be. There is much modern in-filling, which is best avoided altogether, but the heavily ornamented President's Lodgings on the north of the Front Quad, built by Thomas Jackson around 1850 (half 'Jacobean', half 'Elizabethan') are much admired.

Much admired too in the seventeenth century was the home-brewed beer for which Trinity became famous — 'excellent beer, not better to be had in Oxon', according to John Aubrey. He also tells us, in his *Brief Lives*, about the President, Ralph Kettell, whose 'fashion was to goe up and down the college, and peepe in at the key-holes to see whether the boys did follow their books or no'. The worst sort of scholar was referred to by Kettell as a turd; more amenable boys were merely scobberlotchers. He paced up and down the Hall with a pair of scissors, snipping away at hair he considered too long, but if he thought a boy was short of cash he would surreptitiously slip some money through his window.

Two high-spirited seventeenth-century undergraduates one night dressed up as Roman senators, climbed a ladder and stood in niches intended for statues. The Dean and some of the Fellows were informed that the college was haunted, and the whole prank got hopelessly out of hand when another undergraduate, somewhat the worse for drink, began to pelt the 'statues' with bits of brick. In 1794 Walter Savage Landor, 'a mad Jacobin' in the opinion of his fellow poet Robert Southey, who was in residence at Balliol next door, was expelled for firing his gun at the shutters of an undergraduate he despised.

When Newman arrived at Trinity in 1817 he was immensely impressed with the meals served in Hall. 'Tell Mama there was gooseberry, raspberry and apricot pies,' he wrote home. These puddings had been preceded by 'beautiful salmon, haunches of mutton, lamb &c, fine strong beer — served up in old pewter plates and misshapen earthenware jugs'. Yet he strongly disapproved of the pastimes of his companions. 'I really think,' he wrote, 'if anyone should ask me what qualifications were necessary for Trinity College, I should say there was only one, Drink, drink, drink.'

Newman was actually a bit of a prig. Pestered, in vain, to leave off work and relax by taking some wine, he informed the other undergraduates that their conduct was not that of gentlemen, and ordered them out of his rooms. One of those thus dismissed was apparently about six feet three inches tall 'and stout in proportion', and Newman said 'he would knock me down, if I were not too contemptible a fellow'. Newman was fortunate not to have had his room ransacked.

He complained bitterly about the lack of tutorial assistance he received at Trinity, and although he read twelve hours a day he was shattered when he only got 'a common pass, but of honours nothing'. The scholarship he was awarded he attributed entirely to the efficacy of prayer.

Richard Burton, the explorer, followed Newman to Trinity in 1840, and said later that he felt he had 'fallen among grocers'. He rode round Oxford in a dog-cart and got himself rusticated, which means he was temporarily expelled from the college; as he felt tolerably certain his family did not know what rusticated meant, he explained that he had been given an extra holiday because he had taken a Double First.

If Christopher Hollis is to be believed, tutoring at Trinity left something to be desired in the early years of this century. In *Oxford in the Twenties* he recounts that Lionel Hedges arrived at Trinity with a tremendous reputation as a schoolboy cricketer (he had been at Tonbridge), so that when, one morning, a 'seedy looking middle-aged gentlemen' called on him, he thought he must be a newspaper reporter. It turned out the man was not a reporter but Hedges's tutor, 'with whom he was not otherwise acquainted'.

A horizontal cross set in the road in the middle of Broad Street, a few yards west of Trinity, marks the spot where Latimer, Ridley and lastly Cranmer were burnt. It is right opposite Balliol, but the bishops would not recognise the college today. Probably the third oldest college in Oxford, Balliol began life with a house standing roughly where the present Master's Lodgings in Broad Street are now, in which, by 1266, John de Balliol was doing penance for insulting the Bishop of Durham by providing accommodation for poor scholars. But the college's present buildings are predominently Victorian — and some are quite hideous.

John Wycliffe, a translator of the Bible into English, was Master in about 1360. Archibald Tait, Archbishop of Canterbury from 1869

146

to 1882, was one of Balliol's earliest scholars. Another was Benjamin Jowett, who in 1870 became perhaps the college's most famous Master and certainly one of the best-known men in Victorian Oxford. His house was said to be 'the meeting point of the University and the outer world'. Jowett, who coined the phrase so often attributed to others, 'never regret, never explain, never apologise', was known – as Master – to Matthew Arnold (who became Professor of Poetry), Hilaire Belloc, Gerard Manley Hopkins and Swinburne; to Frederick Temple and another Archbishop of Canterbury, Cosmo Lang, who was vicar of St Mary the Virgin from 1894 to 1896, served as Dean of Divinity at Magdalen and declared, 'Balliol was my mother, All Souls was my lawful and loving wife, and Magdalen my very beautiful mistress'; and to Asquith, Curzon, Grey, Lansdowne and Milner. It was Asquith who unfortunately remarked that it was 'effortless superiority' which distinguished his Balliol contemporaries, a remark the college has never succeeded in living down. Just as wealth and privilege have tainted Christ Church, so an aura of academic snobbery seems to hover permanently over Balliol.

The ghastly pale porter's lodge by which you enter was built in 1867 by Alfred Waterhouse, and in the north-east corner of the Front Quadrangle stands Butterfield's chapel of 1857, not of course built on anything like the scale of his later chapel at Keble. It is in fact the third chapel to have stood on this spot, the first dating from 1328, the second from 1525. In 1929 the majority of Butterfield's furnishings and decoration were replaced: the wonderfully sinister 1630 lectern in the shape of a crowned eagle and the Jacobean pulpit were rescued from the second chapel. Among the names of the dead inscribed outside the chapel doors is that of Adam von Trott, executed in 1944 for plotting against Hitler.

Beside the chapel, in the north range, is the original fifteenth-century library, and on the west is what used to be the Hall and is now the College Library, again fifteenth-century but much altered by James Wyatt. You walk through the Library Passage between the library and the tower, built in 1852 by Anthony Salvin, into the Garden Quadrangle, and here you are faced by an amazing jumble of buildings ranging in date from 1720 to 1968. But the oldest objects are the gates flanking the Library Passage; they were hanging in the Broad when the bishops were burnt and were themselves at one time sold for firewood, but earned a reprieve and were returned to the college in 1926.

147

The Hall (Waterhouse again, and it is perfectly awful) dominates the scene from the north-east corner of this restless site and contains portraits of Harold Macmillan, at one time Chancellor of the University, Jowett by G. F. Watts, and King Olaf V of Norway, a grandson of Edward VII. Uniquely, it also contains an organ, installed by Jowett for concerts.

It is hard, faced with so much architecture that speaks of tasteless riches, to conjure up images of Balliol's history. But of course it abounds. In 1452 George Nevill, whose brother was Earl of Warwick, celebrated his MA by inviting 900 guests to a two-day banquet. In 1680 'White, a servitour of Balliol College' was killed by Thomas Hovell, and Hovell 'was hanged on the gallows against Ball. Coll. gate: died very penitent and hang'd there till 2 or 3 in the afternoon'. Southey arrived at Balliol in 1792, was told by his tutor, correctly as it turned out, that he would not learn anything at his lectures, and recalled, 'There is no part of my life which I remember with so little pleasure as that which was passed at the University'.

In 1637, when he was sixteen, John Evelyn, who was to become a respected courtier, learned writer and one of the great diarists of the seventeenth century, was admitted to Balliol as a Fellow Commoner. Balliol was then hard up, and a Fellow Commoner was expected to present the college with plate to the value of £10. Evelyn very wisely gave books. 'Mine was in Books to the value of the *plate*,' he recorded, 'which was all Coin'd into mony to inable the King to maintain his Forces, and Court, which was quartered about Oxon: the Plate was Gon but my Books remaine in the Library'. He would have been called a Gentleman Commoner elsewhere, and because of his status he was given a bedroom to himself. Soon after his arrival he attended Communion in chapel, and 'the greatest part of the following Weeke I spent in Visiting the Coleges, Scholes, Publique Library and Curiositys, which much affect young Freshmen as they are called'.

Evelyn's tutor found him 'a very ingeniose young gent', but he seems at an early age to have been more curious about the world outside Oxford than within, and did not take a degree. At twenty-one, for example, he was present at the execution of the Earl of Strafford. But he maintained close and important ties with Oxford. In 1654 he took his new young wife on a visit, supping at Balliol 'where they made me extraordinarily welcome', and it was John

Evelyn who encouraged Lord Henry Howard to give the Arundel Marbles to the Ashmolean Museum.

The nineteenth-century architects chosen to work at Balliol may have let down the college (they all did better work elsewhere), but for all his own particular faults (he was an atrocious snob) Benjamin Jowett did create within the Victorian walls of Balliol a climate of academic excellence for which it remained renowned long after his death. His pay as Regius Professor of Greek had been £40 per annum in 1861. It was increased to £400, which says something about current estimates of his talent. In 1881 a group of undergraduates produced forty rhymes relating to members of Jowett's college, swiftly withdrawn under ludicrous threats of libel, but the Master's own squib seems innocuous enough:

> First come I. My name is J-W-TT.
> There's no knowledge but I know it.
> I am Master of this College,
> What I don't know isn't knowledge.

Jowett had no small talk, was much given to snubbing people, was often grossly insensitive to the feelings of the young, tried to pretend that the Greek idealisation of homosexual love had something to do with men and women (he himself was a life-long bachelor who professed to an infatuation for the most formidable spinster of her time, Florence Nightingale), and was almost incapable of praising good work. But perhaps his worst fault, as recorded by J. A. Symonds, was drinking lukewarm tea 'out of a large metal pot, in big clumsy cups'. Many people admired him. 'I was profoundly grateful to Mr Jowett,' A. J. C. Hare wrote in his autobiography, 'but being constantly asked to breakfast alone with him was a terrible ordeal. Sometimes he never spoke at all . . . Walking with this kind and silent friend was even worse.' Perhaps the truth is that Jowett was profoundly lonely.

The don who, in the opinion of Sir John Betjeman, dominated Balliol in the early years of the twentieth century was Francis Urquhart, always known as Sligger. He 'held court in summer on a lawn in the garden quad', and was as big a snob as Jowett, but more interested in young men, taking numbers of them on chaste reading parties to a chalet he owned in Switzerland. 'He liked people to be well-born, and if possible Roman Catholic,' Betjeman has

149

written. Evelyn Waugh used to taunt Urquhart by chanting loudly, 'The Dean of Balliol sleeps with men,' sung to the tune of *Here we go gathering nuts in May*, which was pretty rich considering that at Oxford Waugh himself slept with men. It was also strictly untrue. Urquhart's relations with the undergraduates always remained platonic.

Sligger Urquhart was a much nicer man than Jowett. In his biography of Harold Nicolson, who went up to Balliol in 1904, James Lees-Milne has written, 'Sligger talked to these unfledged undergraduates on absolutely equal terms, without the slightest patronage or censure. Yet he managed to humanise their arrogance, and render their superiority less vulgar.' Nicolson, who was made an Honorary Fellow of Balliol in 1953, came to love and revere Urquhart, and in a broadcast in 1951 he said, 'Balliol is, I suppose, a rather bleak and certainly an ugly college, but it remains dearer to me than any institution on this earth'.

A future biographer of Byron and editor of the *Cornhill Magazine*, Peter Quennell, a precocious young poet who had already caught the eye of Edith Sitwell and of Churchill's squeaky private secretary Eddie Marsh, arrived at Balliol in 1923 from Berkhamsted, where Graham Greene's father was headmaster and Greene himself was a pupil. Alas, Quennell's Oxford career came to an untimely end when he decided to conduct a prolonged affair with a lady called Nina in, of all places, Maidenhead. Night after night a friend ruffled Quennell's bed so that his college scout would think it had been slept in. One night, however, he forgot to do so, and Quennell was sent for by the Vice-Chancellor.

He wrote in his autobiography, *The Marble Foot*: 'I could scarcely have played my cards worse; for, instead of affecting submission and regret, I adopted an attitude that was described by the authorities as "contumacious", referred to the rights of the citizen like a modern John Wilkes, and – still more absurdly and inappropriately – defended Nina's good name . . .

'The Oxford I knew was still a semi-monastic institution; some of the dons clearly detested women; and the only kind of moral offence they condoned were discreetly managed homosexual passions, for which they often felt a secret sympathy. I myself had committed a number of crimes; I had fornicated, broken bounds and told the Vice-Chancellor outrageous lies. My sentence was quickly pronounced: I was condemned to rustication – sent down

37 The Radcliffe Camera, built by James Gibbs between 1737 and 1749 with money bequeathed by John Radcliffe, a scholar and Fellow of Lincoln College. It originally housed a library also endowed by Radcliffe, and in 1860 became part of the Bodleian. Gibbs studied in Rome, and his Camera, one of the most exciting buildings in Oxford, is strongly influenced by Italian taste.

38 The south front of the Schools Quadrangle, seen from Radcliffe Square. It dates from the very early years of the seventeenth century. The ground and first floors were intended for lectures, the second floor as part of the Bodleian Library, named after its great benefactor Sir Thomas Bodley.

39 The Schools Quadrangle. The statue is of the 3rd Earl of Pembroke, to whom Shakespeare dedicated his first folio. The tower above the ceremonial entrance is known as the Tower of the Five Orders of Architecture, and between the Corinthian columns sits James I, presenting copies of his own works to Fame and to the University.

40 The fan-vaulted ceiling of the Divinity School. Entered from within the Schools Quadrangle, the Divinity School was built between 1426 and 1483 and the ceiling, one of the most exquisite medieval achievements to be seen in Oxford, was added almost as an afterthought. It was paid for by Thomas Kemp, Bishop of London.

41 In 1810 Percy Bysshe Shelley was expelled from University College for writing a book on atheism. After he was drowned, a marble effigy was commissioned from Edward Onslow Ford. When the work was rejected by the Protestant cemetery in Rome it came to rest at University College, a romantic and rather moving reparation to one of England's greatest Romantic poets.

42 Mob Quad at Merton College, the oldest quadrangle in the oldest college in the oldest university in the world. The first floor houses a library open to the public, dating from 1371, and adjoining the library is a room containing mementos of Max Beerbohm, who had rooms in Mob Quad between 1890 and 1894. The dormer windows were added in the sixteenth century to admit more light.

43 Charles Patey, born in 1829, was seven years old when he went to work at Merton College under his father. He became butler in 1869 and died in harness in 1916, aged eighty-five, after serving the college for seventy-eight years. *Photograph by courtesy of the Warden and Fellows of Merton College.*

44 The extraordinary sundial in the Front Quadrangle of Corpus Christi College commemorates the fact that in 1517, the year the college was founded, a Bavarian astronomer and mathematician, Nicholas Kratzer, was elected a Fellow. It was he who established in England horology — the science of measuring time.

45 Thomas Rowlandson's impression (a watercolour *circa* 1810) of the Radcliffe Observatory, built in 1771 by James Wyatt. Its telescope has been disposed of but the building remains one of the most original eighteenth century constructions anywhere, one of Oxford's most perfect buildings and Wyatt's masterpiece. There were plans in 1927 to knock it down but John Betjeman, still only an undergraduate, successfully campaigned for its preservation. *Photograph by courtesy of the Leger Galleries, Ltd.*

46 Sir Godfrey Kneller's portrait of Sarah Churchill, wife of the 1st Duke of Marlborough, for whom Blenheim Palace at Woodstock was built by John Vanbrugh, and where the painting can be seen in the Green Drawing-Room. She wanted Christopher Wren as architect, quarrelled violently with Vanbrugh, and pronounced the Palace 'too big and unwieldy'. *Photograph by courtesy of His Grace the Duke of Marlborough.*

47 The Thames at Oxford, often called in that region the Isis, offers a variety of pleasures, punting, rowing or gently pleasure cruising. Modern boathouses have taken the place of college barges. From one of them an undergraduate is about to set out in a skull.

for a single term – and would then be gated, as soon as I reappeared, for the remainder of my Oxford life. I must leave immediately. And so I did.'

One of Quennell's contemporaries at Balliol was Cyril Connolly, who had arrived from Eton perhaps too full of promise and did very little at Oxford except convince Kenneth Clark that he was 'without doubt the most gifted man of his generation'. And that was praise indeed, for the undergraduate intake of the early 1920s almost certainly constituted, taken overall, the most brilliant generation ever to arrive at Oxford *en masse*. But Connolly recalled in later life that, 'To me Oxford was no celestial city but a place where I was unhappier than I had ever been before. I could have got a good first in nervous breakdowns.'

Nevertheless he drew on his disappointment with Oxford (being a sensitive and creative person he had almost certainly gone to an inappropriate college) to write a clever poem which he called, simply, *Oxford*.

> When days are long and sunny
> the flower of youth is blown.
> We waste our parents' money
> and time that is our own.
> The days grow dark and colder
> beyond the summer's prime.
> We, before time is older,
> are old before our time.

Perhaps Balliol itself has received and trained more famous men this century than any other college in Oxford, so it hardly seems fair that among their undergraduates between 1922 and 1925 was Graham Greene, himself the greatest English novelist of his generation. He learned his initial trade as a journalist sub-editing for the *Oxford Outlook*, now defunct, whose editors included such disparate talents as Beverley Nichols and L. P. Hartley; and he got in some early practice as a novelist at Balliol by writing there his first book, which not surprisingly remained unpublished. The plot concerned 'the unhappy history of a black child born to white parents'.

From his aesthetic fastness at Christ Church, Harold Acton thought Greene looked 'puritanical and rather disapproving', and needless to say they did not click. In 1964 Greene wrote to Evelyn

151

Waugh with subtle irony to explain why *their* paths had not crossed at Oxford. 'I was not suffering from any adult superiority . . . but I belonged to a rather rigorously Balliol group of perhaps boisterous heterosexuals, while your path temporarily took you into the other camp.' The Balliol club to which Greene owed allegiance was called the Mantichorean Society, and sported a blue and silver tie with black stripes. He later admitted that many of their exploits were rather below those of normal adolescents. One night, for instance, they went out armed with screwdrivers to see who could collect the most plates inscribed 'No hawkers, no tradesmen, no circulars' or 'Beware of the dog'.

Greene was admonished by his tutor, Kenneth Bell, to learn to take his drink like a gentleman, and soon developed an appreciation of good food. 'One could arrange a really topping lunch,' he wrote to his future wife after he had come down. 'One got a card from Sligger authorising it & then went down into the kitchens & interviewed the chef & collaborated in a fascinating menu.'

Greene confessed to Evelyn Waugh that he drank a great deal at Oxford, and in *A Sort of Life* he wrote of his final year, 'For nearly one term I went to bed drunk every night and began drinking again immediately I woke'. Things reached such a pitch that he was drunk first thing in the morning when he was due to take part in an end of term ceremony called the Handshake, when the undergraduates, in turn, sat in front of the Master and Dean while their tutor commented on their work.

'I was helped as far as the door,' he remembered in *A Sort of Life*, 'by two of my friends, Robert Scott and George Whitmore, who held me on a steady course through the quad. Then I slumped into a chair beside Kenneth Bell and faced the Master and the Dean. I don't think it occurred to either of these two that an undergraduate would appear before them drunk at that early hour and on such a serious occasion and they probably put down any strangeness in my manner to nerves.'

Seven

BUILDINGS THAT TAKE THE BREATH AWAY

Brasenose College (open 10.00 a.m. to 5.00 p.m.), Radcliffe Camera (closed), Old Schools Quadrangle and Divinity School (open Monday to Friday, 9.00 a.m. to 5.00 p.m., Saturday, 9.00 a.m. to 12.30 p.m.), Convocation House, Chancellor's Court and Duke Humfrey's Library (guided tours only, March to September, Monday to Friday, 10.30 a.m., 11.30 a.m., 2.00 p.m., 3.00 p.m., Saturday, 10.30 a.m., 11.00 a.m., admission charges; no children under fourteen), Sheldonian Theatre (open Monday to Saturday, 10.00 a.m. to 4.45 p.m., admission charges), Clarendon Building.

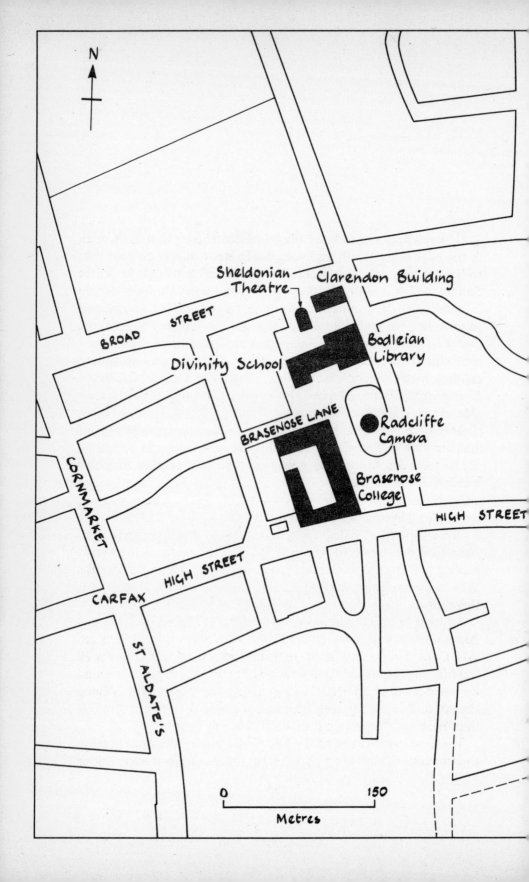

N

Sheldonian Theatre

Clarendon Building

BROAD STREET

Divinity School

Bodleian Library

BRASENOSE LANE

Radcliffe Camera

Brasenose College

CORNMARKET

HIGH STREET

HIGH STREET

CARFAX

ST ALDATE'S

0   150

Metres

Turl Street, opposite Balliol College in Broad Street (it runs through to the High Street), will lead you past Exeter College, on your left, to Brasenose Lane. Turn left into the lane and you enter Radcliffe Square, which is really the heart of the University. In front of you is James Gibbs's monumental rotunda, the Radcliffe Camera, and to the north the Old Schools Quadrangle, the Divinity School, the Old Bodleian Library and the Clarendon Building. But before exploring these unsurpassed examples of Tudor, seventeenth- and eighteenth-century architecture, first visit the oddly named Brasenose College (often referred to as BNC), whose entrance is on the west side of the square.

Brasenose was founded in 1509 by William Smyth, Bishop of Lincoln and Chancellor of the University for three years, and by Sir Richard Sutton, a lawyer who was the first layman to found a college at Oxford. An explanation for this dual foundation, albeit a slightly embroidered one, was supplied in 1662 by Thomas Fuller, writing in *The Worthies of England*:

'It happened that William Smyth Bishop of Lincoln began Brazen-Nose-Colledge, but dyed before he had finished one Nostrill thereof, leaving this Sutton his Executor, who over-performed the Bishops Will, and compleated the Foundation with his own liberal Additions thereunto.'

Another 'worthy' whom Fuller thought worthy of mention was Alexander Nowell, born in 1510, who was 'admitted into Brazen-nose College in Oxford [and] studied thirteen years therein'. Nowell went fishing one day and left a bottle of beer in the grass. 'He found it some days after, no bottle but a gun, such the sound of the opening thereof and this is believed (casualty is mother of more inventions than industry) the original of bottled ale in England.'

The first two storeys of the Old Quadrangle date exactly from the foundation, and are a particularly fine example of early Tudor domestic architecture. The top storey of dormer windows, out of which you feel you may expect to see some old lady emptying a pail, were added early in the seventeenth century, when student numbers began to increase. The sundial on the north side was placed there in 1719.

The Hall, on the south, is small, with pretty panelling dating from 1684 and an eighteenth-century plaster ceiling. It contains two of Oxford's more distinguished modern portraits: an excellent study by Richard Smith of Robert Runcie, Archbishop of Canterbury from 1980 to 1991, and Derek Hill's portrait of H. L. A. Hart, Principal from 1973 to 1978. But perhaps the less said about the unrestrained painting of the renowned novelist Sir William Golding the better.

The famous Brazen Nose knocker hangs over the Principal's chair, beneath a portrait of William Smyth, wearing his episcopal ring on his thumb.

Staircase Seven in the south-east corner of the Old Quad will take you into what is ironically known as the Deer Park, because the area is so small, and to the chapel, entered through a strange, tiny cloister built in 1657. The glory of the chapel is its wooden hammerbeam roof, dating from about 1440 and thus 200 years older than the building itself. It was removed from an Augustinian chapel on the site of Frewin Hall in New Inn Hall Street, property Brasenose has owned since 1580. Painted very successfully at the end of the nineteenth century, this ceiling, so unexpected in the setting of a seventeenth-century chapel, alone justifies a visit to Brasenose.

John Foxe, whose 'Book of Martyrs', properly called *Actes and Monuments*, written in 1563 to celebrate those who had died for the Protestant faith, was a member of the college. So was the author of *The Anatomy of Melancholy*, Robert Burton, and one of Oxford's greatest benefactors, Elias Ashmole, founder of the Ashmolean Museum. The seventeenth century also produced one of the college's most eccentric dons, Thomas Frankland, who became Vice-Principal in 1667. Said to be 'haughty, turbulent and disagreeable,' he took to forging documents and ended up in the Fleet Prison. Even worse was to befall an eighteenth-century common room butler, who was found guilty of stealing wine from the college cellar. 'The sentence of death prefaced by a few words upon the enormity of the prisoner's crime, aggravated as it was by the circumstances of stealing the property of his masters, was,' so a contemporary newspaper recorded, 'most solemn and pathetic.'

An undergraduate who matriculated in 1774, Henry Addington, became Prime Minister, and in addition to William Golding, Brasenose has produced writers of the calibre of John Middleton Murray, Charles Morgan and John Buchan. They can also lay claim to a soldier of dubious distinction, Earl Haig, and to one of the most influential of Victorian academics, Walter Pater, a Fellow from 1864 to 1894. Pater, whose elegant prose inspired several generations of undergraduates throughout the University, has a tablet in the chapel. So has Mervyn Prower, an undergraduate killed in 1857 by a butcher's knife during one of the last serious squabbles between town and gown: *Inter tumultum plebis abdormivit*.

Radcliffe Square – cobbled, and no place for high heels – is almost a microcosm of English architecture, with sixteenth-century Brasenose on the west, St Mary the Virgin and its fourteenth-century spire dominating the south (this is by far the best view of the University Church, marvellous though it is from the High), Hawksmoor's eighteenth-century towers clearly visible in the North Quad of All Souls, and his cloisters' gatehouse and the twin ends of his library and chapel forming the east side of the square. Across the north side of the square is the stupendous south range of the Bodleian Library and Schools Quadrangle, dating from 1613.

The circular Radcliffe Camera in the centre of the square, originally called the Radcliffe Library, was built by James Gibbs between 1737 and 1749, not only with John Radcliffe's money but in order to house a library he had endowed. It only became part of the University's Bodleian Library in 1860, and now contains two reading rooms, mainly used by undergraduates. As you walk across the lawn to the north of the Camera you tread but a few feet above an underground book-store, built in 1912.

British and foreign government publications are housed in the Camera, along with material on history, art history and education. A spiral staircase leads to the upper floor, with its splendid gallery, stone-carving, plasterwork and internal view of the dome, but for obvious reasons no part of the building, which Sir Nikolaus Pevsner called 'England's most accomplished domed building', is open to the public. As the whole conception of the Camera may instantly indicate, Gibbs studied in Rome. His best-known and most famous church is St Martin-in-the-Fields in Trafalgar Square, but his greatest architectural triumph is a building it is almost impossible to stop marvelling at, the Radcliffe Camera.

When you enter the Schools Quadrangle through the south gateway you stand in one of the great courtyards of the world. Notice boards enjoin silence, but any civilised person should automatically be struck dumb by such unostentatious grandeur. On your left is a bronze statue of the 3rd Earl of Pembroke, Chancellor of Oxford University from 1617 to 1630, made originally for the family home, Wilton House, and presented to the University in 1723 by the 7th Earl, but it has only stood in its present position since 1950. His coat of arms can be seen above the south entrance.

It was to the 3rd Earl of Pembroke and his brother that Shakespeare dedicated his First Folio, and Oxford's indebtedness to Pembroke includes a gift, made in 1629, of 250 Greek manuscripts.

On your right is the ceremonial entrance, emblazoned with the crests of the seventeen colleges in existence in 1619. Above the entrance is what is called the Tower of the Five Orders of Architecture (Tuscan, Doric, Ionic, Corinthian and Composite), and between the Corinthian columns sits James I, 'the wisest fool in Christendom' as Henri IV of France is aptly reputed to have called him, presenting copies of his own works (he was no mean theologian) to Fame and to the University. The inscription claims he was 'of Kings the most learned, most munificent and altogether best', a contemporary judgement some modern historians might want to dispute.

When this quadrangle was built, between 1613 and 1619 (and it is hard for us to comprehend that no one knows who did build it), the first two floors were designed as lecture rooms and 'schools', and you only have to decipher the Latin inscriptions above each door to step back into the academic world of the seventeenth century. The Seven Liberal Arts were considered to be Grammar, Rhetoric, Logic, Arithmetic, Geometry, Music and Astronomy; Greek and Hebrew served for foreign languages; and the study of Natural, Moral and Metaphysical Philosophy were all part of a day's work for a Master of Arts. Faculties of Theology, Medicine and Law existed too.

The upper floor of the quadrangle became the core of the Bodleian Library, that part now known as the Old Library, the Bodleian today being spread across the University, with two dozen reading rooms and seating for 2,133 readers. The first University library, founded by Thomas Cobham, Bishop of Worcester, was housed adjacent to the University Church, and was certainly in existence by 1320. Later benefactors included Henry IV and his sons, most notably Humfrey, Duke of Gloucester, who has a part in Shakespeare's *Henry V*. By 1426 the University had decided to build (in the west wing of the Schools Quad) a new Divinity School, and when the Duke began to donate matchless gifts of manuscripts to the University they decided also to build above the new Divinity School a library in which to house his texts. This is now called Duke Humfrey's Library.

By the middle of the sixteenth century, at a time of financial stringency, the entire library had been dispersed (just three of the Duke's books have been retrieved), and for about half a century the University had no library at all. It was in 1599 that Sir Thomas Bodley, a Fellow of Merton and a former diplomat, decided to put matters to rights. 'I concluded at the last,' he explained, 'to set up my Staff at the Librarie dore in Oxon: being throwghly perswaded, that in my solitude, and surcease from the Commonwealth affayers, I coulde not busie myselfe to better purpose, than by dedusing the place (which then in every part laye ruined and wast) to the publique use of Studients.'

And so Sir Thomas restored the Duke of Gloucester's neglected library, restocked it with books and encouraged donations from other sources. A gift of books arrived in 1600 from Thomas Sackville, 1st Earl of Dorset, who had been elected Chancellor of the University in 1591. He it was who had welcomed his cousin Queen Elizabeth I on her visit to Oxford in 1592, and in 1605 he held open house for a week at New College during a visit by James I, when he sent to every college gifts of money and venison, the venison no doubt procured from his park at Knole.

The restored Library was opened in November 1602, and by 1612 an extension had to be built. One year later − the year of his death − Bodley was helping to finance the building of the quadrangle, and from the first the top floor was set aside for the ever-expanding library. One reason its collection of books now increased so rapidly was because in 1610 Bodley arranged with the Stationers' Company that a copy of every book they published should be sent to the library at Oxford, and to this day the Bodleian, like the British Library in London and the Cambridge University Library, is entitled to a copy of every book published in Britain. Sir Thomas Bodley died too soon to see the eventual setting for his library completed;

unaware, too, that he had inspired and made possible the creation of one of Europe's great research institutions, a seat of learning only rivalled in this country by the British Library.

By 1849 the number of printed volumes at the Bodleian was estimated to be 220,000 (today there are 5,300,000, plus 1,013,000 maps) and the number was dramatically increased when the Bodleian took over the Radcliffe Library. With the opening in 1882 of the New Examination Schools in the High Street it was possible for all three floors of the quadrangle to be used by the Bodleian (the library had in fact been steadily encroaching on the schools for a century) and in 1947 work began on converting the top floor – the original storage space – into reading rooms.

Sixteen thousand readers' tickets are issued every year for the Bodleian but it is not possible to borrow a book, even if you are a king. Desirous of a good read while living in Oxford, in 1645 Charles I sent over to the library for a copy of *Histoir Universelle du Sieur d'Aubigné* and had to be told politely that he could not have it. He quite understood. Nine years later Cromwell wanted to lend the Portuguese ambassador a manuscript in the Bodleian, and he too had to be reminded that the Statutes forbad the removal of any book or manuscript whatsoever.

Those Statutes, drawn up in 1610, are pretty comprehensive, requiring readers on entering the library to frame their minds so as to 'study in modesty and silence', and to use 'the books and other furniture in such manner that they may last as long as possible'. It went without saying that it was expressly forbidden to 'steal, change, make erasures, deform, tear, cut, write notes in, interline, wilfully spoil, obliterate, defile, or in any other way retrench, ill-use, wear away, or deteriorate any book or books'.

What had been overlooked was any express way of preventing a misfortune at the laying, in 1634, of the foundation stone for an extension to the library, when apparently some scaffolding collapsed, throwing at least 100 'Proctors, Principals of Halls, Masters, and some Bachelaurs' to the ground, the under-butler of Exeter College suffering a broken shoulder.

With its stark, uncompromising lack of windows, the west wing of the quad makes an impressive entrance into what is called the Prosscholium, built between 1610 and 1612 and now largely given over to the sale of cards and literature. Straight ahead is presumably the most exquisite medieval building in Oxford, the Divinity School, begun in 1426 but not completed until 1483, for Henry VI kept diverting his workmen to Eton College and Windsor Castle. Here theologians engaged in complex dispute, and lectures were given for those attending the Theology Faculty. The low, elaborate fan-vaulted ceiling, added almost as an afterthought and paid for by Thomas Kemp, Bishop of London, is breathtaking. 'The chiefest Wonder in Oxford is a faire Divinitie School,' Sir Roger Wilbraham wrote in 1603, 'with church windoes: and over it the fairest librarie.'

A paved floor adds to the cool effect, and through the windows on the left can be seen dappled trees, through those on the right nothing but a glimpse of the Sheldonian Theatre and the Old Ashmolean Building; one is somehow encased in perfection. Wren cut the Gothic doorway in the north wall in 1669, to allow access to his new Sheldonian, and left his initials entwined inside and out: CWA, which stands for Christopher Wren, Architect. His father, another Christopher, with whom presumably he did not wish to be confused, had been Dean of Windsor. A chair placed on the left of the entrance was given to the Bodleian in 1662 by John Davies, keeper of the naval stores at Deptford Dockyard; it is constructed from timbers taken from Sir Francis Drake's ship when it was broken up.

Entry to the Convocation House (built in 1634), the Chancellor's Court and Duke Humfrey's Library may only be obtained if you go on a guided tour, and children under fourteen are not allowed in at all. These tours are intelligently conducted, take about forty minutes and assemble in the Exhibition Room, in the south-west corner of the quadrangle. First port of call is the Divinity School, open in any case to everyone. The Convocation House was built on to the west end of the Divinity School between 1634 and 1637, to take the place of the old Convocation meeting place at St Mary's, and here all is dark and sombre (there is not even any electric lighting), the plainly carved Jacobean stalls and equally plain fan-vaulted ceiling providing a striking and rather agreeable contrast to the light and airy atmosphere of the Divinity School. It is very much a place for sober meetings, and no matter where you sit you will undoubtedly be residing on the spot occupied by some former politician, for during the Civil War those members of Parliament loyal to Charles I met here, as did Charles II's short-lived Parliament of 1681. In this room are two rare stained-glass sundials, inserted into the windows, and it is here that Convocation meets once a week during term.

Just off the Convocation House is a smaller chamber, the Chancellor's Court, again with a fan-vaulted ceiling, and with suitably dark and forbidding furnishings. A trek back through the Divinity School to the Prosscholium takes you up a modern staircase to one of the most remarkable buildings in England, the library named after Humfrey, Duke of Gloucester, and rescued from decay by Sir Thomas Bodley.

This library has been open to readers since 1488 but the present book presses only date from 1602. They were originally stacked with works on theology, medicine, law and the arts, and the gallery giving access to the upper shelves was the first to be built in any library in England. The east window of what is called the Arts Extension provides a magnificent view of the Tower of the Five Orders of Architecture (you rather have to crane your neck to study it from ground level), and in the smaller window can be seen four beautiful seventeenth-century Dutch panels. But the overriding magic of this library is the painted rafters. They are unique and quite mesmeric.

Leave the Schools Quadrangle by the north gate, beneath the University's coat of arms, and you have the back of the Clarendon Building in front of you, the Sheldonian Theatre on your left. It is worth walking round between the Sheldonian and the Divinity School to see close up the side door – originally presumably the front door – of the Old Ashmolean Museum, a great pile of steps, pillars and carvings.

The Sheldonian Theatre, semi-circular at the north, was commissioned from Wren in 1663 as a setting for ceremonial occasions. Today it frequently serves as one of the most uncomfortable concert halls in the world; at least, it certainly does if you sit on a bench upstairs. Take your own cushion and fire extinguisher. It was named in honour of Gilbert Sheldon, Archbishop of Canterbury and a former Warden of All Souls, who paid the bill, but oddly enough refused ever to set foot in the place.

Wren, already Savilian Professor of Astronomy, was only thirty-one when he designed the Sheldonian, and he surely built it back to front, for the semi-circular section facing Broad Street is far less interesting than the classical façade facing south. But whatever reservations one may have about the exterior of Wren's youthful efforts, the Sheldonian is still far better viewed from without than within, where there is little to engage one's interest. Muddy brown and gold benches flank the Chancellor's chair, on which reposes a notice asking that it should be treated with respect. The painted ceiling by Robert Streater, Serjeant Painter to Charles II, is the least inspired of its kind for many miles around. Samuel Pepys went to view Streater's work in progress, and remarked that critics thought it 'better than Rubens at Whitehall but I do not fully think so'. Those whose bent it is can climb to the cupola or lantern, which is said to provide the best bird's-eye view of Oxford.

In 1942 James Lees-Milne found viewing the Sheldonian itself a bit of a trial. He wrote in his diary on 11 July that year, 'An old, bent woman sold me an admission ticket and would follow me, sitting and breathing heavily whenever I stopped to look at the ceiling. This irritated me profoundly and I asked acidly if visitors were never left alone. She said No, they weren't. Thereupon I lost my temper, and walked straight out. In one way and another the Sheldonian leaves something to be desired.'

The Sheldonian is generally thought of as the place where honorary degrees are conferred, but in 1675 it got tainted with a touch of pornography. At that time the University Press was assembled there, and surreptitious plans were laid to produce an edition of the engravings Giulio Romano had produced with which to illustrate the sonnets of Pietro Aretino, sometimes referred to as 'Aretino's postures'. Apparently the miscreants thought the printer had gone home. 'How he tooke to find his presse workeing at such an imployment I leave you to imagine,' Humphrey Prideaux of Christ Church wrote to a friend.

Degree ceremonies had been enlivened when they were held at the University Church by the medieval custom of getting a sort of licensed satirist known as *Terrae-Filius* (Son of the Soil) to provide a scurrilous commentary on University affairs, and the tradition was transported to the Sheldonian, but the rather strait-laced John Evelyn took exception to the performance at the opening of the Theatre in 1669. '*Terrae-Filius* entertained the auditory with a tedious, abusive, sarcastical rhapsody,' he wrote, 'most unbecoming of gravity of the University.' He thought it was 'rather licentious lying and railing than genuine and noble wit', and within a few years the office of *Terrae-Filius* had faded out.

While staying at Hertford College, then known as Magdalen Hall, Evelyn had seen the Sheldonian under construction, and was shown the model by Christopher Wren, 'not distaining' his advice. The opening ceremonies lasted from eleven in the morning until seven at night. 'Divers Panegyric Speeches both in prose and verse' were delivered by students, bells rang and a good deal of food was consumed. In gratitude for his services in securing the Arundel Marbles, the University conferred an honorary doctorate on Evelyn. 'So formal a Creation of Honorarie *Doctors*' had 'seldome ben seene.'

In 1695 a banquet was laid on at the Sheldonian for William III, but he refused to touch a mouthful of food in case it had been poisoned, and never well known for gracious manners, he left the city within an hour.

A century later Haydn was awarded an honorary doctorate of music. During the second of three concerts he gave in the city his Symphony Number 92 was played, and it has been known as the *Oxford* ever since. The visit proved an expensive one. 'I had to pay 1½ guineas for having the bells rung in Oxforth in connection with my doctor's degree,' he wrote in his Notebook, 'and ½ guinea for [hiring] the robe. The trip cost six guineas.' But despite the cost, Haydn was so proud of his degree that when on his return home an impertinent Austrian prince addressed him in the third person, at that time an intentional slight towards anyone you considered your social inferior, Haydn protested that now he was a Doctor of Music at Oxford University he ought to be shown greater respect.

The University disgraced itself in 1809 when two idiotic dons voted against an honorary degree for Sheridan, whose masterpiece *The Rivals* had been produced in 1775. Nevertheless Sheridan turned up at the Sheldonian, to the delight of the undergraduates, who cheered him until they were hoarse, shouting, 'Sheridan among the Doctors!' Eventually he was at least given a seat where he rightly belonged.

The Sheldonian has witnessed many moving moments – and some comical ones; when Tennyson entered to receive an honorary doctorate of civil law, his locks hanging round his shoulders, so that he looked poetic but unkempt, a voice from the gallery called out, 'Did your mother call you early, dear?'

Few moments have been more moving than the occasion in 1834 when Wellington was installed as Chancellor. 'The whole audience rose to their feet, cheered, waved hats, handkerchiefs, and anything else at hand, for some minutes,' an undergraduate wrote home to his brother. 'The Iron Man seemed quite non-plussed, and did not know what to do; at last he rose, gave the old military salute, and raised his trencher. This of course produced a fresh round of cheers.'

A good deal of Wellington's tenure as Chancellor was taken up with trivia, and when he was importuned for the post of cook at Worcester College his temper very nearly snapped. 'The Duke suggests to Mr Dyson,' he wrote, 'that if he has a female relative unmarried, who is desirous of being married, he might as well desire the Duke to recommend her as a wife!'

He paid his last visit to Oxford in 1844 when he was seventy-five, obliged to escort the heir to the throne of Germany. On a visit to the Radcliffe Camera the Duke remained below while Prince Wilhelm climbed to the roof. 'I'm afraid Your Grace is tired,' said Lord Westmorland, the British Ambassador to Germany. 'Well,' said the Duke, 'this sightseeing is damned tedious work.'

Alongside the Sheldonian stands the Clarendon Building, the work in 1712 of Nicholas Hawksmoor, who at the age of eighteen had become 'secular and domestic clerk', in other words a pupil, to Wren. Wren himself was only regarded as an amateur architect, and before the early eighteenth century there was really no such person as an architect at all. This is why we do not know who built the Schools Quadrangle. It was from the Sheldonian to the Clarendon Building that the University Press was transferred (they moved out of the Clarendon Building in 1829), and in 1975 the Clarendon was incorporated into the Bodleian to provide office accommodation. Hence of course it is not open. Part of the cost of this splendid building was met from the profits of Lord Clarendon's *History of the Rebellion and Civil Wars in England*, which must have sold well. A statue of Clarendon, Vice-Chancellor from 1660 to 1667, whose daughter Anne secretly married James II when he was Duke of York, stands in a niche on the west wall. If you walk through the arched passageway from the Schools Quadrangle you will emerge with your back to the impressive front of the Clarendon, its huge Doric columns rising two storeys to support a portico at roof level, the roof itself adorned with statues of the nine muses. But the best view of the Clarendon Building is obtained from the corner of Catte Street and New College Lane.

What can one say about the New Bodleian Library on the north side of Broad Street, so reminiscent of the worst excesses of the Third Reich? The man responsible for this steel and concrete abortion was Sir Giles Scott. Did Queen Mary, who had pretty good taste, realise what it would look like when she laid the foundation stone in 1936? By 1939 it was finished, but the opening ceremony, by George VI, was delayed until 1946. It was a memorable and somehow altogether appropriate occasion. When the King attempted to open the door, the key broke in the lock.

If you retrace your steps beneath the Hertford bridge in New College Lane, and turn immediately left into St Helen's Passage (once changed to Hell Passage, then changed back again), you will end up at the Turf Tavern. Alternatively, just stand outside Hertford, and to your right are Wren and Hawksmoor. Opposite is the 1613 Schools Quadrangle, to your left the Camera (1735), and squeezed into vision and jostling for attention is the soaring fourteenth-century spire of St Mary the Virgin. All one panorama. Fantastic. Then walk once more into the quad, this time through the ceremonial entrance, for this is a place made for wandering in and out of. How anyone could ever tire of it defies belief. Move to the south exit and there is the Camera, framed for you as you walk out into Radcliffe Square; once you are in the square it fills the whole space. *Quite* fantastic!

Eight

MERTON: THE OLDEST COLLEGE IN THE WORLD

University College (open 10.00 a.m. to 6.00 p.m.), Merton College (open Monday to Friday, 2.00 p.m. to 5.00 p.m., Saturday and Sunday, 10.00 a.m. to 5.00 p.m.; Hall closed; Old Library open Monday to Saturday, 2.00 p.m. to 4.00 p.m., guided tour of Library), Corpus Christi College (open 1.30 p.m. to 4.30 p.m.; Hall closed), Oriel College (quadrangles only open, 2.00 p.m. to 5.00 p.m.), The Bear.

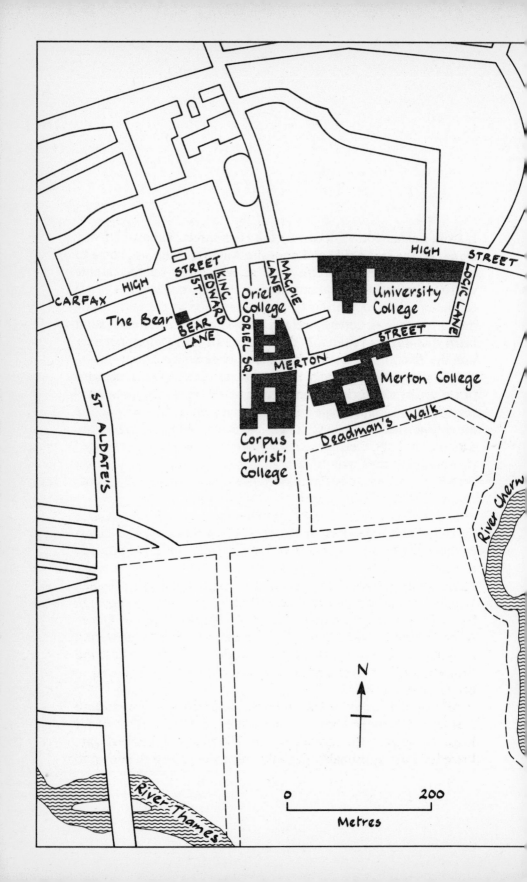

If from Carfax you walk east up the High Street, almost half-way along, on the south side and opposite All Souls, you will come to the steps leading into University College, whose long-running dispute with Merton and Balliol about which is the oldest college in Oxford continues unabated. University College even display notices insisting they are the oldest college, a claim at one time based on the quaint belief that they had been founded by King Alfred. Merton however was the first college in which students were resident.

Like so many of Oxford's medieval foundations, nothing remains of University College's original buildings, although the seventeenth-century Front Quadrangle certainly stands on a site occupied by the college since about 1332; it was founded by William of Durham, who died in 1249. One of the quad's oddest aspects will be revealed if, when you enter, you turn straight round, for above the tower stands the incongruous figure of a man much disliked in Oxford, James II – wearing a toga.

The quad is wide and spacious and almost exactly square, with the chapel and Hall taking up the whole of the south range. Building of the Front Quad went on from 1634 to 1677, but it has retained a remarkable consistency of style. James owes his commemorative statue, set up in 1687, to the fact that the Master at the time, Obadiah Walker, was a Roman Catholic convert. Ironically, on the High Street front there is a statue of James's younger daughter, Queen Anne (placed in position in 1709, where once stood King Alfred himself), whose treasonable activities, and those of her husband Prince George of Denmark and her sister Mary II, contributed to her father's downfall.

All that remains of the Hall as it was conceived in the seventeenth century is the roof. Above the door hangs a large portrait of Sir Roger Newdigate, the baronet who in 1806 endowed the Newdigate Prize for Poetry, probably the only university prize well known to the general public. It has inspired some amazingly bad poetry – so bad that at times it is difficult to distinguish genuine entries from parodies.

It was Newdigate's original intention that poems submitted should be no longer than fifty lines and restricted to the subject of ancient Greek and Roman architecture, sculpture and painting. At least in 1826 these somewhat restrictive provisions were lifted. Four famous lines which are undoubtedly a fake went as follows:

> While at these words the wise men stood appalled,
> Someone suggested Daniel should be called.
> Daniel was called and just remarked in passing,
> 'O Mene, Mene, Tekel and Upharsin.'

It is sad to have to record that a poem on General Gordon failed to please the judges, when you consider it contained lines worthy of the incomparable Alfred Austin himself:

> When winter came again we find this man
> Made Governor-General of the whole Sudan.

On one occasion the Pilgrim Fathers provided inspiration:

> Then by the blessings of Almighty God
> With bellying sails the Fathers made Cape Cod.

Matthew Arnold and Lawrence Binyon were awarded the Newdigate Prize. Swinburne was not. The vast majority of winners have failed to develop true poetic talent, although some, like Margaret Stanley-Wrench, who won in 1937, became very fine minor poets.

Newdigate's is the only portrait at University College which the college bothers to identify. Others include yet another uninspired painting of Lord Wilson and a less than brilliant example of Oswald Birley's work in his study of a previous Labour Prime Minister, Earl Attlee. But above the High Table can be seen one of two definitive portraits of Lord Goodman, an energetic Master of the College, executed between 1973 and 1974 by Graham Sutherland. This is quite simply a work of genius.

The chapel also contains works of genius: eight miraculous seventeenth-century windows in the north and south walls, designed in 1641 by Abraham van Linge. Also to be admired is the carved screen which dates from 1694, and the unusual altar-table of sixteenth-century carved and inlaid oak. In 1862 Sir Gilbert Scott decided to mess about, and he is to blame for the lifeless east window.

Staircase Seven to the left of the chapel leads to the Radcliffe Quadrangle, which at first sight seems like a smaller, quieter version of the Front Quad, which indeed it is, except that it was built 100 years later, between 1716 and 1719. It is in precise imitation of the earlier quad because it was paid for with a bequest of £5,000 from John Radcliffe, on condition that the new buildings 'be answerable to the old'. Above a Gothic fan-vaulted archway on the north side stands the great benefactor himself, holding the staff of Aesculapius. His is one of the very best statues in Oxford — and deservedly so. This archway, if opened, would lead on to the High Street, and on the street front can be seen a statue of Mary II, which means that University College commemorates the last three Stuart sovereigns.

In 1810 an excitable young man of eighteen, Percy Bysshe Shelley, became an undergraduate at University College. One day he went for a walk before dinner, and on Magdalen Bridge seized some poor woman's child, saying, 'Will your baby tell us anything about pre-existence, Madam?'

According to Thomas Jefferson Hogg, who was with Shelley at the time and later wrote his Life, 'The mother made no answer, but perceiving that Shelley's object was not murderous, but altogether harmless, she dismissed her apprehension, and relaxed her hold.

' "Will your baby tell us anything about pre-existence, Madam?" he repeated, with unabated earnestness.

' "He cannot speak, Sir," said the mother seriously.

' "Worse and worse," cried Shelley, with an air of deep disappointment, shaking his long hair most pathetically about his young face; "but surely the babe can speak if he will, for he is only a few weeks old. He may fancy perhaps that he cannot, but it is only a silly whim; he cannot have forgotten entirely the use of speech in so short a time; the thing is absolutely impossible."

' "It is not for me to dispute with you gentlemen," the woman meekly replied, her eye glancing at our academical garb; "but I can safely declare that I never heard him speak, nor any child, indeed, of his age." '

Magdalen Bridge has witnessed some strange encounters, but none so strange as this. Shelley's fertile brain soon got fed up being told to read Euclid and Aristotle's *Ethics*, and he busied himself instead with writing what he later described as a 'little syllabus', which unfortunately bore the title *The Necessity of Atheism*. It fell into the hands of the Master and Fellows, and although Shelley refused to admit he was the author, on 25 March 1811, still only in his second term, he was sent down.

Poor Shelley was deeply affected, and sat on a sofa in Hogg's room 'repeating, with convulsive vehemence, the words, "Expelled, expelled!" his head shaking with emotion, and his whole frame quivering'. He left for London after breakfast the next morning. Eleven years later, when he was only twenty-nine, he was drowned.

If you go to the north-west corner of the Front Quad and sneak into Staircase Three you will discover what University College did to make amends. You may also get rather a shock. There, laid out in marble nakedness, lies the dead poet, or rather, an effigy of him, carved in 1894 by Edward Onslow Ford. Shelley is mounted on a plinth of dubious merit, in front of which a bare-breasted muse of poetry mourns. The whole ensemble looks rather lost behind an iron grille embossed with gold leaf, in a mausoleum too big for it. The bars of the grille are set so far apart that any slender student can easily squeeze through, and those barbarians intent on profaning the effigy, usually with paint, have all too frequently been able to do so. Ford's romantic work had been intended for the Protestant cemetery in Rome where Shelley is buried, but they refused it, perhaps because nothing of the poet's youthful, albeit flaccid, anatomy is left to the imagination.

In 1990 the Bodleian paid £22,000 for a newly discovered collection of thirty-one letters relating the drama of Shelley's expulsion, some of them written with first-hand knowledge by Thomas Hogg.

Shelley was not the first undergraduate of University College to be expelled. In 1774 Joseph Hawkins, who like Shelley was aged eighteen, was discovered 'carousing with some low-life People'. He was conducted back to the college and, according to James Woodforde's diary, 'he was terribly frightened & cried almost all the Way'.

A vivid description of the accommodation an undergraduate was likely to be given at University College in Victorian times is contained in a letter written by Augustus Hare in 1853. He told his mother he was on 'No 2 Kitchen Staircase' and that his room was 'long and narrow, with yellow beams across the ceiling, and a tall window at one end admitting dingy light, with a view of straight gravel-walks, and beds of cabbages and rhubarb in the Master's kitchen garden. Here, for £32 16s 6d I have been forced to become the owner of the last proprietor's furniture − curtains which drip with dirt, a bed with a ragged counterpane, a bleared mirror in a gilt frame, and some ugly mahogany chairs and tables. "Your rooms might be worse, but your servant could not," said Mr Hedley when he brought me here.'

In 1880 some sixty undergraduates were summarily sent down when, after a riotous supper, the Reverend A. S. Chavasse and various other dons found the doors to their rooms had been screwed down and they were locked in. According to an eye-witness who recounted events to the *Oxford Mail* fifty-three years later, 'Mr Chavasse called through the narrow window which looks out on to High Street to some people and asked them to fetch a policeman . . . Presently a fire-escape was secured and the sight of several portly gentlemen descending naturally attracted a large crowd. There was nothing for Chavasse and his friends to do but to make a dash across the street to Queen's College, and the sight of these men rushing hither and thither was unique.'

Eventually one of the culprits admitted his responsibility, and the Master hastily recalled all those who had been sent home.

A hundred years after Shelley, another budding poet and anarchist, Stephen Spender, arrived at University College. 'I became affected,' he confessed in his autobiography, *World Within World*, 'wore a red tie, cultivated friends outside the college, was unpatriotic, declared myself a Socialist, a genius . . .

'One day the other freshmen decided that the time had come when they should break up my rooms. They decided this not out of enthusiasm but on principle, because it was the correct thing to do.' Spender was reading Blake when they arrived, and when he confounded them by continuing to sit quite calmly, and read out loud, they left in embarrassment. 'The hearties despised the aesthetes,' he wrote, 'and regarded anyone who showed any tendency to interest himself in the arts as an aesthete. At Univ. the two or three college aesthetes were certainly sickly young men. They called one another "dear" and burned incense in their rooms.'

173

If you turn right out of University College and right into Logic Lane this will lead you to Merton Street, cobbled and one of the prettiest and least explored streets in Oxford. In front of you will emerge the impressive tower of Merton College Chapel, nothing like so tall as the bell tower of Magdalen but similar in effect. And here most people will accept that you have reached the oldest college in the oldest university in the world. Within it stands the oddly named Mob Quadrangle – the oldest quad in the oldest college in the oldest university in the world.

Anthony Wood, who was a Merton man, had no doubt that his Alma Mater, founded in September 1264 by Walter de Merton, later Bishop of Rochester, 'craves the first place of all colleges in Oxford'. Its Hall, always closed, so that you cannot see where rumour has it the best food in Oxford is served, sports a thirteenth-century door, and much else remains from the earliest days. What remains a mystery is why such an immense chapel, reached by walking straight past the Hall and through the first arch on the right, was begun in 1280.

Much music is performed in Merton College Chapel, and as you enter the ante-chapel you might be forgiven for thinking you were about to enter a cathedral. The painted wooden ceiling is extraordinarily high. The transepts, cross and choir were built between about 1330 and 1451, and that was that: the nave, which would have produced a cruciform building, was never added. Perhaps by the fifteenth century they thought the chapel really was big enough. The glass in the choir windows is fourteenth-century, and the brass lectern is medieval too.

But in some ways the ante-chapel is more intriguing. There is a strange carving of John Pattesan, a Fellow of the college and first Bishop of Melanesia, in the Church of the Provence of New Zealand, who was murdered at Nurapu in 1871; he seems to be having a siesta. On the north transept wall is a richly ornamented monument to Sir Thomas Bodley, and on the south transept wall a memorial to Sir Henry Savile, appointed Warden of Merton in 1585 and founder of the Savilian Chairs of Geometry and Astronomy.

According to John Aubrey, Savile was 'a very severe governour, the scholars hated him for his austerity. He could not abide *witts*: when a young scholar was recommended to him for a good witt, *"Out upon him. I'le have nothing to doe with him; give me the ploding student. If I would look for witts I would goe to Newgate, there be the witts."* '

Behind a spectacularly beautiful green marble font is Anthony Wood's memorial tablet. He died in 1695 aged sixty-four. 'Imprimis,' he wrote in his will, 'I commend my soul into the hands of Almighty God, who first gave it (professing myself to die in the Communion of the Church of England), and my body to be buried in Merton college church, deeper than ordinary, under, and close to the wall (just as you enter in at the north on the left hand) as the place will permit, and I desire that there may be some little monument erected over my grave.' Could any instructions be plainer? And they were carried out to the letter.

The font was a gift in 1816 from the Tsar of Russia. Nicholas I gave an even bigger malachite urn to Queen Victoria, which can be seen in the Grand Reception Room at Windsor Castle.

On the way to the chapel you pass through Mob Quad, with its large dormer windows on the south side, added in the sixteenth century to let more light into the library, for candles were forbidden. The quad was built between 1304 and 1378, and why it is called Mob Quad nobody knows. Any connection with riots or mob rule seems far-fetched. The library, which occupies the first floor of both south and west wings, dates from 1371. Its bookshelves were probably suggested by Bodley at the end of the sixteenth century, and the ceiling, of Spanish oak, is very early sixteenth-century. A verger is generally available to show you round, and a visit to this atmospheric and intimate enclave of learning is highly recommended.

The east window is painted German glass of 1598, depicting the Passion of Christ. Other treasures include Epstein's bust of T. S. Eliot, an undergraduate at Merton, and the first Bible to be translated into Welsh, printed in 1588, housed in a Bible box made during the reign of the covert Catholic, Charles II. Max Beerbohm, whose tragi-comic *Zuleika Dobson* (published in 1911 with illustrations by Beerbohm himself) came to be regarded as the quintessential Oxford novel, had rooms in Mob Quad from 1890 to 1894, and a selection of his books and drawings can be seen in an adjoining room, together with the writing table he used at the Villino Chiaro, and William Rothenstein's famous and very amusing portrait.

'I was a modest good-humoured boy,' Max Beerbohm wrote when he was twenty-seven, 'it was Oxford that has made me insufferable.' No one else ever thought him insufferable; when he first arrived at Oxford from Charterhouse, taking over rooms from Randolph

Churchill, his college servant said he seemed so shy he could hardly bring himself to give an order, and he developed into one of the most entertaining wits and dandies of the Edwardian era. Most of his time at lectures was spent drawing caricatures of the dons, including the Warden of Merton, the Hon. George Brodrick, who still dressed as though the year was 1850 and spoke as he imagined Dr Johnson might have done. It was at Oxford, which he loved, that Max Beerbohm (who for some odd reason had signed the Warden's book Maxwell Beerbohm, when his real name was Maximilian) formed the closest friendship of his life, with another Merton undergraduate two years older than himself, Reginald Turner; both Beerbohm and Somerset Maugham rated Reginald Turner, by any stretch of the imagination almost unbelievably ugly, the most amusing man either had ever met in their lives.

After the chapel and Mob Quad there is something a bit anticlimactic about the rest of Merton. The less said about the building Butterfield put up in 1864 (blocking out the view of Christ Church Meadow from the chapel) the better; he destroyed a grove of trees in the process so the building is called Grove Building. In 1930 the Fellows repented by removing the top floor — and adding two wings. A spacious archway in the cobbled Front Quad, on the left of the Hall, leads to the Jacobean Fellows Quadrangle, built in 1610, which somehow fails to hold one's interest, and twin arches in the north-east corner of the Front Quad reveal a three-sided extension called St Alban's Quadrangle, provided by Basil Champneys in 1904; clearly he imagined he was living in 1504. On the south side of the quad is the Fellows' Garden, held in place by the old city wall; in the eighteenth century the garden was open to the public by night as well as day and its reputation became such that today it is firmly closed by day as well as night.

Discipline at Merton was in some disarray as early as 1338, when the 'chief offender on this occasion was John the Chaplain, who wore unfitting boots and dress. He quarrelled daily with his servant and called him a thief.' It seems he was also 'negligent in church'. There were complaints that some of the Fellows kept dogs 'and by their laziness hindered study. Some talked at table.' The Warden 'quarrelled with the Fellows, talked too much, neglected his financial duties, and absented himself without good cause'.

Yet Merton produced six Archbishops of Canterbury in the fourteenth century, and it was at this time that a Fellow called

William Merle (he died in 1347) spent seven years recording the weather, the first person in the west ever to do so. In the seventeenth century William Harvey, who discovered the circulation of the blood, was Warden of Merton.

James Wilding, who took his degree at Merton in 1687, left a list of rather weird expenditures, weird not so much on account of the cost as the nature of his necessities. It included charges 'for a purge for being let blood', 'for carrying my surplice', for two lobsters, 'mending my shoose' and 'To Mary'. Whoever Mary was, she earned herself 6d.

In 1726 disaster struck, according to the irascible Thomas Hearne of St Edmund Hall. 'Last Sunday Morning,' he noted on 16 August that year, 'between 8 & 9 Clock when they were at Prayers, at Merton College, one Mr Gardiner, MA & Fellow of that College, cut his own Throat in his Chamber, and died of the Wound last Night. He was a pretty Man, & was about 25 Years of Age . . . He hath two Sisters, wch for a good while together lived at Dr Gardiner's at All Souls Coll., & used to go to the College Chappell. One of them was observ'd to be very rampant & wild, & mighty desirous of Men, so as to be ready to leap out at Window after them.'

In his Life of his father, Sir Winston Churchill records the occasion when Lord Randolph Churchill was sent for by the Warden 'to be rebuked for some delinquency'. Apparently the interview began with the Warden standing before the fireplace and the young son of the Duke of Marlborough in the middle of the room, and ended with their positions reversed.

Louis MacNeice was at Merton as well as Eliot, and the experience inspired a wonderfully sarcastic section in his 1938 *Autumn Journal*:

But in case you should think my education was wasted
    I hasten to explain
That having once been to the University of Oxford
    You can never really again
Believe anything that anyone says and that of course is an asset
    In a world like ours;
Why bother to water a garden
    That is planted with paper flowers?

It was while he was at Merton, from 1936 to 1938, that Leonard Cheshire learned to fly. Then he won a Victoria Cross, three DSOs

177

and the DFC and ended the war by dropping the first atomic bomb, on Hiroshima.

Turn left out of Merton and on your left is Corpus Christi, one of the smallest and prettiest colleges in Oxford, a most restful and satisfying sort of place. Who could not marvel at the extraordinary sundial placed in the centre of the Front Quadrangle in 1581? It commemorates the fact that in 1517, the year the college was founded, a Bavarian astronomer and mathematician, Nicholas Kratzer, was elected a Fellow; it was he who established in England horology – the science of measuring time.

The founder of Corpus Christi was Richard Foxe, a man of many parts, the spelling of whose name remains a matter of opinion. He baptised Henry VIII, and occupied at one time or another the sees of Exeter, Bath & Wells, Durham and Winchester, but he admitted he had never set foot in either Exeter or Wells Cathedral. He was Bishop of Winchester when he founded the college. He was also blind.

In 1577 it was reported that Foxe had thought it sacrilege 'for a man to tarry any longer at Oxford than he had a desire to profit', but so long as Foxe's scholars did tarry at Corpus Christi they were subjected by him to a strictly regimented way of life. At dinner 'a portion of the Bible' was to be read, and everyone was to 'earnestly and reverently listen and attend to the reading, and not engage in any talk, story-telling, din, laughter, disturbance, noise, or other enormities'.

After dinner, 'every one of the Seniors, of whatsoever degree or estate they may be, shall forthwith, without any interval, betake themselves to their studies, or elsewhere, and not allow the other younger sort to loiter there any longer, except when either debates of the house, or other arduous business regarding the College, is required to be immediately taken in hand'. However, on saints' days a fire was permitted in the Hall, and the Fellows and scholars were allowed to remain there 'for the purpose of temperate recreation, by means of songs and other reputable sports'. They could 'read, and recount poems, histories, and the wonders of the world, and other things of the same kind'.

Foxe was obviously a puritanical old tartar, decreeing that anyone who broke the college rules was to be 'punished, harassed, and most bitterly afflicted with the penalties of the Statutes, without pardon'.

But by 1556 complaints were being made against the President himself, Thomas Greenway. It was alleged he was pocketing college funds and 'is noted of many men to have had connection with viii Infamous women'. He was also, it seems, 'a common drunkard, a mutable papist and an unpreching prelate and one of an Italian faith'. When in London he attended bear- and bull-baiting and 'In Christmas last past he, comming drunke from the Towne, sat in the Hall amonge the Schollers until i of the clock, totering with his legge, tipling with his mouth, and hering bawdy songes with his eares as, My Lady hath a prety thinge, and such like'. Not only did he keep six horses when only five were allowed, he was 'a faithfull frende to all the papistes and a mortall enemy to all the protestants in this house'. These complaints were listened to by the Chancellor to the diocese of Winchester, who confirmed him in his office.

It all sounds a bit chaotic, but in the early years Corpus Christi educated Cardinal Pole, Nicholas Udall, who became headmaster of both Eton and Westminster and wrote one of the earliest English comedies, *Ralph Roister Doister*, and the influential Bishop Jewel of Salisbury.

The Hall, which is always closed, once witnessed the humiliation of a scholar aged eighteen, Edward Anne, who had had the temerity to write a poem attacking the Mass. 'The act was undoubtedly a bold one,' according to Thomas Fowler, 'for they were written after the Mass had been already re-established. But the youthful poet and zealot was made to smart for having the courage of his opinions. Never, surely . . . was a poet more sharply taught the merit of brevity. Mr Walshe, the Dean of the College, inflicted a public flogging on him in the College Hall, laying on a stripe for every line, and as the lines were probably numerous, and Mr Walshe was a zealous Catholic, the youth's fortitude must have been sorely tried.'

The chapel can be found easily enough in the south-east corner of the Front Quad. It is on a miniature scale with only one row of pews. Equally compact is the Fellows Quadrangle into which you emerge. It is hardly a quadrangle at all. Along one side is an unexpected cloister, and it is not until you go into the garden and look back that you see Fellows Building at its best. It is rather grand, in fact, and it was here, on the first floor of Staircase Two, with rooms looking over Christ Church Meadow, that John Ruskin, a Gentleman Commoner at Christ Church in 1836, chose to live when he returned to Oxford in 1870 as Slade Professor of Fine Art.

In a sheltered corner of the garden — small, like everything at Corpus Christi — is a bench in memory of Russell Crockford who, we are told, 'Did all that he could'.

Opposite the entrance to Corpus Christi lies Oriel Square, and occupying the whole of the east side of the square is Oriel College. The square was only named after the college in 1953, and in case you have slightly lost your bearings, the wall on the west side is that of Christ Church's Peckwater Quad, and the large gateway in the south-west corner leads to Canterbury Quad and the art gallery.

The Front Quadrangle of Oriel was begun in 1619 and completed in 1642, replacing, as so often, the original medieval buildings, Oriel having been founded in 1326 by Adam de Brome, Rector of the University Church of St Mary the Virgin and Almoner to Edward II. The true name of the college is the House of the Blessed Virgin, and how it came to be called Oriel is a bit of a mystery. There seems to have been some ancient building known as La Oriole, not even L'Oriole, but all is lost in the mists of time. There is certainly an oriel window above the gateway, but who in Oxford has not got an oriel window?

The Hall is immediately in front of you, approached up a small flight of steps under an open portico, but it is always closed. During the Civil War meetings of the Privy Council were held at Oriel, and the words *Carolo Regnante* above the porch refer to Charles I, in whose reign the Hall was built. The King is reputed to stand in one niche next to Edward II, although the statues could represent almost anybody. Above them is the Virgin and Child. The whole effect of the Front Quad is heavy Jacobean, and not entirely enticing.

Like the Hall, the chapel is always closed, but the other two quadrangles are worth a visit. From the north-east corner of the Front Quad a passage leads to the Middle Quadrangle where, although built a century later, the east and west ranges (1719 and 1730 respectively) repeat the style of the Front Quad. Best of all is the newest building in the quad, James Wyatt's elegant free-standing Palladian library of 1788, on the north.

A mysterious tunnel located to the right of the library will lead you to a surprising mixture of architecture in St Mary's Quadrangle, once the site of a medieval hall called St Mary's. On the south, with its back to Wyatt's library, is a seventeenth-century range incorporating the old chapel and Hall of St Mary's, now an undergraduate library and junior common room, and on the east is an incongruous but rather delightful timber-framed house with sash windows and dormers. All these ancient buildings have had to accommodate themselves to what is called the Rhodes Building, erected along the High Street side in 1908.

Cecil Rhodes gave his address in his will as Oriel College, Oxford. He also left the college £100,000, obviously not holding it against them that it took him eight years to get a degree. 'All the colleges send me their failures,' the Provost had muttered. Being of a paternalistic frame of mind, Rhodes firmly believed that a good understanding between England, Germany and the United States would secure the peace of the world, and that the strongest ties would be formed through education. When it came to endowing scholarships for Germans, Americans, and men from the colonies, he went into something of a rigmarole. He did not want these men merely to be bookworms, as he put it, and directed his trustees to make sure they had 'fondness of and success in many outdoor sports such as cricket, football and the like'. They were also to have qualities of 'manhood, truth, courage, devotion to duty, sympathy for the protection of the weak, kindliness, unselfishness and fellowship,' and while at school they should have exhibited both 'moral force of character' and 'instincts to lead and take an interest in their schoolmates'.

He went on to emphasise that no student was to be disqualified from a Rhodes Scholarship on account of his race or religious opinions, and just in case others had not got the hang of selecting paragons of virtue who might benefit from his money and Oriel's teaching, he spelt out his criteria for election in 1902 in *The Review of Reviews*: 'You know I am all against letting the scholarships merely to people who swot over books, who have spent their time over Latin and Greek. But you must allow for that element which I call "smug", and which means scholarship. That is to stand for four-tenths. Then there is "brutality", which stands for two-tenths. Then there is tact and leadership, again two-tenths, and then there is "unctuous rectitude", two-tenths. That makes up the whole. You see how it works.'

By the time Cecil Rhodes arrived at Oriel, life was sedate compared to the fifteenth century, when some very strange appointments seem to have been made. A Fellow called Bedmyster pinched books from the library, brought strangers into the college

181

at night, having 'purloined the key from the President in whose custody it was,' and indulged in 'the most violent horseplay' during meals, 'dragging the tablecloth with the things laid on it down to the floor'. He 'snatched the food away from the Dean as he sat, and generally behaved like a wild beast or a demented schoolboy . . . Worse still, he had drawn a knife in controversy with one of the Fellows, and had several times struck the Dean.'

Rhodes thought that Oxford dons were 'children in matters of finance', and he may have been right. Henry Beeke, a Fellow of Oriel and Regius Professor of Modern History, has generally been credited with suggesting to Pitt the introduction of income tax.

Fellows who have brought rather greater lustre to the name of Oriel include the diarist Gilbert White of Selborne, who graduated in 1743 and was a Fellow for half a century, the poet Matthew Arnold, and his father, Thomas Arnold, the controversial headmaster of Rugby. Appropriately enough, Thomas Hughes, who wrote *Tom Brown's Schooldays*, was also an undergraduate at Oriel.

It was as Fellows at Oriel of course that John Keble and John Newman talked through their dissatisfaction with the Church of England until the Oxford Movement materialised. Keble's rooms were in the Front Quad, on the first floor of Staircase Two, and Newman's were on the first floor of Staircase Three.

The unfortunate Walter Ralegh studied at Oriel, often, it was reported, 'under streights for money'. He once borrowed another undergraduate's gown which he failed to return, and consorted with 'boysterous blades, but generally those that had witt'. John Aubrey tells us that at Oxford Ralegh was tall, handsome and bold, but 'damnably proud'.

If you cross Oriel Square you will find Bear Lane at right angles to Edward Street, the ugliest street in Oxford, not worth inspecting unless you wish to see Number 6 where Rhodes had rooms in 1881. It is best to walk up Bear Lane. On the corner of Alfred Street is the Bear, which claims to have been in business since 1247. There are two small bars and it tends to get crowded at night, but in the summer one can always overflow on to the pavement. A genuine old pub, as yet unspoilt.

Nine

OFF THE BEATEN TRACK

Worcester College (open 9.00 a.m. to 12 noon, 2.00 p.m. to 6.00 p.m., quadrangle and gardens only), Oxford University Press, St Paul's, St Barnabas Church, St Sepulchre's Cemetery, Radcliffe Infirmary, Radcliffe Observatory, Pitt Rivers Museum — Balfour Building (open Monday to Saturday, 1.00 p.m. to 4.30 p.m., admission free), Park Town, Cherwell Boathouse Restaurant (open 12 noon to 2.00 p.m., 7.00 p.m., closed Monday, Sunday evening), Canal Towpath, St Bartholomew's Chapel, Iffley (St Mary the Virgin).

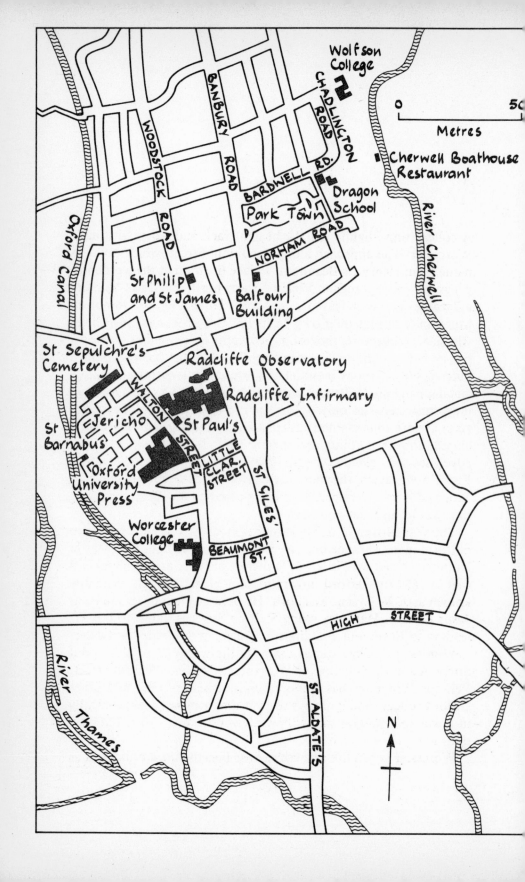

A college only slightly off the beaten track and worth visiting is Worcester. The approach along Beaumont Street, which takes its name from Henry I's Beaumont Palace (it stood at the west end), where his great-grandson Richard I was born, could not be more agreeable. You soon leave the Randolph Hotel and the Ashmolean Museum to display their own variety of Gothic Revival and Greek Classical architecture; the rest of Beaumont Street retains fine town houses built around 1825, with pretty first-floor balconies. Although much colonised today by solicitors, estate agents, dentists, doctors and acupuncturists, Beaumont Street has retained its late Georgian uniformity, broken only by the Oxford Playhouse on the south. As a theatre this has had rather a chequered career; one minute closed, the next billing star performers. In 1948, when it was advertised as England's Newest Theatre and was home to the Oxford Repertory Players, the most expensive seat cost the equivalent of 32p, and if you were prepared to risk finding an unreserved seat, that would have set you back 6p.

The first turn right off Beaumont Street is St John Street, also uniform in appearance but consisting of smaller houses. It was at Number 12 that MENSA was launched in 1946, and at Number 4 that in 1837 the Oxford historian John Richard Green, generally known as J. R. Green, was born. He became an undergraduate at Jesus College. Half-way along St John Street is a turn to the left leading to Beaumont Buildings, a charming domestic backwater.

Worcester College stands opposite the west end of Beaumont Street and at the junction of Worcester Street and Walton Street. Perhaps Worcester has a more complex history than any other Oxford college, and it always seems rather isolated geographically in a way that Magdalen, at the eastern extremity of the old city, does not.

Worcester began life as a college for Benedictine monks, and as

185

such it was certainly in existence in the thirteenth century, but was dissolved in 1541. A Worcestershire baronet, Sir Thomas Cookes, expressed a desire to found a college at Oxford. He died in 1701, but in 1714 Worcester was refounded as he wished, retaining many of the old monastic buildings, the best of which can be seen on the south side of the Main Quadrangle.

Ornamental iron gates, with the chapel and Hall at right angles on either side (both are generally closed), lead to a fifteenth-century gateway, and this, rather surprisingly, gives straight on to an eighteenth-century loggia, with nine rounded arches and, on the first floor, the library. Below is a sunken lawn. The north wing too is eighteenth-century, long and rather dull. Staircase Twelve in the south range leads to the main garden, which provides an excellent view of the back of the south range known as the Mansions, the original lodgings – cottages really – of the Benedictines. The garden however (at any rate until you reach the lake) is much over-rated, a frightful mess to the west that no spread of ancient trees can do anything to disguise.

The first Bishop of Oxford is thought to have lived at Worcester from 1542 until 1546 (when it was still known as Gloucester Hall) before moving into his new palace in St Aldate's. In 1560 Sir Thomas White purchased the property before deciding to found St John's College in St Giles'. This was also the year when Amy Robsart's body lay, so tradition has it, on the first floor of Staircase Eleven while awaiting burial at the University Church. The poet Richard Lovelace, 'then accounted the most amiable and beautiful person that ever eye beheld,' became a Gentleman Commoner in 1634 when he was sixteen, and in the sixteenth century a man of letters in more senses than one, Thomas Coryat, had been resident. He wrote a travel book, the title of which must have taken up at least a page: *Coryat's Crudities hastily gobled up in five Moneth's Travells in France, Savoy, Italy, Rhetia commonly called the Grisons country, Helvetia alias Switzerland, some parts of High Germany and the Netherlands; newly digested in the hungrie aire of Odcombe in the County of Somerset.*

Sir Kenelm Digby, author, philosopher, scientist and professional turncoat, whose father, Sir Everard Digby, was executed for his part in the Gunpowder Plot, was a scholar of the old college. Thomas Allen, who lived for nearly sixty years at Gloucester Hall, was consulted by Elizabeth I about the stars, but many believed him to be a magician. In 1694 a well-intentioned ecumenical scheme, perhaps a little ahead of its time, resulted in boys from the Greek Orthodox Church taking up residence, but Anglicans and Roman Catholics alike made a concerted effort to convert them, and by 1707 only one Orthodox student remained.

A twentieth-century graduate of Worcester College was Rupert Murdoch, who became the publisher of the *Sun*, one of Britain's most illiterate newspapers, dedicated to reinforcing ignorance and prejudice. In 1990 he offered the University three million pounds to establish a Chair in Language and Communications. They accepted.

Walk north up Walton Street and on your left, on the corner of Worcester Place, is Ruskin College, built in 1899. It was founded by an American, Walter Vrooman, with the admirable intent of providing higher education for working-class men, but it looks a bit like a workhouse. Bernard Shaw distinguished himself by refusing to lecture at Ruskin College because he thought 'a workman ought to have a vulgar prejudice against Oxford'. On the right, opposite Richmond Road, is a hideous house, 142 Walton Street, in which at one time, as an undergraduate, John Betjeman had rooms. Then comes a delightful terrace on the left. Enid Starkie lived here, at Number 23, from 1963 until her death in 1970 but apparently it is beyond the wit of Oxford City Council to provide a commemorative plaque.

As Walton Street bends to the left you come upon the smart classical building dating from 1826 into which the Oxford University Press moved in 1830. In 1989 the OUP ceased to print books themselves, but they have been publishing since 1584, when the University lent £100 to Joseph Barnes, an Oxford bookseller, to start a press. They still employ over 2,000 people, and are proud to publish worthwhile books which are financially unviable, a policy taken to extremes in 1990 when they brought out a biography of the art collector Charles Ricketts priced at £50. In 1716 the OUP published an edition of 500 copies of the *Coptic New Testament*, and managed to sell the last copy in 1907. They signed a contract in 1901 with a young chemist called Harold Hartley for a book to be called *Studies in the History of Chemistry*. Seventy years later they got their manuscript; by this time the author was Brigadier-General Sir Harold Hartley, CH.

The Oxford University Press once hit on a novel method of coping with a scandal. In the eighteenth century an employee, Dr William Delaune, embezzled £2,000 from the proceeds of the first two editions of Lord Clarendon's *History*. In order for him to earn enough to repay the money, the University appointed him Lady Margaret Professor of Divinity.

In addition to their general list, the OUP produces publications dealing with music, languages, electronics – almost any subject any modern school or university would have on its curriculum. Perhaps its best-known and most well-thumbed reference book, apart from its dictionaries, is the invaluable *Dictionary of National Biography*.

Opposite the Press is one of the casualties of parish amalgamations, the former St Paul's Church with its 1835 Greek Revival Portico. Holman Hunt painted the ceiling in the apse, now a sad and sorry sight. In 1990 music, dancing and licensed drinking were instituted in the nave.

The complex of streets lying roughly to the west of the Oxford University Press is an area known as Jericho, and as its tiny terraced houses indicate, it was built as a community for artisans, college scouts, domestic servants, printers and shopkeepers. Oxford is packed with churches, and one of the most unusual, St Barnabas, amalgamated in 1963 with the now defunct St Paul's, is situated in Jericho. It can easily be seen by walking down Great Clarendon Street, which runs beside the OUP. Canal Street is the fourth on the right, and the church stands in Cardigan Street, on the left. It was built about 1870 by Thomas Combe, the Superintendent of the OUP, whose widow gave *The Light of the World* to Keble. He intended the church to serve the community that had grown up in Jericho with the removal of the Press from Broad Street. The style is Italian-Byzantine, based on the island cathedral of Torcello in Venice and, like many Victorian churches constructed in working-class areas, it gave expression to the Oxford Movement, and thus, through colourful liturgy, brought drama and pageantry into the drab lives of the poor. The interior may be locked during the day, but the south porch is left open, and through a glass screen you can get a good conception of a liturgical setting for what is modestly billed as a Sung Eucharist. On Sundays, with candles flickering and the clergy and choristers mustered on the altar steps, enveloped in clouds of incense, the effect is rather splendid.

Much of any town's social history is to be unearthed in its

churchyards and cemeteries. St Sepulchre's Cemetery is at the end of Walton Street, just before the junction with Walton Well Road, with an entrance lurking behind rusty iron gates. Its academic ties are strong.

An organist from St John's lies near John Wilson, porter at Worcester for forty-four years, who died in 1850 at the age of sixty-nine. Edward and William, the infant sons of Edward Marshall, a Victorian Fellow of Corpus Christi, share a grave not far from the octogenarian George Pope, lecturer in Tamil and Telugu and chaplain of Balliol. A Fellow of Trinity and Corpus Professor of Latin, Robinson Ellis, who died in 1913 at the age of seventy-nine, was, his tombstone informs us, 'a great scholar'.

As cemeteries go, many will find that St Sepulchre's is a pretty depressing place, and you can always give it a miss, cutting back instead to the Woodstock Road from St Barnabas Church, there to admire the eighteenth-century façade of the Radcliffe Infirmary, once again a gift to Oxford from John Radcliffe. Its courtyard fountain is a copy of Bernini's Triton fountain in Rome, and the chapel on the right was provided by Thomas Combe before he embarked on St Barnabas. The foundation stone of the Infirmary was laid in 1759 and the first patients were admitted eleven years later. Although for many years the Infirmary acted as an ordinary county hospital, today it has an international reputation for research and teaching. Lord Nuffield provided the funds to pay no fewer than seven professors, and it was here, in Beevers Ward, that penicillin was first administered to a patient.

Walk past the Radcliffe Infirmary and make your way through a disagreeable jumble of hospital outbuildings, and you will find the Observatory – again named after John Radcliffe – built in 1771 by James Wyatt. It is one of the most original eighteenth-century constructions to be seen anywhere, many people regard it as Oxford's loveliest building, and it must certainly rate as one of Wyatt's absolute masterpieces. Sir Nikolaus Pevsner thought it architecturally the finest observatory in Europe, and it seems hard to imagine where any competition lies. Signs of the zodiac adorn its ashlar limestone walls, and an irregular octagon tower decorated with architectural sculptures of the winds sits above a balustrade; on top of the tower are the figures of Hercules and Atlas supporting a copper globe.

A covered way links the observatory to the Astronomer's House, and the whole conception is deceptively simple — and quite enchanting. Two mahogany desks designed by Wyatt survive, but its eighty-four-inch telescope was sent in 1935 to South Africa. It seems almost impossible to believe that in 1927, because the observatory itself had outlived its usefulness, it was proposed that the building should be destroyed. Although still only an undergraduate, John Betjeman successfully fought for its preservation.

If you carry on up the Woodstock Road for about 600 yards, on your right you will come to a mid-Victorian church, St Philip & St James, much crooned over by Gerard Manley Hopkins. Turn right into Church Walk, cut through to North Parade Avenue, a pleasant little street full of pubs, restaurants and antique shops, and you will be in the Banbury Road. Those whose appetite for museums cannot be sated will find at 60 Banbury Road the Balfour extension to the Pitt Rivers Museum. The entrance is at the left-hand side of the house, and you can listen through headphones to musical instruments from around the world.

If you prefer architecture to artefacts, cross over the road to Park Town. Behind the public lavatories is a residents' garden and a pair of three-storey crescents later even than one thinks; they look late Georgian but are in fact early Victorian, with scroll windows and balustrades. At the far end, screened by trees, is a more modest terrace. The whole enclave is very stylish and peaceful.

One turn further on off the Banbury Road, Bardwell Road, will lead you to the Dragon School and the Cherwell Boathouse (clearly signposted), where you can hire a punt, have a drink or an ice-cream, or lunch at a restaurant where, depending on the time of year, you may be entertained by boys from the Dragon School learning to scull and canoe.

The Dragon is Oxford's most famous preparatory school (although Summerfields, who send a lot of their little lads to Eton, might dispute this). Known in the past as Lynam's, for two brothers called Lynam were headmasters, its most renowned old boy is John Smyth, who won a Victoria Cross in 1915. They are proud too that John Betjeman was at the school from 1917 to 1920. He published accomplished verse in the school magazine when he was thirteen, managed to get beaten with a gym shoe, and made friends with a boy called Hugh Gaitskell. Another future Labour politician at the Dragon School with Betjeman and Gaitskell was Sir William

Mallalieu, who challenged John Betjeman to a fight behind the bicycle shed. Betjeman got out of it by pretending his mother was ill.

There is an enticing bridge across the Cherwell just upstream from the Boathouse, but to cross it you need to walk back to the lane that leads to the Boathouse, turn right into Chadlington Road and walk through the grounds of Wolfson College. The bridge will give you access to lovely walks in meadowland along the Cherwell or inland, and will lead you back by gentle paths to the bridge leading over the river to the University Park.

Oxfordians once spent much of their time earning their living on the canal, one of the first to be constructed in England, and completed in 1790. But the Victorian railway killed it commercially, and today it serves merely for animals − human as well as those described in *The Wind in the Willows* − to potter about on it in boats, not barges. The walk along the towpath south from Osney, with its sad memorial to Edgar Wilson, who in 1889, at the age of twenty-one, saved two boys from drowning and then lost his own life, has little to commend it. But the longer and more varied walk north, behind the gardens of Jericho and out to the playing fields of King Edward's School at Summertown, makes a pleasant diversion from the bustle of the city.

Those of an even more adventurous spirit should make their way across Magdalen Bridge to the junction called the Plain, and there take the second exit and walk about a mile up the Cowley Road. (There are buses, of course.) Just after Southfield Road, on the left, the second unmarked footpath will lead you to Bartlemas House, now a private residence on the site of Oxford's medieval leper hospital, founded in 1126 by Henry I. In those days the hospital would have been on the old road from London to Oxford that came in over Shotover Hill: it took into quarantine up to a dozen lepers at a time so that they might not infect the inhabitants of the town.

In 1329 Edward III attached the hospital and its chapel of St Bartholomew (which still stands in the garden of Bartlemas House) to Oriel College, whose members used to stay at the hospital to escape the plague in Oxford. By the sixteenth century a policy of rigid segregation had virtually abolished leprosy in Europe, and the hospital became an almshouse. William Temple preached in the fourteenth-century chapel when he was Archbishop of Canterbury. It is now annexed to the parish of St Mary & St John, and is kept in use for Evensong once a month, and an occasional celebration of the Anglican Mass. The key can be obtained from Bartlemas House or Bartlemas Cottage. The chapel was re-roofed by Oriel in 1649, and the oak chancel screen, later atrociously restored, was inserted in 1651. By 1870 the building had become a cowshed, and in 1926 Sir Ninian Comper got his hands on it, installing vile electric candelabra and pointless unadorned shields in the ceiling; the sooner all these come down the better.

The second exit from the Plain is the Iffley Road, and this leads within only about two miles to the remnants − quite well preserved − of the village of Iffley, now really a suburb of Oxford. Where the Iffley Road becomes Henley Avenue, Iffley is signposted to the right. Turn immediately right into Church Way, and carry on until you reach St Mary the Virgin. If this building does not stop you in your tracks, nothing ever will.

It is a Romanesque parish church, almost hidden from the road, built in the twelfth century during the reign of Henry II, with yellow limestone walls and a stone slate roof. Alec Clifton-Taylor thought it 'without doubt one of the best Norman village churches in England'. All three doorways, on the north, west and south, are Norman, although you might think the door on the south side too unweathered to be so old, but until 1807 it was in fact protected by a porch. It was originally the main entrance. The top of the tower with its Norman windows looks less than ancient too, for it was restored in 1975. In the churchyard are two venerable objects; in front of the west door is an outdoor font, the date and origins of which are unknown, and on the south a yew said to be 'of great antiquity'.

Immensely impressive and heart-stopping though the richly decorated west door is, it scarcely prepares you for what lies within. First of all you walk, unless you take care, slap into a square-shaped font large enough in which to baptise babies by total immersion, supported on twelfth- and thirteenth-century spiral columns. But what really strikes you are the Romanesque tower arches. A close inspection in the choir will reveal magical carvings, including, on the south, a bird protecting its nest. The sanctuary is possibly an extension of the Norman chancel, and is a wonderful example of early thirteenth-century craftsmanship. The carving of a lamb on the north wall, more correctly a 'circular *Agnus Dei*', may be fourteenth-century and originally part of a churchyard cross. In the south wall is an aumbry where the Communion vessels were kept, and a piscina or basin in which the priest abluted.

192

What look like the remains of wall paintings in the tower and nave are four surviving Consecration Crosses, and it is thought there may once have been coloured decoration throughout the church. The tiny pulpit was installed in 1907, designed by the versatile Ninian Comper, although what so intimate a building as this needs with a pulpit at all it is hard to say; few English parish churches of any sort had a pulpit before 1603. Most of the glass is Victorian, and it makes what should have been an airy church too dark, but the south-east window in the nave is worth attention; it contains the fifteenth-century arms of John de la Pole, Duke of Suffolk, a great-grandson of Geoffrey Chaucer.

Ten

AWAY FOR THE DAY

Shotover Hill, St Michael's Chapel at Rycote (open Good Friday to 30 September, 10.00 a.m. to 6.00 p.m., 1 October to Maundy Thursday, 10.00 a.m. to 4.00 p.m., closed Mondays in Winter, admission charges), Boars Hill, North Leigh Roman Villa (open 1 April to 30 September, 10.00 a.m. to 6.00 p.m., admission charges), Burford, Bladen (St Martin's Church), Woodstock (Blenheim Palace, Park open daily, 9.00 a.m. to 5.00 p.m., admission charges, Palace open mid-March to 31 October, 10.30 a.m. to 5.30 p.m., admission charges), Broughton Castle (open 18 May to 14 September, Wednesdays and Sundays, Thursdays in July and August, 2.00 p.m. to 5.00 p.m., admission charges), Garsington Manor (gardens open only, one Sunday afternoon in September, admission charge).

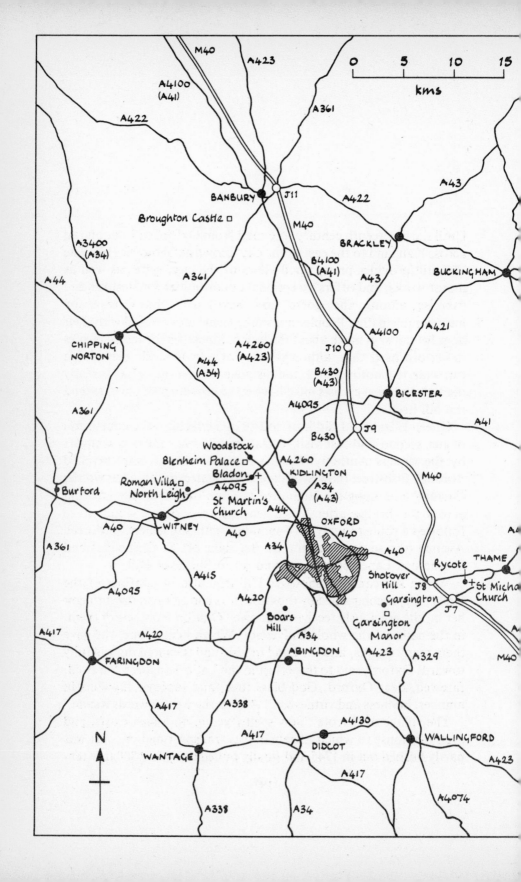

Until the nineteenth century, the road from Oxford to London ran across high land to the east of the city known as Shotover Hill. The Hill still provides pretty good views of the city, spires as well as motor works, and offers exceptional opportunities for fresh air and exercise among the gorse and hawthorn, criss-crossed by innumerable paths. People run, walk, picnic and gambol with their dogs here: it says much about the lack of amenities for such activities in Oxford itself that, although those of a truly hardy disposition can walk to Shotover Hill, the distance is such that a car is really needed, and even cyclists must have extraordinary stamina to ascend the hill itself.

Queen Elizabeth I did it of course in a coach, at the conclusion of her second and last visit to Oxford in 1592. She was seen off by the tireless Anthony Wood, who tells us that she travelled 'through Fishstreet [now St Aldate's] to Quatervois [in other words, Carfax]' and along the High Street. From the Plain, the junction across the bridge after Magdalen, her procession would have followed a route roughly corresponding with St Clement's, Morrell Avenue (the seventh turning on the right off St Clement's) and Warneford Lane, on, on, up and up to Shotover Hill.

'When she came to Shotover Hill (the utmost confines of the University) accompanied by those Doctors and Masters that brought her in, she graciously received a farewell Oration from one of them, in the name of the whole University. Which being done, she gave them many thanks, and her hand to kiss; and then looking wistfully towards Oxford, said to this effect in the Latin Tongue: "Farewell, farewell, dear Oxford, God bless thee, and increase thy sons in number, holiness and virtue, &c." And so she went towards Ricote.'

The village of 'Ricote', now spelt Rycote, no longer exists, and even the house to which Elizabeth was transporting her court was partly burned out in 1745 and finally pulled down in 1800 (the ten-

197

year-old heir to the estate perished in the blaze). But what does remain is the fifteenth-century chapel of St Michael & All Angels, which stood next to the house and which the Queen knew well from previous visits to Rycote. It was later viewed by Charles I when in residence in Oxford in 1625. The chapel is now maintained by English Heritage and can be found without difficulty down a lane off the A329, nine miles east of Oxford and three miles south-west of Thame.

When Elizabeth arrived in 1592 she was received by the incumbent of the manor, Lord Norreys, whose father-in-law, Sir John Williams (later created Lord Williams), the first owner of Rycote, had been a benevolent guardian when Elizabeth was held captive by her sister Queen Mary at Woodstock Palace. 'I meane not to recount my service but to tell your Majesty that I am past al service, save devotion,' Norreys informed his royal guest. 'My horse, mine armour, my shielde, my sworde, the riches of a young souldier, and an old souldier's reliques, I should here offer to your Highnesse; but my four boies have stalled them from me, vowing themselves to armes, and leaving me to my prayers. This is their resolution, and my desire, that their lives may be imployed wholy in your service, and their deathes be their vowes sacrifice.'

The chapel in which old Lord Norreys was wont to pray is an extraordinary place: nothing of the fairly conventional fifteenth-century exterior (the building was consecrated in 1449) really prepares you for the unique seventeenth-century interior fittings. The western gallery, the two large pews and the pulpit with its canopy date from about 1610; the reredos was placed in position around 1682. Far earlier – fifteenth-century in fact – is the wooden seating in the nave and chancel, the base and cover of the font and the base of the rood screen. The plain circular font itself, which stands beneath the gallery, is twelfth-century.

The wagon-roof is original and hence fifteenth-century, but it was decorated in the seventeenth century. Beneath the tower are the Commandments, inscribed with gold paint in 1610. The two compartments in which the Commandments are contained are surmounted by arches, and the spandrels of the arches are filled with carvings – of acorns and pomegranates, and a bird which looks like a pheasant.

You can reach the gallery up a very steep spiral staircase, and those with a head for heights can go on up to a priest's room with a fireplace, then the belfry, and finally on to the roof of the tower. From the gallery there seems to be so much to see and enjoy in a very small space: a second gallery for musicians, the wonderful rough-hewn pews, the strange dome erected, it is said for Charles I, on the south side. In what remains of the churchyard stands a yew believed to have been planted in 1135, the year King Stephen usurped the throne. Few small ecclesiastical buildings have been so faithfully preserved or grip one's imagination so firmly.

When it comes to obtaining a panoramic view of Oxford, many people forget about Boars Hill, a stiff three mile walk (uphill, needless to say) south-west of the city. Buses do go there, but a car or bicycle is best. Here sixty-four acres of fields, wild gardens and woodland walks are administered by the Oxford Preservation Trust. They made their first purchase in 1928 of the Old Berkeley Golf Course, with undulating fields that afford one of the most commanding views of any city in England. A year later the Trust bought a field associated with Matthew Arnold, who apparently drew inspiration from it for his *The Scholar-Gipsy*.

A leading light in the early work of the Trust was Sir Arthur Evans, better known for his excavations at Knossos on Crete; it was he who laid out a wild garden at the foot of a mound of uncertain safety which he threw up, now known as the Jarn Mound. From the top, if you are agile enough to reach it, you can see the city to the north and Shotover Hill to the east.

It was to Boars Hill that students from Christ Church used to come to hunt. Two fields were acquired by the Oxford Preservation Trust from local residents in 1937; in 1941 Evans left to the Trust a five-and-a-half-acre site between his garden and the Matthew Arnold Field; and there are plans to create another wild garden on land recently bequeathed by Mr. A. A. Daryush, son-in-law of Robert Bridges.

Oxford itself lies on the eastern border of the Cotswolds, and to explore the area's stone-built villages you need to travel west. Their most distinctive feature is perhaps the amazing degree to which they have been preserved; almost all modern housing estates have been forced to blend in with the roof lines and building materials favoured for centuries, and apart from the installation of telephone wires, cars and television aerials, many of the smaller villages remain almost entirely as they always were.

If one Cotswold town must needs stand in for all, it has to be

Burford. Over-crowded in summer though it is, architecturally and historically it is a show-case. Just twenty miles west of Oxford, it can be reached swiftly on the A40 from a roundabout at Summertown, or by a more leisurely saunter through countryside to the south of Witney, where at one time every field was partitioned by Cotswold stone walls, most of which in recent years have been allowed to fall down.

On the way to Burford, signposted north off the A4095 to East End (this is north-east of Witney), is the site of North Leigh Roman Villa; this is a diversion not to be missed by anyone with an imagination vivid enough to reconstruct in their mind's eye what must have been an extremely large fourth-century country house. There is no parking at the site, so leave your car on the road and trudge down a rough country lane. On your right, in a field provided with water from the River Evenlode, some descendant of a Roman invader decided to farm. What is known as Akeman Street, a couple of miles north, would have provided transport for farm produce to St Albans and Cirencester, and timber from nearby Sturt Wood and stone from two local quarries were all to hand.

The villa was probably only one storey high, but contained some sixty rooms, including a grand dining-room with a mosaic floor, some of which is protected from the weather in a shed. The floor is abstract in design, and consists of red tiles, and blue, grey and white limestone. Remains of a bath house have been disclosed, and the house had under-floor heating. Discovery of this important building was first noted in 1783, but no proper excavation was attempted until 1815, when souvenir hunters arrived and did a good deal of damage, carting off one entire mosaic pavement. The University acquired a lease on the land in 1921, and between 1956 and 1976 exploration was consolidated. Like St Michael's Chapel, the villa is now in the care of English Heritage.

It was the wool trade that brought so much prosperity to Burford, reflected in quite grand town houses. There is one such, not inappropriately named The Great House, in Witney Street, where two friends of Dr Johnson once lived — Mrs Ann Crisp and her sister, Mrs Sophia Gast. Both ladies are commemorated in the north transept of the parish church by a round marble tablet in the floor. When Mrs Gast died it was recorded that she could speak French, Latin, Greek and Hebrew, and that 'her society, which was at once entertaining and instructive, was courted both by young and old.

She expended half her income (£300 per annum) in feeding, clothing and instructing the poor, and in donations to worthy, but distressed families.'

Another occupant of The Great House was W. H. Hutton, an Oxford don who became Dean of Winchester. In the High Street the Methodists have an eighteenth-century chapel behind iron railings that could well be mistaken for the elegant dwelling of some fat alderman, but essentially the houses and cottages in Burford are seventeenth-century, and the variety of their doors and windows adds constant interest and enchantment to the whole haphazard layout.

The centre of Burford lies in a deep hollow, so test your brakes before descending the hill; to walk up it is no light undertaking. The ground floors of many of the houses have inevitably become shops, some selling expensive antiques. None is offensively garish, and one, the Red Lion Bookshop, although extremely small, is stocked it seems with every new hardback and almost every intelligent paperback you might need. Pubs of varying quality abound (there were twenty in Victorian times), and the one thing you will not do in Burford is starve.

The *Countryman* magazine has its offices in Sheep Street, in a former fifteenth-century Temperance hotel which for many years served as a staging post for teetotallers travelling from London to Gloucester. You are at liberty to wander into their garden through an archway that used to lead to the stables. As this is Burford you will not be surprised to find the garden terraced. Connoisseurs of roses will discover crimson Parkdirektor Riggers and Hamburger Phoenix, pink Kathleen Harrop and yellow Leverkusen. A small croquet lawn is shaded by a walnut tree, and there is a fine tree peony and a mulberry tree near the top. It is a small and intimate garden, and the chief reason for a visit is to sample from it a vista of the grey tiled roof-tops of Burford's snug domestic dwellings.

Burford's *pièce de résistance* however is the church of St John the Baptist, one of the great parish churches of England. Some strange and terrible deeds have been enacted here. On 17 May 1649, in the aftermath of the Civil War and just two days before the Commonwealth was declared, three Levellers were executed in the churchyard, and forty-eight years later one John Pryor was found murdered in the priory garden. He lies buried in the south transept. Pryor was guardian to two young boys whose mother had eloped with a groom. When the affair petered out and her husband, William Lenthall, conveniently died, she married the 5th Earl of Abercorn, and it was he who was arrested for the murder of John Pryor.

It seems the boys' guardian and their step-father had an argument over William Lenthall's estate. The future Bodleian librarian, Thomas Hearne, who was only nineteen at the time, attended the Earl's trial in Oxford, and wrote: 'The Murderer was clear. Yet the Jury, being bribed, gave a verdict of Not Guilty. They were drunk, especially the Foreman. Lord Abercorn had many friends to speak for him. The Duke of Norfolk said a man related to the Royal Blood in all three Kingdoms would not commit such a horrid crime; while the Bishop of Oxford praised his former life & his honest, sober and peaceable living. Yet, this Lord Abercorn had before threatened several times to murder many others and, after his aquital, he committed another Murder and soon came to an untimely end in Ireland, as I have heard.' (Abercorn died in 1701.)

Architecturally, St John the Baptist spans 300 years. Work on the church commenced around 1175, and the zig-zag Romanesque west doorway with its original door and hinges survives from about that date. Inside, the tower is supported by two superb Romanesque arches. Just east of the main door is a chapel dedicated to St Thomas à Becket, where the Sacrament is reserved; this is a fourteenth-century addition. There is a south chancel chapel dating from 1400, and a beautiful chantry with a partially concealed fourteenth-century stone canopy above the altar. At one time there were at least eight altars in the church, with six priests to serve them.

A rare conglomeration of people are buried or remembered here. Henry VIII's barber, Edmund Harman, who witnessed the King's will, has a monument whose oddest feature is the inclusion of four figures believed to be members of an Amazonian tribe. Another sixteenth-century memorial in the south choir aisle notes, 'I go to sleep before you but we shall wake together'. Sir Lawrence Tanfield (a judge) and his wife were both deeply unpopular in Burford, but posterity has bequeathed to us in the north chancel their masterly Jacobean tomb, complete with a carved skeleton underneath it and effigies of their daughter and grandson.

William Lenthall, the Speaker who defied Charles I when he so rashly went to the House of Commons to try and arrest five members, who was also, incidentally, great-grandfather to the boys entrusted to the care of the murdered John Pryor, is buried in the north transept, yet all trace of his actual burial spot has been obliterated.

Perhaps the most poignant inscription at Burford is to be found on the font. It reads: 'Anthony Sedley, Prisner'. Sedley was one of about 340 disaffected Parliamentary soldiers, known as Levellers, who were rounded up at the Crown on the corner of Sheep Street and locked up in the church. A large number escaped, so Cromwell ordered a summary execution. It was while awaiting his fate that Sedley left his inscription for us to contemplate today. However, he survived.

First, Cornet Thompson was led out to be shot. Then Corporal Perkins, 'accounting it a great mercy that he was to die for this quarrel'. Then John Church 'stretched out his arms, and bade the soldiers do their duty, looking them in the face, till they gave fire upon him, without the least kind of fear or terror'. Just as the leader of the mutiny, Cornet Deene, was being taken into the churchyard to be executed, the gallant Oliver Cromwell sent a pardon. He then forced Deene to preach a sermon justifying all the crimes Cromwell had committed, against which the Levellers had been protesting. The three murdered men were buried in unmarked graves. Christopher Fry based his play *A Sleep of Prisoners* on this intolerable event, and in 1979 the Labour politician Anthony Wedgwood Benn unveiled a memorial tablet on the outside wall of the Lady Chapel.

Dreadful things still go on at Burford's parish church. In recent years the poor boxes have been broken into, and the verger's wand, a silver crucifix, two silver candlesticks, three carpets and a Persian mat have all been stolen.

The records of parish clergy go back to 1214. They have been a mixed lot, as one might expect. Charles Knollys, vicar from 1747 to 1776, laid claim, not very successfully, to the Earldom of Banbury. John Eykyn, parish priest from 1701 to 1718, was reported by the churchwardens to be a common drunkard, a man who terrorised his wife, seduced his maid, refused to catechise the children, and would not live in the vicarage, preferring to lodge 'at a barber's in a mean manner'.

Oxfordshire's greatest country house – a palace, in fact – is Blenheim, at Woodstock, only eight miles north-west of Oxford. The town of Woodstock itself is worth a visit, and if you are going on there from Burford, the A361, and then the first right to

Charlbury, will take you over high ground affording spectacular views of the Cotswold countryside.

But first it is worth making a detour to the village of Bladen, on the A4095 just two miles south of Woodstock, where St Martin's doubles up as parish church of Bladen and Woodstock. Here the Spencer Churchill family are buried in some numbers. Chief among them of course is the Rt. Hon. Sir Winston Churchill, KG, OM, CH. He lies beneath a plain and dignified slab simply marked 'Winston Leonard Spencer Churchill, 1874–1965'. In 1977 he was joined by his wife, Clementine, Lady Spencer Churchill, created, after Churchill's death, a baroness in her own right.

Churchill's parents lie just behind him. One of the many divorced duchesses of Marlborough, Consuelo Vanderbilt, is nearby, as is Churchill's unfortunate son Randolph and the ashes of his even more unfortunate daughters, Diana and Sarah. Here too are the remains of Churchill's loyal brother John and his devoted son-in-law, Lord Soames.

St Martin's Church itself, almost entirely reconstructed in 1804 at the expense of Churchill's great-great-great-grandfather, the 4th Duke of Marlborough, is not up to much, but following Churchill's interment the bellringers certainly did their stuff, ringing a peal of 5,040 Plain Bob Minor half muffled for two hours forty minutes. Campanologists will know what that means.

The town of Woodstock is a pleasant jumble of Georgian architecture, with an abundance of very expensive antique shops, very expensive hotels and very expensive restaurants. Rolls-Royces purr around looking for somewhere to stop, and you may prefer to park and picnic in the spacious grounds of Blenheim Palace, a house you will scarcely need instructions to find.

Blenheim is not at all typical of the English country house, being just too palatial and Baroque for many people's taste. Even the family have had doubts about it. 'So terribly gloomy', was how Laura, Duchess of Marlborough, widow of the 10th Duke, described it. 'I never liked any building so much for the show and vanity of it as for its usefulness and convenience,' Sarah, the wife of the first Duke, wrote, 'and therefore I was always against the whole design of Blenheim, as too big and unwieldy, whether I considered the pleasure of living in it, or the good of my family who were to enjoy it hereafter.'

As a family home, the house never had a hope, for it was always intended as a memorial to John Churchill's military feats, and in particular his victory in 1704 at Blenheim; hence it was furnished with state apartments. Although we can now appreciate these as some of the most splendid rooms in Europe, their upkeep has at times very nearly ruined the family.

Churchill was created Duke of Marlborough in 1702 with a pension of £5,000 a year during Queen Anne's lifetime. But the house was never endowed (arrangements even to pay for the cost of building it were quite simply chaotic), and the family were not enriched on a scale commensurate with their status; Sarah was Mistress of the Robes to Queen Anne and Ranger of Windsor Park, and John went on to consolidate his military reputation (with Wellington, he was one of the two greatest generals who have ever lived) with stunning victories at Ramillies, Oudenarde and Malplaquet. But everything must have seemed rosy enough on the day the foundation stone was laid:

> About six o'clock in the evening, was laid the first stone of the Duke of Marlborough's house, by Mr Vanbrugge, and then seven gentlemen gave it a stroke with a hammer, and threw down each of them a guinea. There were several sorts of musick, three morris dances; one of young fellows, one of maidens, and one of old beldames. There were about a hundred buckets, bowls and pans, filled with wine, punch, cakes and ale. From my lord's house all went to the Town Hall where plenty of sack, claret, cakes, etc, were prepared for the gentry and better sort; and under the Cross eight barrels of ale, with abundance of cakes, were placed for the common people.

It was in 1705 that an Act of Parliament was passed granting to John Churchill the estate at Woodstock which had been in royal hands since before the Norman Conquest. Sarah wanted Christopher Wren appointed architect, but John Vanbrugh, with whom she later quarrelled violently, got the job. He was ably assisted by Nicholas Hawksmoor, who was one of the seven men who tapped the foundation stone, and until money became such a problem that workmen had to be laid off, men of genius like Grinling Gibbons were cheerfully chiselling away.

To describe the contents of so enormous a place as Blenheim it would be necessary to write a separate book. The hall stands sixty-seven feet high, with a ceiling painted by Sir James Thornhill. The saloon has murals by Louis Laguerre. There is a delicious ceiling by Hawksmoor in the Green Writing-Room. Kneller's portrait of Sarah Churchill hangs in the Green Drawing-Room, and there are priceless tapestries in the State Rooms. And of course on view is the bedroom in which the only true heir in seven generations to the first Duke's brilliance, Sir Winston Churchill, was born. The gardens, like the palace, have gone through many vicissitudes. Today there is an orangery and a formal Italian Garden, water terraces and a lake, but the great success outdoors is 'Capability' Brown's landscaped park. This at least presents the very heavy, ornate house with a setting as English as it could ever hope to have.

A house of a very different kind, Broughton Castle, is the finest medieval house in the country, and can be found at the village of Broughton, about three miles south-west of Banbury on the B4035. And it is signposted off the A361, a mere twelve miles or so north of Woodstock. Although Broughton has a moat, battlements and a gatehouse, it is really a fortified house, not a castle, and is approached through a park to which, in the time-honoured tradition of civilised country folk, the owners, Lord and Lady Saye & Sele, allow the public access.

There has been a manor house here since 1306. It was considerably enlarged in the sixteenth century, and played a minor role in the Civil War: the family sided with Parliament and got the gatehouse damaged for their pains. The second owner was William of Wykeham, founder of New College, but Broughton Castle has been in the family of the present owners since 1447, the year the barony of Saye & Sele was created. The present peer, whose family name is now a famous tongue-twister, Twisleton-Wykeham-Fiennes, is the 21st, and it was one of his ancestors, Celia Fiennes, who rode from Land's End to Newcastle. The manuscript of her journals is in the house but, in danger of decay, no longer on display.

The Great Hall is a bit distracting, with an eighteenth-century pendant ceiling and sixteenth-century windows competing for attention with the bare stone walls of the original medieval room. But off the Hall is a modest dining-room with fabulous seventeenth-century double-linenfold panelling that goes very well with both Regency furniture and the original quadripartite rib-vaulted ceiling of what originally was simply the undercroft or storage room of the medieval house. At the other end of the Hall is an oak-panelled

Elizabethan drawing-room, light and lofty but so cold in winter that the family escape elsewhere. In this room is a portrait by Lely of Celia's mother, Mrs Nathaniel Fiennes, but the house lacks any great works of art; they were sold off in 1837 to meet pressing family debts.

James I and his wife stayed here in 1604, and Queen Anne's bedroom contains a Hepplewhite four-poster and a peep-hole overlooking the fourteenth-century chapel. There is a charming late eighteenth-century painting by Angelica Kauffmann of Maria, wife of the 14th Lord Saye & Sele, and a lively contemporary portrait of Queen Anne herself. The room in which James slept (and, 300 years later, Edward VII), is virtually unfurnished, but retains interesting eighteenth-century hand-painted Chinese wallpaper. The enormous sixteenth-century French stone and stucco chimneypiece is rare, to say the least; it is also much admired but far too big for the room, and may at one time have been intended to warm the Gallery as well.

The Gallery is decorated in the Gothic style, contains a mishmash of family portraits, and some nice Newhall, Spode and Crown Derby. You can go on to the leads (tours are arranged, or you may wander round the house on your own) to look down on a compact Tudor boxed garden with archways to the moat, and examine at close quarters the wonderful Stonesfield slates on the roof. Your abiding impression, however, may well be of the lovely grey-green golden stone, quarried only a few miles away, with which this most unusual and welcoming house was built.

In 1913 Philip Morrell, a solicitor, Liberal Member of Parliament and a member of the brewery family whose pubs dominate Oxford, purchased Garsington Manor with its gardens and 200-acre farm. Two years later, when the house became vacant, he and his wife, Lady Ottoline Morrell, moved in. She was the half-sister of the 6th Duke of Portland (a title which has since become extinct), and a much-maligned hostess to the Bloomsbury Group.

Garsington Manor is easily located in the village of Garsington, just off the B480 road to Cowley; you leave Oxford over Magdalen Bridge and take the second exit from the Plain. The house remains in private hands, but on one Sunday afternoon in September the gardens are open to the public. The day is announced in the national press, tea is available, and if you happen to be in Oxford on that annual occasion, do not fail to go.

Garsington became an extension of the London salon Lady Ottoline had previously run at her house in Bedford Square. Many of those who drifted over to this ravishing Tudor manor house to laugh at Lady Ottoline (she dressed exotically and looked a bit like a horse) and to avail themselves of her food, drink, luxurious surroundings and sincere interest and sympathetic encouragement, came from the University: Edward Sackville-West, David Cecil, L. P. Hartley, Anthony Asquith. Here they would meet up with literary lions already established: T. S. Eliot, Lytton Strachey, Virginia Woolf, Bertrand Russell.

The Morrells lived at Garsington until 1927. The house is approached through double wrought-iron gates and sits cosily inside a small gravelled courtyard. Lady Ottoline painted one of her drawing-rooms Venetian red, the other sea-green, and hung them with paintings by her Bloomsbury friends: Augustus John, Mark Gertler, Henry Lamb, Duncan Grant. The gardens fall away behind the house, enhanced, in the Morrells' day, by strutting peacocks. Lady Ottoline re-landscaped in the Italian style, blending lake, statues and hedges to provide unexpected vistas. Kyrle Leng, an amusing undergraduate at Oxford in the 1920s and an excellent photographer, was one of many welcome visitors whose ghosts rustle so evocatively through this magical place. He wrote one day to Eddy Sackville-West to say, 'I seem to have spent half the term at Garsington. Tennis is still a sort of Alice in Wonderland nightmare. The net breaks, Pung runs off with the balls, one hits down a shower of laburnum with one's service, the balls fall among the pigs. Croquet is much the same, there are few of us strong enough to hit the ball across the full length of the meadowland lawn.'

There were no Cowley motor works to mar the view in Lady Ottoline Morrell's day. But then, there was no penicillin either. Oxford produced them both.

INDEX

212